6.95

Gender and Sex in Society

Gender and Sex in Society

by

LUCILE DUBERMAN

with chapters by
Helen Mayer Hacker
and
Warren T. Farrell

PRAEGER PUBLISHERS • New York

Published in the United States of America in 1975
by Praeger Publishers, Inc.
111 Fourth Avenue, New York, N.Y. 10003

Library of Congress Cataloging in Publication Data

Duberman, Lucile, 1926–
  Gender and sex in society.

  Bibliography: p.
  Includes index.
  1. Sex role. 2. Socialization. 3. Feminism. 4.
Interpersonal relations. I. Title.
[DNLM: 1. Psychology, Social. 2. Sex behavior.
BF692 D814g]
HQ1154.D79   301.41   73-10658
ISBN 0-275-52110-9
ISBN 0-275-85070-6 pbk.

Printed in the United States of America

To my daughter, Nanette Faughnan, and my son-in-law, Richard Faughnan, with love. I hope they will help their children, Jeffrey and Lisi, to be human beings first and a man and woman second.

Of course men play roles, but women play roles too, blanker ones. They have, in the play of life, fewer good lines.

IRIS MURDOCH, *The Black Prince*

Contents

Preface and Acknowledgments

The women's liberation movement is only the latest phase in a long struggle to obtain equality for women. It is to be hoped that those who are involved in this struggle realize that freedom for women is not enough; our society must also free its men. This book is one tiny part of that wider struggle. It is addressed in particular to the younger men and women in our society, for it is with them that our hopes for the future lie. If they gain some insight into themselves and into the members of the opposite sex from reading this book, and if they will implement those insights to improve their personal relationships, I will have made my contribution to the movement to free humanity from the tyranny of gender type-casting.

The study of gender roles is new in American universities. Until 1968 there was hardly a course that could properly be subsumed under such a category. Today, however, almost every discipline—biology, history, English, anthropology, political science, economics, psychology, and sociology—is rushing to offer a "woman's course" within its area of expertise. We are still searching for the best way to deal with this material. This book is an effort to bring together current theory and research in the sociology of sex status and gender roles.

Clearly ours has been, and largely still is, a sexist society. But societies do not come by their characteristics, or ethos, in some mysterious way. Each society indoctrinates its young to carry on the traditions of the past, to pursue the same goals, to believe in the same values, to hold the same attitudes. During the early part of this process, which is called socialization, we also learn self-identity, including gender identity.

The first chapter in this book gives a brief historical overview of the roles and statuses of women. Chapter 2 deals with socialization in general, then with how Americans learn to differentially identify, rank, and deal with masculinity and femininity. What accounts for sex differentiation in society? Is it rooted in the biological differences between males and females or in differences in the ways in which males and females are trained? As corollaries to this question, human sexual behavior and human sexuality are also discussed.

Chapter 3 considers the personal interactions between men and women, a topic with which one branch of the current women's movement is vitally concerned. The other major branch of the movement is more interested in inequality of economic and political opportunity for women. This is analyzed in Chapter 4.

American sociologists have frequently been accused, with some justification, of being ethno- and temperocentric. In Chapters 5 and 6, Helen Mayer Hacker fills a major gap in our knowledge by presenting the sex-differential theme from the cross-class, cross-race, and cross-cultural perspectives.

Chapter 7, by Warren T. Farrell, addresses the problems of men and their attitudes toward the feminist movement. Men, we know, are as culture-bound and as rigidly tied into their roles as women, but too much of the study of sex differentiation has focused on women only, thus excluding one half of the human race.

I could not have written this book alone. Two of the people who helped immensely, Helen Hacker and Warren Farrell, are "officially" recognized, but there are many others. My students, for example, contributed innumerable ideas and insights during confrontations in my classroom between the feminists (many of them male) and the male chauvinists (many of them female). Paul Bryant, a graduate student at Rutgers University, was kind enough to read the section on the psychological and biological approaches to sexuality. Arthur Vidich generously read and criticized an early version of the entire manuscript. My friend and colleague Clayton A. Hartjen also read the manuscript and offered many useful suggestions and several wisecracks. Gladys Topkis was, as always, more than editor and can never be thanked enough. My husband, Ralph Kaminsky, was wise enough to stay totally outside the project. To all these people, my thanks and my love.

New York   Lucile Duberman
February 1975

Gender and Sex in Society

1

Women Then and Now

In the past few years there has been a profusion of books and articles devoted to women's rights. Several of them are historical, dealing with the leaders and issues of the first women's movement, which began in the nineteenth century and culminated in the passage of the Nineteenth Amendment in 1919. This focus is an important and necessary aspect of the current movement, for women should gain a sense of the continuity of the battle for female rights in the stream of time, thus acquiring an awareness of their own significance and value as part of the flow of humanity.

Until now, women have usually been subsumed under the category of "man." We speak of man in the generic sense—mankind—and women are included. We use the term *his*tory, which is also *her* story. Women have, in truth, been deprived of a story of their own, and this in turn has deprived individual women of the chance to identify with other women as a group.

The world has previously been defined by men and in terms of men and their actions. Now it is time to include women, not as adjuncts or appendages but as living, breathing human beings who have always been there but rarely visible. Just as participants in the civil rights movement came to realize that blacks needed to develop pride in their heritage and in their blackness, women now need to develop pride in themselves and in their sex. Women need to see themselves clearly in the story of humankind and be able to point directly to heroes—better, heroines—of their own. It is essential to recognize that women do have a story that is both independent of men and their story, and bound together with it. For a true picture of the human race, it is time for both sexes to learn about women who have shared in and contributed to its growth and development.

PRIMITIVE SOCIETIES

From what little is known about societies that existed before recorded time, most anthropologists conclude that males have always and everywhere been dominant.[1] Two biological factors are largely responsible for this state of affairs: the superior physical strength of the male and the exclusive reproductive function of the female. Primitive man contributed to society by providing protection against enemies and by hunting animals for food; woman contributed by producing and nurturing offspring. Logically this division of labor should have made them equals* because each benefited from the participation of the other. However, primitive man probably made no connection between sexual intercourse and the birth of a child, because of the time differential; thus, he thought woman controlled life itself (and, conversely, death). To assuage his fear of this female power, man used his heavier muscles to enforce taboos that reduced women to an inferior status, giving him dominance over her. Thus man, in his desire to control woman's mysterious sexual power, took advantage of her biological handicaps to subject her to his will.[2]

ANCIENT SOCIETIES

There are two basic types of kinship systems. The prevailing system in Western societies is *bilaterality*, which reckons a child's descent from both parents. An American child, for example, inherits everything except the surname from both parents. The second type, called *unilaterality*, takes one of three possible forms. In *double-descent* systems, the child inherits certain things from the mother's family and certain things from the father's; he or she may inherit the father's occupation and the mother's name, for exam-

---

* Most anthropologists agree that in terms of economic importance women were not considered inferior to men because the berries and roots they gathered were as necessary to the tribe's continued existence as the meat the men hunted. (Colin Turnbull, *The Mountain People* [New York: Simon and Schuster, 1972], p. 26.)

ple, but not the other way around. In a *matriarchal* system, the mother is the formal, nominal head of the family, but usually the real power is vested in the mother's brother, and the child inherits through this uncle. The third form is the *patriarchal* system, which characterized almost all ancient societies, such as the early Hebrew, Indian, Chinese, and Japanese.

In the patriarchal family, the outstanding characteristic from which all else flows is that the authority resides in the oldest male and passes from him to *his* oldest son. Power, wealth, property, and title pass through the male line directly. The father is the only significant ancestor; the mother is valued merely as a breeding machine. Thus, marriage in a patriarchal system is obligatory. "The effect of marriage in the eyes of religion and the laws was the union of two beings in the same domestic worship, in order to produce from them a third who would be qualified to continue the [ancestor] worship."[3]

All notions about women flowed from this basic concept of patriarchy. Marriage was for procreation only; the chastity of the wife, therefore, had to be beyond question. Unfaithful wives could be put to death. A promiscuous woman threatened the entire social structure, so almost all known ancient societies insisted on premarital virginity and marital chastity for women. Furthermore, a barren woman or one who produced only daughters (which amounted to the same thing) could be put aside; her husband could take additional wives and concubines.

In addition, women had no civil or social rights. They could own no property; any dowry they received from their fathers passed to their husbands. They were legally categorized with minor children, slaves, and strangers. Because they were considered unclean, they were not permitted to share in holy rites or touch religious articles. In short, in ancient patriarchal societies women were no more than chattels.

PREMODERN SOCIETIES

Until very recently, scholars disagreed as to the amount of freedom women in Greek society had before the fifth century A.D.[4] Today, however, most historians believe that women had much more freedom than earlier writers suggest. "It seems impossible," says Raymond Bloch, "that the Greeks, among the most civilized of people, could have failed in this 'one most important mark of civilization,' the elevation of women."[5] Elizabeth Gould Davis adds:

. . . the writings of the ancient Greeks themselves do not indicate any suppression of the rights of women. The contemporary Greek writers, as well as Plutarch a little later, betray the essential freedom of Greek women in their casual revelations of daily life. From these writings the evidence is inescapable that Greek women enjoyed a high degree of independence.[6]

It seems clear that Roman women were equally misunderstood.[7] In fact, both Greek and Roman women were important to their societies, were greatly admired and active, and had many rights and privileges. They were welcome to attend plays and to join intellectual discussions in the salons. They had access to birth-control devices and abortion. Women owned property and could divorce their husbands as readily as they could be divorced. Women educated the children during the early years, and no distinction was drawn between boys and girls. Both sexes were trained in philosophy, the classics, history, and logic. Females as well as males were encouraged to participate in sports.

Plato summarized the position of Greek women, which differed little from that of Roman women:

No calling in the life of the city belongs to woman as woman or to man as man; by nature the woman has a share in all practices, and so has the man. For a woman to hold the guardianship she will not need special education. We will be dealing with the same nature in woman as in man and the same education will be required for both.[8]

THE EARLY CHRISTIANS

When the Christian Church came to power, women lost the status, freedom, respect, and authority they had attained during the Greek and Roman eras. The early Christians reverted to the notion of their predecessors, the early Hebrews, that women were basically evil because they could tempt men to perform sinful and "unnatural" acts.

The writings of the founders of Christianity reflect this view of women. Clement of Alexandria wrote that "every woman ought to be filled with shame at the thought that she is a woman."[9] Tertullian told women, "You are the devil's gateway."[10] The Council of Macon in A.D. 584 debated whether or not women had souls. Paul, who was most outspoken in his contempt for women, wrote, "For the man is not of the woman, but the woman is of the man. Neither was the man created for the woman; but the woman for the man."[11]

Thus, women during the early Christian era experienced strong discrimination. They were considered dangerous, unclean, vicious, and depraved. As Christianity spread around the world, so did this attitude toward women. Ultimately, women could not avoid accepting it themselves.

THE MIDDLE AGES

Three major institutions, Christianity, chivalry, and feudalism, influenced attitudes and values throughout the Middle Ages, which extended roughly from A.D. 500 to 1500.

The Church by the end of the thirteenth century had complete control over the institution of marriage. In the early Christian period, divorce had been almost completely a male prerogative, but the church prohibited divorce completely. This helped women because it meant that their husbands could not easily discard them.

During the twelfth century, when chivalry was at its height, the concept of romantic love crystallized. Romantic love was unlike sexual love and unrelated to marriage inasmuch as it meant the devotion of the knight to the unreachable, idealized Lady. Marriage, on the other hand, was an obligation, arranged for social or economic reasons. In one sense, chivalry raised the status of upper-class women by creating the notion that there could be gratification between men and women beyond the sexual. However, the position of ordinary women was hardly changed. Women were still considered the embodiment of evil because the values of the Church were widely circulated and accepted and had greater impact for the masses of people than chivalry.

The third important institution was feudalism. In return for his services to the lord, the serf won protection for himself and his family. If the serf was accorded no respect, the status of his wife was even lower. It was even the privilege of the lord of the estate (*le droit du seigneur*) to have sexual intercourse with the bride of any of his serfs on her wedding night. Thus, chivalry and feudalism were a mixed blessing for women in general. "A courtly lover might rape a peasant girl after serenading his Lady, but at least he now knew two ways of loving rather than one."[12]

Thus, the three institutions that were dominant during the Middle Ages were based on differing views of women. The Church protected them from divorce but still treated them as inferior beings. Feudalism demeaned them even more. Only the romantic notions of chivalry gave promise of some respect and affection for women; and that was confined to the upper class.

THE RENAISSANCE AND THE REFORMATION

Toward the end of the fourteenth century, feudalism declined, urban areas began to develop, and population density increased around centers of communication. Trade and commerce meant increasing wealth, allowing the upper classes enough leisure to direct their attention to education and the arts. By the sixteenth century women were welcome in these areas of intellectual and social life, which had long been closed to them.[13]

In the brief period between Luther and Calvin, women enjoyed a life-giving respite from the abuse and bondage of the past thousand years. The ban on women's brains was also for a time lifted, with the result that the sixteenth century witnessed a remarkable blossoming of feminine intellectualism and creativeness that far outshone, relatively, the Renaissance itself.[14]

At the same time that the arts were being rediscovered, the Church was undergoing reform, beginning in Germany under Martin Luther and spreading through France, Switzerland, and Scotland. The forces of the Renaissance that elevated women were countered by the forces reforming Christianity. Protestants were no kinder to women than Catholics had been.

The concept of predestination was the most destructive of these forces because it is based on the notion that *man*'s fate is predetermined and unchangeable on earth. Women, as God's least valued human beings, could no longer hope for redemption even in heaven. At least Catholicism held out the expectation of forgiveness and a place in heaven. In the sixteenth and seventeenth centuries, then, women both gained and lost. "From Italy to England, for every Renaissance song to woman's goodness and beauty, there was a verse or tract on her silliness, stupidity, malice, and lust."[15] There was a mixture of acceptance and respect for women and a continuation of the old attitudes of restriction and contempt.[16]

THE PURITANS

American ideology concerning women owes much to the seventeenth-century Puritans who came to New England in search of religious freedom. Many of the attitudes and values the Puritans brought with them from England influence us today. The religion of the Puritans and the colonial law were inseparable. Religion was based on the notion that man is naturally evil and must try to repress this flaw in himself by devotion to work, sacrifice, and thrift. Life was difficult in the Puritan colonies, and marriage was a necessary and serious institution for religious, economic, and social reasons. In terms of religion, God had decreed that man must marry. Economically, men and women could not survive separately. Thus, the division of labor was sharp. The men worked on the farms and in the small shops in the towns; women cared for the home and the innumerable children. Socially, men and women needed the companionship they could give each other in the isolated, inadequate houses during the long, cold winters.

The principle of male dominance prevailed in the Puritan colonies as it did all over the world.[17] Only men could be citizens. Women had no legal status apart from their husbands, who were financially and physically responsible for them. The same suspicion, fear, and awe of femaleness obtained, and women were still thought to be morally weak, irrational, and untrustworthy.

Yet, because marriage and family life were so basic to survival, women did have some respect. Furthermore, the religion required men to love their wives. For the first time, then, the concept of love moved out of the realm of extramaritality, where it had been during the age of chivalry, and into marriage and the home. Although men were legally dominant, "this does *not* seem to have been a society characterized by a really pervasive, and operational, norm of male dominance. There is no evidence at all of habitual patterns of deference in the relations between the sexes."[18] Puritan women, then, were in a somewhat better status than they had been in preceding eras, because they were scarce and at the same time essential for survival.

THE VICTORIANS

Because of the difficulty of simply staying alive on the frontier, life in the early Puritan colonies was characterized by a directness and a lack of the prudery and hypocrisy that were typical of the older, more established, prosperous countries in Europe. But by the end of the eighteenth century, the naturalness and openness had practically disappeared.[19]

In New England a striving middle class began to imitate English life-styles. The Puritan woman, who had shared a pioneering life with her man, metamorphosed into the Victorian lady, preoccupied with manners and dress and prudish about her body and its functions. Sexuality was repressed, and medical doctors began to claim that sexual desire in a woman was pathological.[20] Women ascended their pedestals—out of the reach of men. The ancient division between woman as mother and woman as sex object reappeared.[21]

Laws were enacted that purported to protect the now fragile wife but actually made her a prisoner. She could own no property, make no will, sign no contract, cast no vote. Her legal existence was incorporated into that of her husband. Heavy and complicated clothing made movement difficult. Girls' schools taught upper- and upper-middle-class girls how to do beautiful and worthless things so they could be good companions to their husbands, provide comfortable and elegant homes in which men could entertain their business acquaintances, and be beautiful and charming at all times. To be a Victorian lady meant to be idle, intellectually stagnant, and totally dependent.[22]

At the same time there was a strong undercurrent of protest and the faint rumblings of a feminist movement. In 1792 Mary Wollstonecraft wrote *The Vindication of the Rights of Women,* which has become the bible of the new feminist movement.

At first feminists concerned themselves with such issues as divorce, free love, contraception, individualism, and a division of labor based not on sex but on ability and interest. Other radical movements shared these concerns, so for a time at the beginning of the nineteenth century "romanticism, feminism, socialism, free love, anarchy, and birth control were all bubbling together in a world of underground protest and experiment."[23]

THE EARLY FEMINIST MOVEMENT (1840–90)*

By 1840 feminism was a joke. It was amid the laughter of women as well as of men that the first true feminist movement grew up as a response to the pressures to which Victorian women had been subjected. It was a radical movement because it dared to ask, "What is so honorable about being a wife? What is so sacred about motherhood? What is so holy about the family?"

The antislavery movement was the catalyst for the women's rights movement because, in their efforts on behalf of blacks, women discovered their own lowly status. The most blatant example of how women were discriminated against was the refusal, in 1840, of the World's Anti-Slavery Convention in England to seat Lucretia Mott and Elizabeth Stanton, delegates from the American Anti-Slavery Society, on the ground that they were women. Mott and Stanton went home and, in 1848, convened the first women's rights meeting, in Seneca Falls, New York. They were joined by many other women, among them Susan B. Anthony, Angelina and Sarah Grimké, Julia Howe, Antoinette Brown, and Lucy Stone, and by several prominent men of the period, including Henry Stanton, Theodore Weld, James Mott, William Lloyd Garrison, and Wendell Phillips.

During the Civil War these people devoted their efforts to

---

* Most historians divide the fight for women's freedom into two periods: the nineteenth century up to 1920, and the present. In this book, the preference is to define three separate attempts to gain female liberation. The first occurred before the Civil War and continued up to 1890. The second ended in 1920, when the franchise was given to women. The third movement is the current one. These three generations of feminists are distinct because they have had different goals and ideologies.

freeing the slaves. But when the war ended and women had still not been given the status they felt they had earned, interest in women's rights revived. By this time, there were two distinct factions. The National Women's Suffrage Association, led by Anthony and Stanton in New York, focused on domestic problems such as the institution of marriage and the role relations of husbands and wives. The American Women's Suffrage Association, led by such Boston women as Howe and Stone, was concerned with obtaining legal and political rights for women. By 1890 the differences between the two groups were resolved, and they merged into the National American Women's Suffrage Association.

THE MIDDLE MOVEMENT (1890–1920)

The newly formed National American Women's Suffrage Association (NAWSA) centered its interests almost exclusively on obtaining the vote at state and local levels. Ten years of exhausting and generally unsatisfying work had won women the vote in only four states: Wyoming, Idaho, Colorado, and Utah.

At this point social feminism, as opposed to "hard-core" feminism, reached maturity. Concentrating solely on bettering the status of women, women organized local clubs to address the problems of temperance, prostitution, working-class women, female employment, prison reform, and more. By 1910, the General Federation of Women's Clubs had 190 member chapters and over a million members.[24]

The club movement was unique in that, in addition to the social problems it concerned itself with, it served important personal needs of the members. By this time women were finding it easier to get into prestigious universities and colleges; the problem was no longer getting an education but using it. Club work offered myriad possibilities. The Women's Trade Union League, Consumers' Leagues, the Association of Collegiate Alumnae, the National Council of Women, and the Women's Christian Temperance Union, among others, offered women avenues for their reformist ideas and humanistic zeal. They provided activities with which women could fill their time and use their energies constructively. They supplied an "outlet for talents and ambitions that home life could neither satisfy nor healthily contain."[25] During the period between 1890 and 1920, then, the women's movement turned its attention to moderate reforms of American society and the American value system. In many ways it did a tremendous amount of good work; yet it was "probably most important . . . for the good it did women themselves [rather] than for the good women succeeded in doing."[26]

In their efforts to attain equality, women in the movement at first had insisted that there was no difference other than the sexual between men and women. But after 1890 their tactics changed. Now they argued that women should be enfranchised because they were different from men. Women had special qualities, they said, deriving from their experiences as wives and mothers, which would make them particularly capable of raising the moral and spiritual standards of government.

Using this basic argument, the feminists gradually gained power. NAWSA began in 1915 to make an all-out effort to get the vote for women, with Carrie Chapman Catt in charge of the campaign. By 1919 the contest was over. The Nineteenth Amendment passed by votes of 304 to 90 in the House and 56 to 25 in the Senate. Women, after nearly seventy-five years of struggle, had won the right to vote.

The feminists of 1920 believed that they had successfully carried out the dream of their predecessors and had established female freedom. Unfortunately, they overestimated the power of the vote and misjudged women's use of it.

The Lull Between 1920 and 1963

As early as 1924 it was apparent that women were not forming a cohesive voting bloc. Indeed, they were not even exercising their right to vote, and when they did, there was no difference between the way they voted and the way men voted. Women were not very much interested in politics. When they participated, it was along social-class lines and not according to sex.[27]

Not only were women not united; by 1925 they were actually polarized into two distinct, antagonistic groups, one favoring the Equal Rights Amendment and one opposing it. The National Women's Party, led by Alice Paul, supported the Equal Rights Amendment because it favored total, not only political, equality for women and would prohibit all discrimination. The League of Women Voters, on the other hand, was more interested in broad social reforms, not only feminist ones. They believed that women, weaker than men, belonged in the home, and they favored protective legislation that would safeguard females. (Since that time, of course, the League of Women Voters has changed its position, and today it supports the Equal Rights Amendment.) In his brilliant analysis of this period, Chafe writes:

> In retrospect, it seems that the leaders of the woman's movement should have been able to devise a compromise which would have advanced the cause of women's rights while still maintaining the recognition of some sexual differences. . . . The Equal Rights Amendment was certainly not a panacea, but its adoption might well have provided an important vehicle for eliminating legal discrimination as well as for establishing the principle that women deserved the same rights as men. As it was, however, antagonism was so congealed on each side that cooperation was impossible. For both reformers and feminists, defeat of the enemy within was more important than joining together in pursuit of a common purpose.[28]

The Depression also created a strong reaction against any change in the traditional female role. Few people, including women, challenged the idea that whatever jobs there were should go to men. However, when the United States entered World War II in December, 1941, women became the most logical labor pool, replacing the millions of men who went into the armed forces.

The war helped women in many ways. Many of them realized for the first time the pleasure of receiving their own paychecks. They had the best working conditions women had ever enjoyed. Many discovered the advantages of unionization, and their economic status vastly improved. Most important, the public accepted the notion of working women. Not that society approved of women working, but at least it tolerated the idea, and this was better than condemnation. Hope was high: Women had finally come into their own and would henceforth receive equal economic treatment.

However, when the war ended, it rapidly became apparent that women were not welcome in the labor market on a permanent basis. Public opinion polls taken at that time showed that most Americans, men and women, still felt that, if the society were to regain stability and if the family were to remain cohesive, women had best go home. Men should be breadwinners, women homemakers.[29]

Many women did go home, but by 1947 there were a million more employed women than there had been in 1940.[30]

By almost any criterion, therefore, the war represented a turning point for women workers. It was responsible for millions of women joining the labor market for the first time. It forced the substantial elimination of barriers to the employment of wives. And it opened up the opportunity for the second vocation to thousands of older women whose primary homemaking duties were over.[31]

By 1950 it was becoming clear that middle-class white women were facing a problem—the conflict between the traditional women's role and the war-conceived notion of working wives and mothers. The antifeminist stance was articulated by Ferdinand Lundberg and Marynia Farnham,[32] who posited that the family was no longer an important social institution. It had lost most of its traditional functions; the home now served only as a place in which to hang one's hat. Women, Lundberg and Farnham suggested, could revitalize the family and at the same time resolve the woman problem if only they would accept their biology and psychology and recognize their passivity and dependence—nay, enjoy them. Feminists who reject the God-given feminine role were psychologically ill, masochistic, suffering from penis envy, and craving the sexual activities and freedom that natural law reserves for men. Such women demonstrate their neurosis by rejecting their natural status in society. Lundberg and Farnham offered a concrete program to correct the problem. Women should have access to government-subsidized psychotherapy; they should be encouraged to have many children; and the government should undertake a propaganda campaign on behalf of the family and the female role within it.

Feminists, on the other hand, believed that the "woman problem" derived from the very roles Lundberg and Farnham advocated for women. Several social scientists[33] argued that biology need not be destiny, that the society and its cultural norms were mostly responsible for personality development. Women were what they were because they were encouraged to be so. Their unhappiness was the result of the societal norms regarding woman's place. If women were allowed into other spheres of activity, their discontent would be lessened. In short, feminists felt that woman's role in society was determined not by her biology but by the social structure, which confined her to a single acceptable status.

From the point of view of how women actually lived their lives, Lundberg and Farnham and the antifeminists appeared to have won the argument. There was a huge exodus to the suburbs "for the good of the children." Between 1940 and 1960 the birth rate for third children doubled and for fourth children it tripled. Families were building, camping, traveling, and barbecuing like crazy. Now the middle-class woman, in addition to her traditional chores, was responsible for PTA attendance, seeing to it that the children were driven to the dentist, dances, libraries, parties, school games, and meetings. Do-it-yourself gave her a chance to can and preserve food, sew her own and her children's clothes, upholster her furniture, refinish her antiques, and bake her own bread. The "problem" was apparently resolved as women found new satisfaction in enlarged domestic and nurturing chores.[34]

The contradiction that was occurring at the same time that Mom was fulfilling her destiny in the kitchen and in the car went unmentioned in the popular media. More and more women were working. The number of working women doubled between 1940 and 1960. By 1960 the median age for working women was up to forty-one, 30 per cent of the female workers were married, and 39 per cent of all mothers with children between the ages of six and seventeen were employed.[35] If women were so content at home, why were so many of them in the labor force?

Most studies[36] showed that women workers liked their jobs, valuing the psychological satisfactions over the financial ones. Many middle-class white women interviewed complained about the conditions they had experienced when they were "just housewives": social isolation, economic and social dependence, boredom, lack of rewards, lack of demands on their abilities, loss of adult companionship.

In a subtle way, then, the feminists were proved correct in the

1950s. Women were not renouncing their traditional roles, but they were adding the status of worker to that of homemaker, although most waited until their children were at least of school age. Nevertheless, there was no basic change in society's view of woman. Her place was still at home, her primary responsibility still domestic, her status still second class.

THE REVIVAL: SINCE 1963

The revival of feminism was quietly heralded when President John F. Kennedy established the Commission on the Status of Women in 1961. The Commission reported and documented the second-class position of women, at the same time permitting several women with leadership qualities to meet and interact. Two years later, Betty Friedan wrote *The Feminine Mystique*.[37] The book attacked the notion, especially prevalent after World War II, that women could be happy only if they immersed themselves in wifehood and motherhood to the exclusion of all else. Friedan argued that such a philosophy had compressed women into a tiny area of social life and that, in revenge, women had emasculated their husbands and tyrannized their children. Friedan's data are somewhat dubious and her conclusions somewhat overstated. Nevertheless, her book spoke eloquently to thousands of women.

In 1966 some of the women who had served on the President's Commission joined Betty Friedan to found NOW, the National Organization for Women, the first feminist organization in America in almost fifty years. At the same time, several other feminist groups began to form, each with a different value orientation, organizational structure, and set of objectives. Between 1966 and 1970 there was no such thing as a coherent and unified "women's liberation movement." At the present writing, two distinct types of groups have emerged.

One branch, represented by NOW, tends to have a membership of middle-class, white, middle-aged professional women. The organizations tend to be formal and bureaucratic; they address their attention to structural changes in the legal, political, and economic aspects of women's lives through existing channels. The second branch is composed of more radical, less formal, and less bureaucratic organizations. The members are younger; the groups, more heterogeneous, diversified, and creative. Instead of focusing on political and economic issues, the concern of these groups is directed toward interpersonal relations between men and women and between women and women. They devote their attention to attitudinal change, encouraging open communication between women so that they can re-evaluate the female sex and recognize that their problems are collective, not individual, and that therefore the solutions are also collective, not individual. The result has been a tremendous contribution—consciousness-raising.

The prototypical consciousness-raising group is composed of women only, usually people who know each other from the neighborhood, school, or work. Generally, the six to eight members are homogeneous in age, education, and social class. An atmosphere is created in which the women are encouraged to talk about personal issues and problems that are vital in their lives. Most groups meet once a week for two to four hours, rotating in the various members' houses.

Groups try to avoid acquiring a leader, although this is sometimes difficult because some people are naturally endowed with leadership qualities. Nevertheless, leaderlessness is desirable because women are too easily seduced into the familiar roles of passivity and docility. Consciousness-raising is a learning process, and topics for discussion are selected according to members' needs and interests. Usually they include male-female relationships, sex, money, children, the home, work, and the relations between women. The members speak of power, love, marriage, fears, hopes, discrimination, the future—all things human.

Consciousness-raising, through an open airing of what each woman believes to be her personal problems, demonstrates that these problems are really shared and, indeed, are common. Women are learning how society has limited their horizons and narrowed their opportunities, so that what they thought were personal defects are really societal defects instead. The result is that many women are being resocialized. Their sense of the world, their men and children, and themselves is changing. They are beginning to like themselves and other women better.

Women's liberation is now a household phrase. It has received enormous publicity, some favorable and some not. Thousands of women and men of every age, race, religion, geographical location, social class, and ethnic group have discussed it, participated in it, gone to meetings, marched in demonstrations, and signed petitions. Perhaps thousands more have been profoundly affected by the movement although they have not been active in it. Each segment of the movement has its own set of beliefs and priorities. Still, there are two core concepts that all groups accept. One is a feminist posture in relation to society; the other is the notion of sexism.

Traditionally society assumes that there are essential differences between males and females beyond the obvious sex differences and that therefore they should have different statuses and serve different functions. Feminists have the opposing assumption; they say that neither sex has any native ability that is lacking in the other. The feminists do not deny that most males have superior physical strength or that there is a difference in sexual equipment and functioning. But that is all that is conceded. All other observable differences in personality, behavior, or abilities, the feminists claim, are the result of differential socialization. Because these socially induced differences result in differential rewards, efforts should be made to alter the social structures that encourage them. All factions of the women's liberation movement accept this position.

Feminists also agree that sexism is rampant in Western society. Sexism parallels racism in that it

. . . defines a society's discriminatory ideologies and practices as they are reflected in the opportunities given to individuals for self-expression, with sex being the basis for selective acceptance or rejection. Like the term *racism*, it was coined by those who question that the dominant group's, in this case male, standards, values, goals, and strategies are the best, if not the only worthwhile ones, for members of a society.[38]

Discrimination against women is readily visible in our legal, political, social, and economic structures. It is to problems in these aspects of sexism that NOW and similar organizations address themselves. The more radical groups devote themselves to the subtler, less tangible, harder-to-alter matter of sexism in the attitudes of both men and women.

Sexism derives from the concepts that men are superior to women and that women are on earth for the pleasure of men and for the propagation of the species. The first concept stems from the notion that the husband's occupation as breadwinner is more important than his wife's work, whether within or outside the home. It follows that it is more important for a man to be educated, to be promoted, to be well paid.

The sexist idea that women are meant to please and serve or assist men in their important work plays a prominent part in socialization. Girls and boys are taught that female roles are complementary to those of males. They are taught that it is not "natural" for girls to compete with boys, much less to best them. This concept leads to the attitude that women should be dependent on men for social definition and economic support. It explains why women are the secretaries and men the bosses; why women are nurses and men doctors. It explains why women give up their own names when they marry to take on their husbands'. It clearly defines the few roles for which women are socially rewarded—wife, mother, teacher, sex object, helpmate, secretary.

When women reject these roles, refusing to direct their primary attention toward a man, his home, and his children, they are often stigmatized. A woman who does not seek her identity through association with a male seems to threaten the social value system.

Sexism and the supporting concepts of man's superiority and woman's natural subservience are extremely pervasive in our society. Generally we take them for granted, accepting discrimination as normal and justified. It is to be hoped that consciousness-raising will alert women to the destructiveness of these notions and encourage them to do something about them. Again, the various women's organizations offer a multitude of responses. Underlying all the suggestions, however, is the egalitarian ethic that there is no difference between the sexes other than the biological and that therefore all discriminations based on sex must go. The egalitarian ethic sees that both men and women in our society are constrained and confined by social values and institutions. Both sexes need to be liberated. Now that machines have largely eliminated the need for muscles, contraception relieves women of frequent childbearing, and social mores encourage smaller families, it is no longer necessary to assign jobs to people because they are of one sex or the other. Men and women can now develop as individuals. Options and diversity can be unlimited for both sexes if we learn to see biological apparatus in the correct perspective. If we can eliminate "men's work" and "women's work," people and society will benefit because we will then be able to utilize better the talents of all people.

NOTES

1. H. R. Hays, *The Dangerous Sex* (New York: Pocket Books, 1966), p. 7.
2. J. MacDonald, "Manners, Customs, Superstitions, and Religions of South African Tribes," *Journal of the Anthropological Institute*, vol. 20 (1891); Ernest Crawley, *The Mystic Rose*, vol. 1 (New York: Meridian Books, 1960).
3. Fustel de Coulanges, *The Ancient City* (1864), trans. Willard Small (1873). This edition published by Doubleday Anchor Books, New York (no date), p. 51.
4. For a discussion of the controversy, see Elizabeth Gould Davis, *The First Sex* (Baltimore: Penguin, 1971); Jacquetta Hawkes, *The Dawn of the Gods* (New York: Random House, 1968); and Robert Flacelière, *Daily Life in Greece at the Time of Pericles*, trans. Peter Green (New York: Macmillan, 1965). For an example of the position opposite the one taken in this book, see Panos D. Bardis, "Family Forms and Variations Historically Considered," in *Handbook of Marriage and the Family*, ed. Harold T. Christensen (Chicago: Rand McNally, 1964).
5. Raymond Bloch, *The Etruscans*, trans. Stuart Hood (New York: Praeger, 1958).
6. Davis, *op. cit.*, p. 190.
7. Montesquieu, *The Spirit of the Laws*, vol. 1, trans. Thomas Nugent (New York: Hafner, 1949), p. 21.
8. Plato, *The Republic*, trans. W. H. D. Rouse (New York: New American Library, 1956), p. 253.
9. *Paedagogus*, 2:2.
10. *De Cultu Feminarum*, 1:1.
11. *1. Corinthians*, 11:3–10.
12. Arno Karlen, *Sexuality and Homosexuality* (New York: Norton, 1971), p. 93.
13. Myra Reynolds, *The Learned Lady in England 1650–1750* (Gloucester, Mass.: Peter Smith, 1964).
14. Davis, *op. cit.*, pp. 282–83.
15. Karlen, *op. cit.*, p. 106.
16. For a full discussion of this dual attitude toward women during these centuries, see G. Rattray Taylor, *Sex in History* (New York: Ballantine Books, 1954).
17. John Demos, *A Little Commonwealth* (New York: Oxford University Press, 1970), chap. 5.
18. *Ibid.*, p. 95.
19. Page Smith, *Daughters of the Promised Land* (Boston: Little, Brown, 1970), p. 56.

20. Karlen, *op. cit.*, p. 165.
21. Smith, *op. cit.*, p. 63.
22. Duncan Crow, *The Victorian Woman* (New York: Stein & Day, 1971), p. 147.
23. Karlen, *op. cit.*, p. 206.
24. William L. O'Neill, *The Woman Movement* (Chicago: Quadrangle Books, 1969), p. 48.
25. *Ibid.*, p. 43.
26. *Ibid.*
27. Charles Merriam and Herbert Gosnell, *Non-Voting* (Chicago: University of Chicago Press, 1924).
28. William Henry Chafe, *The American Woman* (New York: Oxford University Press, 1972), p. 131.
29. Hadley Cantril, *Public Opinion 1935–1946* (Princeton, N.J.: Princeton University Press, 1951).
30. Chafe, *op. cit.*, p. 181.
31. *Ibid.*, p. 183.
32. Ferdinand Lundberg and Marynia Farnham, *Modern Woman: The Lost Sex* (New York: Harper & Row, 1947).
33. See, for example, Margaret Mead, *Sex and Temperament in Three Societies* (New York: William Morrow, 1935); Viola Klein, *The Feminine Character* (London: Paul, Trench, Trubner & Co., 1946); Elizabeth Nottingham, "Toward an Analysis of the Effects of Two World Wars on the Role and Status of Middle Class Women in the English-speaking World," *American Sociological Review*, 12 (December 1947); Florence Kluckhohn, "Cultural Factors in Social Work Practice and Education," *Social Service Review*, 25 (March 1951); and Mirra Komarovsky, *Women in the Modern World* (Boston: Little, Brown, 1953).
34. Chafe, *op. cit.*, pp. 217–18.
35. F. Ivan Nye and Lois Wladis Hoffman, eds., *The Employed Mother in America* (Chicago: Rand McNally, 1963).
36. Mirra Komarovsky, *Blue Collar Marriage* (New York: Random House, 1962); Jeanne L. Hafstrom and Marilyn M. Dunsing, "A Comparison of Economic Choices of One-Earner and Two-Earner Families," *Journal of Marriage and the Family* (August 1965), 27:403–9; David M. Gover, "Socio-economic Differentials in the Relationship Between Marital Adjustment and Wife's Employment Status," *Journal of Marriage and the Family* (November 1963), 25:452–57; and Robert S. Weiss and Nancy M. Samuelson, "Social Roles of American Women: Their Contribution to a Sense of Usefulness and Importance," *Journal of Marriage and Family Living*, 20, (November 1958).
37. Betty Friedan, *The Feminine Mystique* (New York: Norton, 1963).
38. Clarice Stasz Stoll, ed., *Sexism: Scientific Debates* (Reading, Mass.: Addison-Wesley, 1973), p. 1.

2

Socialization, Sexuality, and Sex

BECOMING SEXUAL: THE PROCESS OF SOCIALIZATION

Sociologists refer to positions in society as *social statuses*. Everyone throughout his life occupies many statuses. Some are concomitant; a female can be a daughter, a sister, a wife, a mother, and a worker all at the same time. Some statuses are sequential; a male is first an infant, then a schoolboy, a college student, a father, and a grandfather. Each status is related to at least one other status; one cannot be a daughter unless someone else occupies the reciprocal status of parent. Similarly, to be a sister, one must have a sibling.

A status always has rights, obligations, and a measure of prestige attached to it, and these factors constitute a *social role*. A role is a set of behavioral expectations related to a particular status. The person who occupies the status has the same expectations about his behavior that others hold. For example, when a man occupies the status of father, both he and his society expect him to support his wife and children. When a woman is in the status of mother, she and her society expect her to care for her children. Thus, people act in ways that correspond to the normative expectations of others and themselves for people who occupy those statuses.

Socialization is the training people are given in order for them to learn what their statuses are and how to perform the roles attached to those statuses. Thus, Brim defines socialization as "the process by which individuals acquire the knowledge, skills, and dispositions that enable them to participate as more or less effective members of groups and the society."[1]

Because we can be socialized only by other human beings, the

23

process always occurs within a social setting and during interaction with others. Moreover, the socialization process is reciprocal. The learner responds to the stimuli of others, and they, in turn, respond to him. The result is that the society is being changed or maintained as each new individual becomes part of it. In other words, while the society creates the human being, the human being is at the same time helping to redesign or preserve the society. People help to create each other, each dependent for existence on the process of socialization.

Until fairly recently, sociologists concentrated on childhood as that part of the life cycle when socialization is most effective. Although we know that socialization is a lifelong process, we still recognize that childhood is its most significant period. It is essentially within the family that socialization occurs, although play groups, teachers, and other *primary groups*, as well as the mass media, are also socializing agents. Cooley defined primary groups as

> . . . those characterized by intimate face-to-face association and cooperation. They are primary in several senses, but chiefly in that they are fundamental in forming the social nature and ideals of the individual. The result of intimate association . . . is a certain fusion of individualities in a common whole, so that one's very self, for many purposes, at least, is the common life and purpose of the group. Perhaps the simplest way of describing this wholeness is by saying that it is a "we"; it involves the sort of sympathy and mutual identification for which "we" is the natural expression.[2]

The family is the best example of Cooley's primary group. There is face-to-face association within a small group that interacts very often. Family relationships are ends in themselves; that is, the members find the relationships satisfying in their own right and not for other purposes. Primary-group interaction, then, is spontaneous, personal, sentimental, and inclusive. It is within the family setting—the primary group—that significant socialization occurs.

George Herbert Mead explained how the process actually works.[3] He began by assuming that people cannot become human unless they associate continuously with other people in a social environment. But humanness also requires the presence of certain biological equipment. *Whether or not* a person learns depends on his or her physical inheritance. People with extremely low intelligence do not learn how to be sociologists, for example, because they are not able to use the facilities of our culture. What a person learns depends on the social system in which he or she interacts. For example, in the United States one cannot become a witch doctor, because the necessary training is not available in our society. The full development of the human being, then, is subject to two interdependent modes: the *biological* and the *social*.

Let us assume, for the purpose of examining how the socialization process works, that the biological equipment is intact. How, then, do we get socialized? Long before we were born, our parents were socialized. They had already learned their social statuses and the attached roles. They had courted, married, and mated (sometimes not precisely in that order) in socially prescribed ways. They were prepared to teach their children the socially approved ways to behave and think. Thus, socialization begins even before we are born, and the self emerges out of a long, gradual process.

The most direct socialization occurs through *role-taking*. This is a process during which the individual imagines himself in the place of the other (the person with whom he is interacting) in order to anticipate reactions and responses. Role-taking permits us to develop a notion of how others see and evaluate us. We guess, often very accurately, how we appear to others and how they judge us. We accept these imagined attitudes and adapt our own behavior to conform to them.

Socialization, then, is a process that allows the human animal to learn to live in his society according to its values. It permits him to develop a social self and to discover his status within the framework of his world. It is a process that encourages people to behave in ways that will gain social approval and the ability to predict the reactions their actions will evoke. Without socialization, society and humanness would disappear.

Statuses have been divided into two categories: *ascribed* and *achieved*. Achieved statuses are "those requiring special qualities, although they are not necessarily limited to these. Achieved statuses are not assigned at birth. They are left open to be filled through competition and individual effort."[4] For example, we can achieve the status of lawyer, husband, mother, electrician, mayor, or friend. We are not born into any of these statuses; we choose to become them and then work to earn them.

Ascribed statuses, according to Linton, are "those which are assigned to individuals without reference to their innate differences or abilities."[5] In our society we acknowledge three ascribed statuses: age, race, and sex. Age, of course, changes, but one can never alter one's date of birth; so in that sense one's age is ascribed for life. Race is also unalterable, unless one's physical characteristics are so ill defined that there is no way to make an absolute identification. Sex, too, is almost always unchangeable.

Sex, therefore, is an ascribed social status referring to the biological differences between people. Males are born with male genitalia; females, with female genitalia. Biology determines maleness and femaleness. This is *sex status*—rarely misperceived, rarely alterable. Like other ascribed statuses, it is acquired at birth and is independent of skill, effort, or ability.

A social role is attached to one's sex status, as roles are attached to all statuses. Here I shall refer to this as one's *gender role*, meaning the socially learned patterns of behavior that differentiate men from women in a given society. Masculinity and femininity are gender roles, acquired during one's lifetime through learning, role-taking, imitation, observation, and direct instruction. They are dependent on skill, effort, and ability.

A society decides what is considered masculine and what feminine, and the individual interprets these decisions and applies them to him- or herself. Gender, then, is learned behavior, usually related to one's sex, but sex status does not necessarily determine gender role. One's degree of proficiency in playing one's gender role depends on how well one has been socialized, how much one seeks approval from society, and how much one's gender-role performance has been reinforced with positive sanctions.

Most children learn their gender roles primarily by role-taking. Within the family the children role-take with their parents. They learn how to be masculine or feminine by imitating their same-sex parent and interacting with their opposite-sex parent in order to learn how to anticipate the normative behavior and responses. They learn the "proper" attitudes, values, behaviors, and goals associated with their sex status. They learn the rights, obligations, and prestige accompanying their sex status. Gradually and irrevocably, the children internalize* their gender roles until the attributes come to seem like the only possible ways to behave and feel.

Jerome Kagan⁶ has demonstrated that cultural definitions of masculinity and femininity are internalized by children as young as three years old. Children of this age can tell us that daddies should be aggressive, big, and strong; mommies should be little, pretty, and cuddly. They understand that little girls are expected to be more conforming and dependent than little boys, and they are likely to become very upset if their peers violate these normative prohibitions.

Thus, to paraphrase W. I. Thomas, we define what is masculine and what is feminine. We teach these definitions to our children, and gradually the definitions become real and have real consequences all through life. Boys are defined as "strong," so they do things to "prove" that they are strong. Girls are defined as "dependent," so they act and feel dependent. This is, once again, a self-fulfilling prophecy.

It is interesting that there are social-class differences among children in the ways in which they describe gender roles. Lower-class children define feminine and masculine characteristics more sharply and perceive a stricter division of labor. (See Chapter 5.) We can assume, therefore, that social classes differ in their definitions of gender roles, because surely there is no biological difference between social-class members. "Proper" behavior for each sex, then, is socially determined. This is significant because it indicates that the biological distinctions can be interpreted loosely and that human beings could alter the existing stereotypes if they wanted to do so.

To summarize, sex is a status ascribed at birth, whereas the gender role considered to be appropriate to a given sex status is learned, just as all roles are learned. Youngsters observe and role-take with adults and finally internalize the gender role to the point where girls "instinctively" love their dolls and boys "nat-

---

* As the word is used by role theorists, to *internalize* means to accept the norms of the group as part of one's self, to adopt the standards of one's society as part of one's self-image, so that the attitudes and behaviors approved by the society appear to have no possible alternatives.

urally" enjoy playing with toy soldiers. We noted before that socialization is a reciprocal process: The person being socialized contributes to the changes or nonchanges in the society. Thus, when the child accepts his gender-role training, he continually justifies its values for the group and, in turn, will socialize his children in the same way. The system, then, is constantly being perpetuated and reinforced.

The problem is that sex status and gender role are frequently confused. In our society men are thought of as biologically (inherently and unchangeably) aggressive and women as biologically nurturant. Gender roles are seen as naturally identical with sex status. Male and female children are treated differentially from birth. They learn very early to accept the relationship between their sex status and their gender role as defined by the society, and forever after the two concepts remain intertwined. It should be clear to the reader, however, that gender-role differences are not based in biology. To be born male does not guarantee masculinity. To be born with a penis does not ensure that one will be brave. The male learns how to act as if he were brave because he believes that such behavior is a display of masculinity. To be born female does not guarantee femininity. Having ovaries does not assure a girl that she will love housework. She will be socialized to act as if she loves housework because that is the behavior socially accepted as feminine. Masculinity and femininity must be learned within a social context. Nevertheless, the differential treatment we receive because of our sex status leads to the development of very real psychological and personality differences between males and females.

SEXUALITY

The sex status into which one is born has profound effects on one's entire life. The important question is whether the gender role that almost invariably accompanies sex status is of biological origin and therefore unalterable or is socially determined and therefore subject to change. There is a correlative problem: Are those characteristics we impute to males and those we impute to females inherently masculine and feminine, respectively? Or is it that the "masculine" ones are displayed more often by males and the "feminine" ones more often by females, either because they are biologically determined or because they are socially induced? All the major theories assume that gender differences have always obtained in human societies and always will. Beyond that, they offer widely differing explanations. Probably all contain some element of truth and, at the same time, all are incorrect and too simplistic.

There are two basically contradictory theories regarding psychosexual development. One is rooted in the Freudian concept of infantile sexuality, which argues that the sex drive is instinctive and that childhood is the most significant time for the development of psychosexuality. Everything depends on childhood experience. The other theory, chiefly supported by Simon and Gagnon, rejects the notion that sexuality is a powerful innate drive and that it evolves out of infantile sexuality. Instead, the authors postulate that adolescent sexual development is disjunctive with infantile or childhood experiences and is the true beginning of adult sexuality. For example, they state that "sexual behavior is socially scripted behavior and not the masked or rationalized expression of some primordial drive."[7]

Freud and his followers posited that infant behavior is sexual and is in a direct relationship with adult sexuality in the sense that "both adolescent and adult sexuality were viewed as being in some measure re-enactments of sexual commitments developed, learned, or acquired during infancy and childhood."[8] This stance assumes that the adult observer is capable of interpreting and understanding children's feelings and actions. For example: "Discovery of the genitals, in particular, appears to arise within the second half of the first year as accidental touching and is followed by *deliberate* poking and tugging"[9] (emphasis added). Or, "Toilet training, usually another educational landmark of the period, lends itself to increased awareness of genital sensation and structure. The youngster's attention is now *specifically directed* to sensations arising from adjacent structures, while wiping further stimulates the anal-perineal area"[10] (emphasis added).

The question Simon and Gagnon (and I) ask of those offering this perspective is: How do these adult observers know that the poking and tugging is "deliberate" or that the attention is "specifically directed"? Surely the six-month-old child cannot tell them. It may be that the adult observer is labeling behavior "sexual" when the actor (the child) has no such motive. In the words of the psychoanalyst, this may be mere projection. "To suggest that infant or childhood genital play is prototypical of or determines adult patterns is to credit the biological organism with more 'natural' wisdom than we normally do in areas where the biological and the sociocultural intersect."[11] In fact, Simon and Gagnon write, "The sexual area may be precisely that realm wherein the superordinate position of the sociocultural over the biological level is most complete."[12]

Simon and Gagnon present a much more plausible description of psychosexual development. They begin by acknowledging that a child's sex status will almost without exception determine his gender-role training, which will then influence his later sexual commitments and capabilities. Aside from that, however, there is discontinuity between preadolescent and adolescent sexual experiences. They note wide cross-cultural variations in the types of training young males and females get and especially pronounced differences between the sexes and between social classes in our own society. (See Chapters 5 and 6.) Although there is probably some link between the differential training of the sexes and their differences in physiology, there can be no link between socioeconomic status and physiology, or between nationality and physiology. This observation strengthens the argument for the significance of social and cultural factors in differential gender-role training. This is the same interpretation Kagan placed on his finding that young children of different social classes characterize their parents differently, in the sense that daddies are more "masculine" and mommies are more "feminine."[13]

In short, Freudians posit a continuity between infantile sexuality, which is biologically rooted, and adult sexuality. Simon and Gagnon, on the other hand, see no relationship between infantile sexuality—indeed, they question its existence—and sexuality in adulthood. Now we will look at specific intermediate explanations of psychosexuality.

The Psychological Explanation

Experiments can be conducted with the lower species that would be impossible with human subjects. Animal studies can be carried out in laboratories, for example, under controlled conditions, while the best data available on human sexuality (except for the findings of Masters and Johnson)[14] come from subjective reports. Therefore, some psychologists study animal behavior and then generalize their findings to human beings, on the assumption that there are linkages and similarities between beasts and human beings. These psychologists stress evolution in their study of gender-role behavior, searching for common characteristics in all species, regardless of function and structure. On the other hand, some animal psychologists simply use animal experiments to gain potentially valuable insights into questions that might be asked about people.

We must, then, interpret the psychologists' findings with caution. Researchers, like all other people, are subject to selective perception and may see the similarities they want to see. Further, it may be, as some scientists claim, that each species develops along separate lines,[15] so that we can only rarely or tentatively extend our knowledge of any one animal to any other, including the human animal.

Studies of animals seem to indicate that there are sex-linked differences in the hypothalamus, the part of the brain that influences the endocrine system. If this is true, it is also plausible that there are sex-linked differences in the central nervous system, because the hypothalamus is part of the central nervous system, and thus constitutional differences between males and females in their responses to stimuli. When R. W. Goy injected pregnant rhesus monkeys with androgen (the male sex hormone), the newborn female infants were either masculinized or hermaphroditic, displaying typically "masculine" characteristics, such as aggression, roughness, chasing, and mounting.[16] When S. N. Levine injected four-day-old female rats with testosterone, they did not develop normal female physiology. Castrated four-day-old male rats injected with the female sex hormone estrogen became feminized.[17] Levine and his associate, R. F. Mullins, concluded that testosterone is the crucial hormone in the period just after birth. Its absence feminizes both sexes; its presence masculinizes both.

Pfeifer substituted testes for ovaries in young rats and found that the female became completely masculine.[18] When he implanted testes and allowed the ovaries to remain, female functioning was prevented. The reverse experiments on male rats showed that the removal of testes and the substitution of ovaries resulted in female functioning. When ovaries were simply added to the body of the rat without removal of the testes, masculinity was not diminished. Pfeifer, then, like Levine and Mullins, found that testosterone is dominant over estrogen.

Young summarized the animal studies that attempt to correlate hormones and sexual behavior.[19] In general, he concluded that the relationship between the timing of hormonal release and sexual activity is a direct one. The evidence seems to show that hormones have a strong influence on sexual behavior. When young males receive additional male hormones, they increase their aggressive behavior; when females receive it, they become masculinized.

Sexual behavior in animals ranges from asexuality among very small marine animals to very elaborate sexual behavior among primates, with tremendous variation among species. No matter how closely the mating activities of some of these higher animals resemble human activities, however, scientists have always believed that there is one major difference: Animal sexuality is always cyclical, dependent upon the female estrous cycle. The newest thinking is that there may be human cycles also. It is, nevertheless, clear that, as we ascend the phylogenic scale, genetic and hormonal influences diminish and learning increases in significance. Sexual activity thus becomes more social and less exclusively related to reproduction.[20]

Studies such as those discussed above are interesting but not conclusive, because most of the work has been done with the lower animals and it is hazardous to generalize from these to the higher primates* and to human beings. Genetic and hormonal explanations are not enough to allow us to understand the sexual behavior of simple animals and are certainly insufficient to describe human sexuality. In short, the comparative psychologist stresses evolution in his study of gender-role behavior, searching for similar characteristics in all species. "Attempts to apply these

---

* In a brilliant article, Naomi Weisstein points out that all primates do not exhibit the same kind of sexual behavior. She notes that researchers who work in this area tend to ignore the many species whose behavior does not provide evidence for their theories. ("Psychology Constructs the Female," in Vivian Gornick and Barbara K. Moran [eds.], *Women in Sexist Society*, New York: Basic Books, 1971, 207–224.)

to human sexual behavior are fraught with difficulty. Though hormonal variables are important determinants of sex-role behavior in animals, they are clearly of diminished relevance in the understanding of such behavior in humans."[21]

The Biological Explanation

Biologists are divided in their explanations of the relationship between biology and gender-role behavior. There are those who argue that psychosexual development is organized by the body—that is, that sexuality is inherently biological. Others argue that people are psychosexually neuter at birth, neither feminine nor masculine. There is nothing new in the notion that gender is constitutional. Krafft-Ebing believed there were actually two different centers in the brain, although he had no evidence to sustain his belief.[22] Broverman and his associates argue that cognitive sex differences are rooted in physiological sex differences.[23] These researchers claim that there are basic biological differences that cause females to be superior at perceptual-motor tasks such as key punching or typing and males to be superior at restructuring tasks like problem-solving and mathematics.

Biological determinists hold that the physical differences between males and females impose constraints on psychological development and limitations on the changes that can be brought about during the early period of socialization. These scientists believe that women are "naturally" subordinate to men and can find fulfillment only if they accept "femininity"—that is, passivity, subjectivity, sensitivity, intuitiveness, dependency, and emotionality. Men, on the other hand, are "naturally" superior and should be rewarded if they are tough, active, objective, independent, controlled, confident, and rational. These traits are biologically derived, and attempts to change them cannot succeed.

Moss, who also subscribes to the notion of a fundamental sexual difference, tried to demonstrate that newborn female infants require more handling than males.[24] Garn's work[25] showed male infants are larger and stronger than females; Garn and Clark[26] showed that males have higher energy levels than females; Knop[27] showed them to be more active as infants; and Lipsitt and Levy[28] concluded that males have a higher threshold of pain than females. In general, basic differences have been observed between the sexes among infants. Males tend to be more extroverted, active, and aggressive; females, more introverted and passive.[29]

Although the studies just described do seem to show differences between male and female infants, there is a paucity of such studies, and they are based on an assumption that may be fallacious. Most of the researchers posit that their subjects are too young to have been socialized at all, and that therefore nothing intervenes between physiology and behavior. However, there is evidence to show that socialization begins at the moment of birth. Girl infants, for example, are held more gently, spoken to more softly, picked up more quickly when they cry, and cuddled more often. An additional problem is that an infant's behavioral repertoire is limited and often apparently aimless, thus not readily subject to interpretation.

The newest attempts to assert the biological theory stress the resemblance of man and ape and try to show that human beings have been genetically programed throughout the evolutionary process.[30] These writers see the male evolving as a killer, instinctively destroying his own kind, stealing or protecting territory, and dominating females, who, according to this kind of thinking, have been programed to seduce the male and then spend the rest of their lives caring for children.

This form of biological reductionism has been amply disproved. The problem lies in its basic assumption that people are naked apes. There are simply no scientific reasons for the assertion that the behavior of the primate is analogous to that of the human animal. Such an assertion totally ignores the influence of society on people. As Weisstein said, "Following this logic, it would be reasonable to conclude that it is quite useless to teach human infants to speak, since it has been tried with chimpanzees and it does not work."[31]

There is other evidence that points to genetic and hormonal influences in gender-role development. Females normally have two X chromosomes, while males have one X and one Y chromosome. Anomalies help to show the genetic influence. In Klinefelter's syndrome, phenotypical males have an XXY combination, typically leading to small testes and sterility. In Turner's syndrome, the female has only one X chromosome, is usually lacking in secondary sex characteristics, such as pubic hair and breasts, and is mentally retarded.

Kallman[32] studied forty pairs of identical twins and forty-five pairs of fraternal twins, one of each pair being homosexual. Among the identical twins, the sibling in every case was also homosexual; among the fraternal twins, the frequency was the same as would be found in the general population. Schlegel's[33] findings confirm Kallman's results. These investigators conclude that homosexuality is, if not genetically determined, at least genetically predisposed.

Hormones are also believed to play an active part in gender-role development. Androgen, originating in the testes, promotes male sexual activity and estrogen and progesterone promote female sexual activity. If a male is castrated before puberty, there is an almost total absence of sexual interest,[34] although, if the operation is performed after puberty, sexual interest and activity continue in some men, at a diminished level.[35] For women, a prepubertal ovariectomy also leads to lessened sexual interest and activity, but the results are not so clear as the results of comparable surgery are for men. When women are castrated after puberty, they may experience either no change, lessened sexuality, or heightened sexuality.[36] The fact that sexual activity sometimes continues after postpubertal castration may well indicate that habit may be extremely meaningful even in the absence of hormones.[37]

We do know that androgen is the prebirth determining hormone. If it is present, the individual will develop into a male; if absent, into a female. This is the position of those scientists who posit biologically determined gender-role development: One's sexuality depends on one's chromosomes and on the kind of hormone present. If the chromosomal pattern is XX and the hormones present are estrogen and protesterone, the individual will behave in "feminine" ways; if the chromosomal pattern is XY and the hormone is androgen, the person will be "masculine." Sexuality is inherent in biology according to these theorists, although they grant some social and cultural influences.

Studies of abnormality seem to substantiate the argument favoring the biological basis of gender-role development. However, just as it is difficult to generalize from studies of infants to adults and from studies of lower animals to higher, it is also difficult to generalize from abnormality to normality. These results should, therefore, be interpreted with extreme caution.

The neutrality theory, on the other hand, contends that people are sexually undifferentiated at birth and posits that gender roles are differentiated by the society. Children can be reared into a gender role that is opposite the sex status into which they were born. Money, Hampson, and Hampson studied hermaphrodites, individuals who possess the external genitalia of one sex and the sex chromatin patterns, gonads, internal structures, or hormones of the other. The investigators concluded that gender role is in accord with sex status as assigned at birth or with the gender role into which people are reared rather than with chromosomal patterns, gonadal sex, hormonal sex, internal reproductive organs, or external genitalia.[38] Hampson wrote:

> Psychologic sex or gender role appears to be learned—that is to say, it is differentiated through learning during the course of the many experiences of growing up. In place of a theory of innate constitutional psychologic bisexuality we can substitute a concept of psychosexual neutrality in humans at birth. Such neutrality permits the development and perpetuation of many patterns of psychosexual orientation and functioning in accordance with the life experiences each individual may encounter and transact.[39]

In short, the neutrality theory argues that from the moment a child is assigned a sex status at birth, on the basis of the external sexual apparatus, his masculinity or her femininity is constantly reinforced. Gender role, then, is the result of social learning, not hormonal, gonadal, or chromosomal sex. Boys are boys and girls are girls because they are reared, not born, that way.

One researcher who rejects the neutrality theory believes that learning is a necessary but not sufficient condition for gender-role development.[40] He says that genetics and learning interact. One's biological makeup predisposes one to learn the acceptable gender role, but biology can be modified by life experience. In short, many modern thinkers believe there is a complex interaction between biology and social factors that is still unclear.

The same criticism that applied to the previously discussed theory is applicable here. Diamond's subjects were abnormal (in this case hermaphroditic), and, although the evidence seems convincing, one cannot with impunity generalize from abnormality to normality.

The Social-Learning Explanation

So far we have looked at explanations of gender-role differentiation from a physiological viewpoint derived from animal experiments and human biological experiments. It is now time to see what social-learning theory tells us.

Learning theory is rooted in stimulus-response theory. However, stimulus-response views the child as passive, totally dependent on reward and punishment. Social-learning theory grants the child a somewhat more active part as he or she imitates role models. It argues that the child is extremely dependent on the maternal figure, associating her presence with comfort and pleasure, her absence with frustration and anxiety. The result is that the child learns to respond to others and to perform those behaviors that will meet with approval. Proper behavior is thus constantly reinforced by reward. As the child matures, this social learning becomes generalized because he or she begins to adopt role models and to imitate them. For example, if parents are aggressive people and want their child to be aggressive, they will reward the child whenever he or she imitates them and displays such behavior. Aggressive behavior becomes internalized as natural behavior.

This theory sees femininity and masculinity as socially acquired, for approval is almost always forthcoming when a child adopts the gender role appropriate to his or her sex status. Sex status is assigned at birth, and the infant is thereafter treated in accordance with it. (This resembles the position taken by the neutrality theorists in biology.) Sex-differential behaviors are rewarded, role models of the appropriate sex are acquired, the child internalizes the approved responses, and gender role is established as it is reinforced. No child will acquire sex-appropriate behaviors unless the members of his or her society reward him or her for displaying them.

One major problem with this theory is that all experiments based on it have been conducted in laboratories under controlled conditions, using behaviors that can be systematically reinforced. It is yet to be demonstrated whether or not other behaviors, those commonly occurring in the real world, are equally susceptible to reward and punishment. This criticism notwithstanding, social-learning theory makes good sense because it helps to explain the ways in which behavior can be molded, at least partially, to meet the requirements of the society. The theory casts considerable light on how children use role models to establish their gender roles. On the other hand, the theory tends to overstress the passivity of early childhood.

The Psychoanalytic Explanation

The psychoanalytic explanation, which was discussed briefly earlier in this chapter, is based on the work of Sigmund Freud, who saw the neonate as a bundle of instincts and drives, with sensitive erogenous zones—the mouth, anus, and sex organs—responsive to manipulation and capable of producing pleasure. Each child during the first five or six years of life passes through a series of stages, concentrating on each zone in its turn, with the cross-sex parent as the object of desire. From about the age of six until adolescence, the child's sexuality is latent, but, during the teen years, the libido (sexual energy or life force) is very active and in healthy children is centered in the genital region. Sexual interest passes from the parents to peers. Thus, psychoanalytic theory de-emphasizes the social aspect of life and focuses on biological drives and the relationship between the individual and his or her parent.

A notable aspect of Freud's thinking was the inferior status he assigned to women. He based his assessment of women on five major assumptions. First, he said that *anatomy is destiny*. Female genitalia determine a woman's basic nature and equip her perfectly to be the caretaker of the home and the children. Second, Freud believed that all women experience *penis envy*. That is, female children regard the male penis as a symbol of power and spend all their lives wishing to have one so that they will be as powerful as males. Third, Freud felt that women are *naturally passive and masochistic*, and that any woman who is not is unhealthy and immature. Freud also said that females have *faulty superego development.* He explained this on the basis of the girl's lack of a penis, for which she blames her mother. Because of her anger at her mother, she attaches herself to her father. The result is failure to resolve fully what Freud calls her "Electra complex"; therefore, her superego cannot develop completely. For this reason, Freud said, women lack a sense of justice, cannot be trusted, and are by nature devious and envious. Finally, Freud claimed that an important indicator of maturity in women is the ability to have *vaginal orgasms.*

This last was his most damaging assumption because it caused great unhappiness for the thousands of women who thought they were failures as women because they could not "achieve" what had been proclaimed to be the sign of maturity. Because they did not find penile penetration sufficiently stimulating for them to reach orgasm, these women were said to be, and in many cases believed they were, infantile, repressed, and man-rejecting.

Kinsey's work began to disprove this assumption. Less than 15 per cent of his gynecological sample were even aware that they were being touched inside the vagina, because the vagina is a very insensitive organ, containing only fourteen nerve endings.[41] It is the clitoris, not the vagina, that is the seat of female sexuality. This organ structurally resembles the penis inasmuch as it is composed of erectile tissue and has the same especially sensitive surface covering as the penis. Furthermore, unlike the vagina, which has reproductive functions, "the clitoris has no other function than that of sexual pleasure."[42] Freud's edict that clitoral orgasm is a sign of immaturity and rejection was "perhaps one of the most infuriating and damaging results of this whole charade. . . . Women who were perfectly healthy sexually were taught that they were not. So in addition to being sexually deprived, these women were told to blame themselves when they deserved no blame."[43]

These, then, were Freud's assumptions about women: They all suffer from penis envy throughout their lives; they have underdeveloped superegos; they are passive and masochistic by nature; and they are immature if they do not have vaginal orgasms. In short, anatomy is destiny, and the true woman accepts her inferior status in life.

We can, in a sense, understand how Freud came to these conclusions and forgive him. He was, like all of us, a product of his time and his society. The Victorian era regarded women as inferior, sexless creatures. Furthermore, Freud treated a limited, biased sample of deeply disturbed females. His major error was in generalizing from them to all women. It is harder—no, it is impossible—to forgive Freud's followers, medical doctors who supposedly have studied anatomy. According to at least one woman in the liberation movement, male psychoanalysts and psychiatrists respond not as doctors but as men. Their masculinity is threatened by the clitoral orgasm, which negates the penis. "Men fear that they will become sexually expendable if the clitoris is substituted for the vagina as the center of pleasure for women. Actually, this has a great deal of validity if one considers *only* the anatomy."[44] Thus, some male doctors tend to react on the basis of Freudian theory, ignoring what they may have learned in medical school about female anatomy.

The Cognitive-Developmental Explanation

This theory is based almost completely on the work of Lawrence Kohlberg,[45] who criticized both psychoanalytic theory and social-learning theory, which stress the child's relationship to the mother and state that her nurturance combines with the child's dependency to determine psychosexual behavior in later life. Kohlberg says, rather, that the parent-child relationship is not the significant factor but that a person's psychosexuality is related to his or her self-categorization. Very early in life a child begins to understand himself or herself as either female or male partly because he or she is identified sexually by society and partly because he or she makes cognitive self-judgments. Once the categorization is made, a child identifies with members of his or her chosen sex and becomes interested in stereotypical toys and objects considered appropriate to that sex. Kohlberg rejects the notion that a judgment of one's sex status is based on parental identification or rewards. Instead, he suggests that children construct their own gender roles in a process interrelating both biology and culture. His theory "assumes that basic sexual attitudes are not patterned directly from either biological instincts or arbitrary cultural norms, but by the child's cognitive organization of his social world along sex-role dimensions."[46] The difficulty with this theory is that it fails to explain how young children manage this self-categorization without influence from parents and peers.

The Anthropological Explanation

Anthropologist Margaret Mead has done a considerable amount of work in the area of gender-role development, addressing herself to the question of whether psychosexuality is dependent on genetic inheritance or whether people are *taught* to behave in ways that are socially defined as "masculine" or "feminine."

Many primitive societies, unlike ours, have more than two possible sex statuses. For example, females can be assigned to marriage and childbearing, to celibacy, or to what we would consider prostitution. Males can become celibates, transvestites, or fathers. A child is watched very carefully before assignment is made into a sex status. There are even some societies that have no sex differentiation, except, of course, to specify that females bear the children. There are other societies that define sex characteristics in a way opposite to that in which we define them in our society.[47]

Mead's research, she claims, clearly shows that gender-role behavior can be and is manipulated to fit the needs of the society, that the community determines behavioral patterns and then, frequently using a system of reward and punishment, teaches children the attitudes and behaviors that will help them adjust to the category to which they have been assigned. Thus, gender-role training is patterned to satisfy the requirements of the society.

Other anthropologists argue that there are some near universals. Barry, Bacon, and Child[48] contend that girls in almost every society are trained to be obedient, responsible, and nurturing while boys are encouraged to be independent and self-reliant. D'Andrade noted that the male usually holds the superordinate position, wielding the power and authority and having greater prestige.[49] In short, most societies defer to the male. These scientists, however, differ as to the meaning of these "universals." Some feel that the patterning indicates cultural agreement as to the logical sex differences; others believe that there must be a biological reason for the near universality.

Most anthropologists feel that primitive societies have less control over their environment and, therefore, make more direct use of biological differences to survive. As societies become more complex and can more readily control the world, they depend less on biological distinctions and are more likely to differentiate members to serve less basic social needs. Cultures, in this view, can either emphasize or de-emphasize biological differences, as required.

The Sociological Explanation

It is difficult to separate the sociological explanation from social-learning theory or from anthropological theory. Both social learning and sociology focus on the relationship between the child and his parent. Both anthropology and sociology focus on the relationship between the child and his or her social group.

Parsons and Bales[50] formulated a theory that personality and gender characteristics are developed in the child's interaction with his or her parents, who act as agents of the society. Because these sociologists recognize the uniqueness of each family in its distinctive cultural setting and era, their theory is more dynamic than the others. Most sociologists are aware of the mutuality of the parent-child relationship, so that, unlike the social-learning theorists, they recognize the influence of the child on the parent, as well as the other way around. Finally, in sociology, the parent and child are seen as a social system with functions that are necessary for the maintenance of the whole society. The family's division of labor is seen as biologically based—the father plays the instrumental role and the mother the expressive one—for the benefit of the society. Socialization, in this view, is a process during which the child internalizes the society's norms. Gender-role socialization is not only socially structured but continuous throughout life, although based on biological differences. Psychosexual development is neither totally instinctual nor totally social but a combination of both.

A Partial Synthesis of the Theories

Rosenberg and Sutton-Smith, synthesizing these theories, claim that psychoanalytic theory and the biological theories are most useful in explaining the genesis of sexuality, that social-learning theory demonstrates the importance of role models during childhood, that sociology points to the continuous nature of gender-role development, and that anthropology highlights the significance of cultural needs. Thus, "one's sex role [gender role] is an outcome of all influences: biological, psychological, and cultural."[51]

Nurture can ignore *nature*, but usually chooses not to do so. . . .
We conclude from this that despite the malleability of the infant organism, most cultures have chosen to satisfy their basic functions by capitalizing on these differences at birth rather than ignoring them.[52]

The important question to Rosenberg and Sutton-Smith, as well as to me, is whether or not sex differences really matter for behavioral development. There is no doubt that,

. . . although there are biological differences between the sexes at birth, the overlap in behavior is so extensive and human malleability so great that both sexes are capable of exhibiting most forms of human behavior. At this time there are few behaviors that may be viewed as solely within the province of one sex. The fact that human cultures throughout history have made use of sex differences need not imply that they will continue to do so.[53]

Real Differences Between the Sexes

The biological differences between men and women unquestionably result in some psychological differences. Surely the menstrual cycle has an effect, as does the fact that during sexual intercourse men *enter* women, while women *are entered*. Undeniably, because of our biological differences, society views our bodies differently, and this, in turn, affects our views of ourselves. For example, menstruation has been and generally still is regarded as "dirty" in most Western societies; surely this must have an impact on the way women see themselves. A man is expected to be sexually "ready" at all times; surely this expectation affects his self-image. Thus, biology must have some effects on personality. However, in Western societies these biological differences have been overemphasized. We tend to differentiate sharply between masculinity and femininity, although the potential for these characteristics is probably close to equal. The clear differences we observe result more from socialization than from biology. Society determines which sex will stress which abilities and talents. Still, the differences are real, and we will discuss what they are.

INTELLIGENCE. Intelligence, we now recognize, is what intelligence tests say it is. It has been known for years that most IQ tests favor the white, middle-class, urban child. Some of these tests also tend to favor males over females, or vice versa. So far, the people who construct IQ tests have been unable to eliminate these biases completely.

In general, girls seem to score higher on IQ tests during the preschool age, but boys test higher during high school[54] and continue to do so in college and adulthood.[55] One explanation is that, beginning in high school, girls come to realize that they will be more "popular" if they do not appear to excel the boys, and so they suppress their intelligence. Matina Horner, in her well-known work on success avoidance in college women, has made this point explicit.[56]

On the basis of standardized tests, girls excel through the early grades in all areas of verbal skills. They speak earlier than boys, use longer sentences, articulate more clearly, and speak more frequently. They read earlier and more often, and they are better at spelling and grammar. However, by about ten years old, boys catch up to girls in all areas except spelling and grammar.[57] Girls also show early skill in arithmetic, but by high school boys pass them and continue to be superior through adulthood.[58] Identical patterns obtain in tests of analytic and spatial abilities.[59]

Despite these facts, girls get generally higher scholastic grades than boys in high school and the early years of college, except in mathematics and the sciences. The question, then, is: If the differences in standard tests are nonexistent or only slight, why do girls get higher grades?

Edwin C. Lewis[60] feels there are at least two explanations. First, girls are generally more skilled in their use of language, oral and written, and they have better handwriting. Teachers, therefore, get the impression that the girls know more than the boys. Second, girls present fewer behavioral problems in school; they are socialized to conform, to avoid taking risks, and to be cautious. The result is that teachers like girls better than boys, especially if the teacher is female. (Women teachers are known to favor girl students, to be more sympathetic toward them, to reward them higher, and to give them special attention if necessary.) Even if the teacher is male, boys do not gain an advantage because male teachers grade both sexes lower than female teachers do.

OTHER BEHAVIORAL DIFFERENCES. We have noted that women are superior at verbal skills and men at numerical skills. We also find that men outperform women in mechanical ability, "although such differences do not appear to be innate but instead are due to differential cultural experiences. As they grow older boys are given more encouragement to develop mechanical interests and, as a result, they come to perform better on tests of mechanical knowledge."[61]

Girls excel in tests of perceptual speed; that is, they recognize and respond to small stimulus changes faster and more accurately than boys. Memory seems to depend on what is memorized: girls remember things related to verbal concepts better; boys remember things related to numerical and mechanical things better. Girls are superior in artistic and musical abilities and judgment. Lewis, however, feels that this is because our society does not encourage males to be "artistic" or musical. Because these are regarded as "feminine" traits, boys repress these interests and abilities, especially during adolescence.[62] The reverse is true of problem-solving. Girls tend to believe, because of the way they are socialized, that it is unfeminine to be able to restructure situations to overcome problems. In creativity, the findings are mixed, although usually boys score higher. Lewis contends that female conformity is the explanation. "Peer group pressure operates . . . to discourage the person who is 'different' and . . . such pressure is put more effectively on girls."[63]

In an excellent book, Eleanor Maccoby summarizes sex differences in selected behavior areas. Of twelve studies on aggression, nine reported more aggression in boys; the rest reported no difference. There were twenty-six reports on dependency; six found that boys showed more dependency, eleven found girls more dependent, and nine found no difference. Of the twenty-seven studies of conformity and suggestibility, only two showed the males to be more conforming and suggestible, fourteen showed this to be true of females, and eleven revealed no difference.[64]

These findings are inconsistent and, at the present time, all are subject to challenge. There seem to be some areas in which girls do better and others in which boys excel. However, our society exerts pressure on children to adopt one set of gender roles or the other by exposing them to differential objects and training. Boys become more familiar with mechanical objects; girls are given more domestic objects with which to play. Those tests with a mechanical bent favor males; those requiring social skills favor females. In short, most tests reveal greater *familiarity* with certain kinds of items or behaviors, rather than any innate sex-linked difference.

One proof of the significance of socialization is the results obtained when scores on the Wechsler Intelligence Scale for Children are compared to scores on the Wechsler Intelligence Scale for Adults. Males generally score higher on tests using numbers and spatial relations; females on perception and verbal skills. However, the differences are significant only on the adult tests, after cultural factors have had a longer time to operate on the individuals.

We must conclude, then, that the perceived differences between males and females are rooted in their biology but that they are related even more strongly to the differential ways in which the sexes are socialized, including the encouragement they receive to become familiar with different kinds of information and objects.

DOING SEX

People have always been interested in social behavior. Two thousand years before Christ, Hammurabi proposed a code of ethics to cover every possible social situation and social act. Plato, in *The Republic*, described the perfect society. In the fourteenth century, Ibn Khaldun suggested that social laws are natural and patterned—if we could understand the rhythm of social life, we could control it. Of all social behavior, however, nothing has held so much fascination as human sexual behavior. And yet, there has been very little new in sexual behavior since earliest history. People apparently are not very inventive about their sexual behavior. Nor have there been real attitudinal changes—far from it.

All Western societies, the United States not excepted, have always ideologically repressed sexuality, confining it to marriage, especially for females. Even within marriage there has really been only one acceptable form of activity—sexual intercourse, using the missionary, or male-superior, position. One reason for the persistence of this theme has been the notion of male dominance, shared by most Western societies and extending into the area of sexual activity. This theme stresses sexuality as pleasurable for men and obligatory for women. It is based on the assumption that males have stronger innate sex drives than women and that, in this as in all other areas of life, women should be passive and receptive and men should be aggressive.

The notion that men are sexually more active than women leads quite naturally to the double standard. If females are regarded as sexually disinterested within marriage, then certainly they would be presumed to be disinterested in premarital and extramarital sex. Males, on the other hand, because they supposedly have almost uncontrollable sex needs, are permitted to seek gratification whenever and wherever it is available. Indeed, during some periods of history, men justified the double standard by declaring that they were actually doing their repressed wives a favor by diverting male "animal" impulses.

Sex researchers agree that during the past fifty years there have been great changes in our sexual mores and behavior.[65] These changes can be observed in the reported increased frequency of premarital sex, in the gradual disintegration of the patriarchal ethos, in the progress toward economic equalization of men and women, and in the shift from a view of sex as primarily procreative to a view of sex as recreational, with all the changes that implies.

John W. Petras has given us an excellent explanation for the changing values of sexuality. He notes that members of societies base their acceptance of norms on authority. The authority patterns in our society are rooted in societal interests that have gradually moved from the sacred to the scientific and finally to the secular, so that today sexuality is considered part of everyday life. Petras uses the phrase "sexualization of society" to refer to

> . . . the process whereby sexuality has become integrated into the everyday life patterns of the society–i.e., has become normalized, so that it is no longer treated as a cultural unmentionable and hidden from open discussion. In other words, as sexuality loses its forbidden aspect, it becomes less mysterious and more "understandable" in the eyes of society.[66]

The religious ideology dichotomized the mind and the body, regarding the mind as the center of spirituality; the body, of sexual desires. Thought and deed were always separate—the mind charged with controlling the evil actions of the body. Religion thus taught people to repress sexuality and to feel guilt when sexual thoughts even entered their minds.

Religion lost out to science for several reasons. There has been a general trend in all areas of social life to turn to science, not to religion, for explanations. Second, organized religion weakened its own authority by trying to make people obey out of fear. That is, it refused to meet scientific findings on sexuality on scientific grounds, preferring to continue to preach to people to refrain from unacceptable sexual behavior. Third, religion itself has become more secularized, so that its own explanations are increasingly scientific.[67]

The scientific study of sex is usually thought to have begun with Kinsey's studies in the late 1940s.[68] However, earlier scientists, notably Freud, Krafft-Ebing, and Havelock Ellis, deserve some credit for bringing the study of sex into an atmosphere of greater openness and freedom. Attention, in these early studies, centered only on the individual. Social factors were acknowledged but given little credence, and there was no interest in cross-cultural or subcultural research. Sexual behavior was seen primarily as generated from within the individual, and sexuality was considered to parallel physiological development.

The secular view of sexuality defines the individual not in terms of his personal experiences and psyche but in terms of his society. Human sexuality, like all other human behavior, is regarded as socially determined, although its biological basis is not denied. A great deal of attention is directed to subcultural differences. Deviance from sexual norms is not seen as individual pathology but as a result of failure in the social-value system or in the socialization process. Thus "normality and abnormality in sexual behavior are defined in terms of the values that are relative to a particular society."[69]

The significant differences among the three perspectives on human sexuality are that religion sees sexuality in moral terms, believing that it can be regulated if people can be taught the morally correct attitudes; science considers sexuality in individual terms, seeking to discover and eliminate personal pathologies; and secularity relates the individual to his society and, in general, seeks answers within the cultural framework.

In fact, we can now detect a convergence of the scientific and secular views, retaining the underlying religious coloration. As Petras points out, "The strength of the secular ideology in its role of defining our thinking about sexuality is found in its ability to reinterpret and thus reincorporate the religious and scientific ways of thinking about sexuality into its own context."[70]

The work of Kinsey and of Masters and Johnson can be credited with bringing the study of sex behavior into the public domain, although it is fair to note that there were earlier studies.[71] Kinsey's research centered on asking people to report on their past and present sexual activities. His work permitted readers to identify with the subjects, as previous psychoanalytic studies did not, and it appeared at a time when Americans were apparently ready for it, although the initial reaction was resistance. Sociological research and societal values frequently show a surprising symbiosis, and the Kinsey studies reflect this. People apparently needed to learn more about their sexual proclivities, and Kinsey was able to satisfy that need in an atmosphere of readiness (or near readiness) to accept his work. Just as Freud, Krafft-Ebing, and Ellis reflected the values of their time, so Kinsey reflected his own.

This is even more true of Masters and Johnson.[72] Large numbers of Americans at first reacted negatively to the Kinsey report because it pointed up the discrepancies between our stated sexual norms and our actual sexual behavior and therefore was thought to threaten the moral fabric of society. If Kinsey could be shown to be wrong, the rent could be magically repaired. The Masters and Johnson report, on the other hand, was received more calmly, even though they used a more inflammatory method to learn about sexual behavior. These researchers observed their subjects (all volunteers) during sexual activity. By 1966 Americans were receptive to research that was explicit and personal.

Thus the study of sexual behavior has wended its slow way through the edicts of religiosity, the individual bias of science, and the recognition of social influences by secularity. As the search for knowledge about sexuality continued, each of these three ideologies left a little of itself behind.

Studies today still have a trace of morality and a tendency to trust too much in clinical evidence. There is no doubt, however, that the major thrust is on the relationship between the individual and his or her cultural world. Furthermore, there is more public recognition of the necessity to study sexuality and more public acceptance of sexuality as part of one's everyday life and experience.

The study of sex has continued to grow and, as we have mentioned, is more and more hospitably received. Such research encounters all the problems any social research must deal with, but in addition it has some special pitfalls all its own.

For one thing, samples of subjects cannot avoid being unrepresentative of the population. This was the chief criticism of Kinsey's work, and it is not without justification. Not everyone is willing to discuss his or her sexuality with a stranger; therefore, the tendency is to get subjects who are urban, middle-class, and educated. A true random-probability sample has so far been impossible to obtain in sex research. Thus, what is true of those willing to participate in the studies may well not be true of those who are unwilling to do so.

Secondly, the fashion in what to study changes over time. Until recently, the stress was on sex in marriage and how to improve it. No one talked about extramaritality or even premaritality. From the early 1960s to the present, there has been some interest in sexual deviance, such as homosexuality, pornography, "swinging," and prostitution. This presents special difficulties because the subjects are frequently involved in behavior that is defined as illegal, unethical, or immoral, and, therefore, they are either hard to locate or unwilling to participate. There seems now to be a trend toward studying sexuality wherever it exists—among teen-agers, in marriage, outside of marriage—and in whatever form—"normal" sex, group sex, homosex. In other words, there is a recognition that sexual behavior is characteristic of all social groups and occurs in many diverse ways. It is all grist for the mill, and no forms are undeserving of serious consideration.

Another common problem in social research, especially sex research, is to ascertain when one's subjects are telling the truth. It is not that people habitually lie to investigators, although surely that occurs, but it is not unlikely that they confuse or deceive themselves about their own sexual conduct. Middle-aged people cannot be expected to recall accurately their teen-age sexual experiences. In addition, males, especially young ones, tend to exaggerate their sexual activities, while females tend to minimize theirs.

Lastly, there is the problem of how to measure sexual satisfaction. Kinsey and Masters and Johnson were criticized for using orgasm as the unit of investigation, omitting the emotional aspect of the sexual response. Is orgasm with a loved partner the same as orgasm with a casual acquaintance? No one can really be sure, and so the criticism has some validity, but it is hard to think of another criterion that could be used for objective measurement.

Apparently there is a good deal wrong with the sex lives of many Americans, perhaps the majority. It is difficult to obtain reliable data on the subject, because most people, given our societal norm of a "good" sex life, will give the socially accepted answer. However, it is clear that all is not rosy in the American bedroom. Dr. William Kroger, executive director of the Institute of Comprehensive Medicine in California, wrote, "Sexual frustration is so widespread in our society that it might well be referred to as the 'emotional plague.' "[73] Dr. Kroger describes the psychological, gynecological, and psychosomatic expressions of sexual frustration. Elsworth Baker, editor of the *Journal of Orgonomy*, comments that Dr. Kroger's article

. . . shows clearly how widespread sexual frustration really is and the disastrous effects it can have on both the emotional and physical life of the individual. . . . It is probable that very few ever find a truly satisfying sexual life. Many are completely unaware of this lack and may only be conscious of diminished joy in living, irritability or a growing hostile attitude.[74]

Of the five social scientists who were asked by *Sexual Behavior* if most people are dissatisfied with their sexual life, three gave an unequivocal "yes," and the other two felt that people were dissatisfied only because the mass media created unrealistic expectations.[75]

Simon and Gagnon have made a major contribution to our understanding of what may well be a basic problem in American life—unsatisfying sexuality.[76] Earlier I mentioned that these authors posit a dysjunction between childhood and adolescent sexuality. They consider adolescence to be the real beginning of sexuality, and they point out that males and females pass through very different processes. Males experience very high hormonal inputs at this age and are, therefore, very easily aroused sexually. To relieve this sexual tension, teen-age boys engage in a great deal of masturbatory activity. "This form of introduction to sexuality tends to give rise to a capacity for detached sexual activity, activity where the only sustaining motive is sexual; this may actually be the hallmark of male sexuality in our society."[77] In addition, Simon and Gagnon note, segregation of the sexes is very common, especially among the lower classes, so that the adolescent boy derives his greatest rewards from homosocial relationships. The audience for his heterosexual activities is his male friends rather than the female or females with whom he has sexual relations. Thus young males, especially in the lower classes, engage in casual and exploitative relations with women. They are unlikely to think of females in "romantic" or even friendly terms; rather, they see women as sex objects.

Girls, on the other hand, do not reach the same high hormonal levels during puberty. They are less stimulated by visual erotica in the environment, and society does not encourage them to be sexual. They masturbate less than males. Preadolescent girls, therefore, learn very early how to use sex to achieve nonsexual goals without really understanding what seduction is. Females are socialized to display sexuality but not to use it directly—to be sociosexual.

Males and females, then, are socialized to regard sex and love in opposing ways. Females are trained to be romantic and nonsexual; males, to be sexually active and nonromantic.

> Males—committed to sexuality and relatively untrained in the rhetoric of romantic love—interact with females who are committed to romantic love and relatively untrained in sexuality. Dating and courtship may well be considered processes in which persons train members of the opposite sex in the meaning and content of their respective commitments.[78]

Simon and Gagnon's theory helps to explain a puzzling finding in research on courtship. When girls are in love they increase their sexual activity and are more likely than boys to want premarital coitus. When boys are in love they tend to avoid sexual relations with their girls. Previous investigators explain this by suggesting that girls need the reassurance that love brings into the relationship while boys still think of females as either "good" girls whom one marries or "bad" girls with whom one has sex.[79] The loved one falls in the first category.

Simon and Gagnon contend that this pattern has to do with socialization—specifically, with the masculine tendency to separate love and sex and the feminine need to bring the two concepts together. Each sex needs time to be socialized toward the other. The problem is that the training each sex gives to the other is not always successful. The result is that adult sexuality is frequently unsatisfactory to both members of the dyad. The female continues to seek romance during the sex act; the male can include romance in the sex act only with difficulty. As a result, both may be frustrated.

There are still many contradictions and paradoxes in human sexuality and in research on our sexual behavior and attitudes. Adults continue to be reluctant to give frank information. There is still ignorance and confusion. We persist in stressing sexual "technique" instead of sexual honesty and freedom. We socialize our children in sexually nonproductive ways. We misuse not only our minds and our bodies but our vocabularies as well. *Sex* is an ascribed status determined by the apparatus with which we are born; *sexuality* and *gender roles* are learned (achieved) and encompass the whole self and personality. It may be that sexuality and gender roles are rooted in biology, but cultural factors impinge to the point where men and women reveal vast differences —perhaps to a very unproductive degree.

NOTES

1. O. G. Brim, Jr., "Socialization Through the Life Cycle," in O. G. Brim, Jr., and S. Wheeler, *Socialization After Childhood* (New York: John Wiley, 1966).
2. C. H. Cooley, *Social Organization* (New York: Scribner's, 1909), p. 25.
3. George Herbert Mead, *Mind, Self, and Society* (Chicago: University of Chicago Press, 1934).
4. Robert Linton, *The Study of Man* (New York: Appleton-Century-Crofts, 1936), p. 115.
5. *Ibid.*
6. Jerome Kagan, "Acquisition and Significance of Sex Typing and Sex Role Identity," in *Review of Child Development Research*, vol. 1, eds. Martin L. Hoffman and Lois W. Hoffman (New York: Russell Sage Foundation, 1964), pp. 137–96.
7. William Simon and John H. Gagnon, "On Psychosexual Development," in *Handbook of Socialization Theory and Research*, ed. David A. Goslin (Chicago: Rand McNally, 1969), p. 736.
8. *Ibid.*, p. 733.
9. Ellen Rothchild, "Emotional Aspects of Sexual Development," in *Sexual Development and Behavior*, ed. Anne McCreary Juhasz (Homewood, Ill.: Dorsey Press, 1973), p. 6.
10. *Ibid.*, p. 7.
11. Simon and Gagnon, *op. cit.*, p. 734.
12. *Ibid.*
13. Kagan, *op. cit.*
14. William H. Masters and Virginia E. Johnson, *Human Sexual Response* (Boston: Little, Brown, 1966).
15. J. P. Scott, "*The Naked Ape:* A Zoologist's Study of the Human Animal by Desmond Morris," *Contemporary Psychology* (1970), 15:374–75.
16. R. W. Goy, "Organizing Effects of Androgen on the Behavior of Rhesus Monkeys," in *Proceedings of the London Conference: Endocrines and Human Behavior*, ed. R. P. Michael (1968).
17. S. N. Levine, "Sex Differences in the Brain," *Scientific American* (April 1966), pp. 84–90; and S. N. Levine and R. F. Mullins, Jr., "Hormonal Influences on Brain Organization in Infant Rats," *Science* (1966), 152: 1585–92.
18. Cited in E. S. Valenstein, "Steroid Hormones and the Neuropsychology of Development," in *The Neuropsychology of Development: A Symposium*, ed. R. L. Isaacson (New York: John Wiley, 1968), pp. 1–39.
19. W. C. Young, "The Organization of Sexual Behavior by Hormonal Action During the Prenatal and Larval Periods in Vertebrates," in *Sex and Behavior*, ed. F. A. Beach (New York: John Wiley, 1965), pp. 89–107.
20. W. A. Mason, "The Social Development of Monkeys and Apes," in

Primate Behavior, ed. I. DeVore (New York: Holt, Rinehart, and Winston, 1965), pp. 514–43.

21. B. G. Rosenberg and Brian Sutton-Smith, *Sex and Identity* (New York: Holt, Rinehart, and Winston, 1972), p. 21.
22. R. Krafft-Ebing, *Psychopathia Sexualis* (New York: Physicians and Surgeons Book Co., 1922).
23. D. M. Broverman *et al.*, "Roles of Activation and Inhibition in Sex Differences in Cognitive Abilities," *Psychological Review* (1968), 75: 23–50.
24. H. A. Moss, "Sex, Age, and State as Determinants of Mother-Infant Interaction," *Merrill-Palmer Quarterly* (1967), 13:19–36.
25. S. M. Garn, "Fat, Body Size, and Growth in the Newborn," *Human Biology* (1958), 30:265–80.
26. S. M. Garn and L. C. Clark, Jr., "The Sex Differences in the Basic Metabolic Rate," *Child Development* (1953), 24:215–24.
27. C. A. Knop, "The Dynamics of Newly Born Babies," *Journal of Pediatrics* (1946), 29:721–28.
28. L. P. Lipsitt and N. Levy, "Pain Threshold in the Human Neonate," *Child Development* (1959), 30:547–54.
29. See, for example, Lois B. Murphy *et al.*, *The Widening World of Childhood* (New York: Basic Books, 1962); J. Kagan and H. A. Moss, *From Birth to Maturity* (New York: John Wiley, 1962); and E. S. Schaefer and Nancy Bayley, "Maternal Behavior, Child Behavior, and Their Intercorrelations from Infancy Through Adolescence," *Monographs of the Society for Research in Child Development*, 28:3 (1963).
30. Konrad Lorenz, *On Aggression* (New York: Harcourt, Brace and World, 1966); Robert Ardrey, *African Genesis* (New York: Atheneum, 1966), and *The Territorial Imperative* (New York: Atheneum, 1966); and Lionel Tiger, *Men in Groups* (New York: Random House, 1969).
31. Naomi Weisstein, "Psychology Constructs the Female," in *Woman in Sexist Society*, eds. Vivian Gornick and Barbara K. Moran (New York: Basic Books 1971), p. 218.
32. F. J. Kallman, "Comparative Twin Study of the Genetic Aspects of Male Homosexuality," *Journal of Nervous and Mental Diseases* (1952), 115: 283–98; F. J. Kallman, "Twin and Sibship Study of Overt Male Homosexuality," *American Journal of Human Genetics* (1952), 4:136–46; and F. J. Kallman, "Genetic Aspects of Sex Determination and Sexual Maturation Potentials in Man," in *Determinants of Human Sexual Behavior*, ed. G. Winokur (Springfield, Ill.: Charles C. Thomas, 1963), pp. 5–18.
33. W. S. Schlegel, "Die konstitutionsbiologischen Grundlagen der Homosexualität," *Zeitschrift für menschliche Vererberung: Konstitutionslehre* (1962), 36:341–64.
34. H. Ellis, *Studies in the Psychology of Sex*, vol. 1 (New York: Random House, 1936).
35. J. Bremer, *Asexualization: A Follow-Up Study of 244 Cases* (New York: Macmillan Co., 1959); and J. Money, "Components of Eroticism in Man: The Hormones in Relation to Sexual Morphology and Sexual Desire," *Journal of Nervous and Mental Diseases* (1961), 132:239–48.
36. W. Filler and N. Drezner, "The Results of Surgical Castration in Women Under 40," *American Journal of Obstetrics and Gynecology* (1944), 47:122–24.

56   *Gender and Sex in Society*

37. Rosenberg and Sutton-Smith, *op. cit.*, p. 29.
38. The first study was by J. Money, J. L. Hampson, and J. G. Hampson, "An Examination of Some Basic Sexual Concepts: The Evidence of Human Hermaphroditism," *Bulletin of the Johns Hopkins Hospital* (1955), 97:301–19. The research was summarized in J. L. Hampson and J. G. Hampson, "The Ontogenesis of Sexual Behavior in Man," in *Sex and Internal Secretions*, ed. W. C. Young (Baltimore: Williams and Wilkins, 1961), 2:1401–32.
39. J. L. Hampson, "Determinants of Psychosexual Orientation," in *Sex and Behavior*, ed. F. A. Beach (New York: John Wiley, 1965), p. 125.
40. M. Diamond, "A Critical Evaluation of the Ontogeny of Human Sexual Behavior," *Quarterly Review of Biology* (1965), 40:147–75.
41. Alfred C. Kinsey, Wardell B. Pomeroy, and Paul H. Gebbard, *Sexual Behavior in the Human Female* (Philadelphia: Saunders, 1953), p. 580.
42. Anne Koedt, "The Myth of the Vaginal Orgasm," in *Liberation Now!* (New York: Dell, 1971), p. 315.
43. *Ibid.*, p. 317
44. *Ibid.*, p. 319.
45. Lawrence Kohlberg, "Stage and Sequence: The Cognitive Development Approach to Socialization," in *Handbook of Socialization Theory*, ed. David A. Goslin, *op. cit.*, pp. 347–480.
46. Lawrence Kohlberg, "A Cognitive-Developmental Analysis of Children's Sex-Role Concepts and Attitudes," in *The Development of Sex Differences*, ed. Eleanor E. Maccoby (Stanford, Calif.: Stanford University Press, 1966), p. 82.
47. Margaret Mead, "Cultural Determinants of Sexual Behavior," in *Sex and Internal Secretions*, vol. 2, ed. W. C. Young (Baltimore: Williams and Wilkins, 1961), pp. 1433–80.
48. H. Barry, M. Bacon, and I. L. Child, "A Cross-cultural Survey of Some Sex Differences in Socialization," *Journal of Abnormal and Social Psychology* (1957), 55:327–32.
49. R. G. D'Andrade, "Sex Differences and Cultural Institutions," in Maccoby, *op. cit.*, pp. 173–204.
50. Talcott Parsons and R. F. Bales, *Family Socialization and Interaction Process* (Glencoe, Ill.: Free Press, 1955).
51. B. G. Rosenberg and Brian Sutton-Smith, *Sex and Identity, op. cit.*, p. 87.
52. *Ibid.*, p. 80
53. *Ibid.*, p. 88.
54. L. W. Sontag, C. T. Baker, and Virginia A. Nelson, "Mental Growth and Personality Development: A Longitudinal Study," *Social Research Child Development Monograph*, 23, no. 68 (1958).
55. Katherine P. Bradway and Clare W. Thompson, "Intelligence at Adulthood: A Twenty-five-Year Follow-Up," *Journal of Educational Psychology* (1962), 53:1–14.
56. Matina Horner, "The Motive to Avoid Success and Changing Aspirations of College Women," in *Readings in the Psychology of Women*, ed. Judith M. Bardwick (New York: Harper & Row, 1972), pp. 62–67.
57. Maccoby, *Development of Sex Differences, op. cit.*, p. 26.
58. Norma Haan, "Proposed Model of Ego Functioning: Coping and

Defense Mechanisms in Relationship to I.Q. Change," *Psychological Monographs*, 77, no. 571 (1963).

59. Maccoby, *op. cit.*, p. 26.

60. Edwin C. Lewis, *Developing Women's Potential* (Ames: Iowa State University Press, 1968), p. 47.

61. *Ibid.*, p. 52.

62. *Ibid.*, p. 55.

63. *Ibid.*, p. 56.

64. Maccoby, *op. cit.*, pp. 323–51.

65. See, for example, Robert R. Bell and Michael Gordon, eds., *The Social Dimension of Human Sexuality* (Boston: Little, Brown, 1972); Ira R. Reiss, *The Family System in America* (New York: Holt, Rinehart, and Winston, 1971); and John W. Petras, *Sexuality in Society* (Boston: Allyn and Bacon, 1973).

66. Petras, *ibid.*, p. 10.

67. *Ibid.*, pp. 42–43.

68. Alfred C. Kinsey *et al.*, *Sexual Behavior in the Human Male* (Philadelphia: Saunders, 1948); and Kinsey, 1953, *op, cit.*

69. Petras, *op. cit.*, p. 27.

70. *Ibid.*, p. 44.

71. See, for example, Katherine B. Davis, *Factors in the Sex Life of 2200 Women* (New York: Harper & Bros., 1929); Gilbert V. Hamilton, *A Research in Marriage* (New York: Albert and Charles Boni, 1929); and Robert L. Dickinson and Lura Bean, *A Thousand Marriages* (New York: Century, 1932).

72. W. Masters and V. Johnson, *op. cit.*

73. William S. Kroger, "Sexual Frustration," *Sexual Behavior* (December 1972), p. 41.

74. Elsworth F. Baker, "Our Sex-Negating Culture," *Sexual Behavior* (December 1972), p. 46.

75. *Sexual Behavior* (December 1971), pp. 52–55.

76. Simon and Gagnon, *op. cit.*, pp. 733–52.

77. *Ibid.*, p. 743.

78. *Ibid.*, p. 746.

79. Ira R. Reiss, *op. cit.*, p. 144; Winston W. Ehrmann, *Premarital Dating Behavior* (New York: Holt, Rinehart, and Winston, 1959), p. 134.

3

Love Thine Enemy:
Male-Female Relationships

Home Sweet Home

It seems hardly necessary to describe the "proper" roles of men and women in the home. Everyone knows perfectly well what they are because most of us have watched our parents enact them and have, indeed, enacted them ourselves.

The conventional pattern for a woman in our society is to enter into a monogamous marriage during her early twenties, live in a nuclear family, and limit her interests and concerns to her husband and children. Even if necessity compels a married woman to work, she must still assume the primary responsibility for domestic chores.

This is a pretty narrow existence, but the man also lives in a restricted world. He also enters into a monogamous marriage, taking on the responsibility of supporting his wife and children. A husband's routine is almost as circumscribed as a wife's, although he certainly has a wider range of career choices and social contacts. While we speak of the "feminine mystique," we must recognize that there is also a "masculine mystique." Women are defined in terms of reproduction and nurturance; men, in terms of protection and occupation. There is a hidden assumption that men and women are irrevocably different. But the truth is that our gender roles are not innate and God-given, nor are they necessarily irrevocable. Society creates gender roles, and society can alter them. Recently a tremendous amount of attention has been given to women's roles, but men's roles have been treated only in terms of reaction to changes in feminine roles. Actually, the roles of both sexes are in transition. Both men and women are

58

confused and troubled, not only because the meanings of "masculine" and "feminine" are in flux but also because men and women today are unsure of how to interact with each other. Before talking about alterations, we will examine closely the traditional roles of men and women—man the provider and father, woman the homemaker and mother.

THE HOMEMAKER

What does it mean to be a wife in contemporary American society? First of all, a wife is a homemaker. Homemaking is defined as an occupation, but it is certainly a peculiar one. For example, it takes more time than other so-called full-time jobs—it is a 24-hour-a-day, seven-day-a-week job. Furthermore, it is a nonpaying job, the remuneration depending solely on the generosity of the employer-husband. Third, short of divorce, it is almost impossible to quit or be fired.

Whether or not they work outside the home, most married women are still primarily engaged in housework. And there are 30 million American women who are classified as "nonworking," "housewife," or "married, not in the labor force."

Ann Scott suggests that the following mock advertisement is an accurate description of the job of housewife:

Help Wanted

REQUIREMENTS: Intelligence, good health, energy, patience, sociability. SKILLS: at least 12 different occupations. HOURS: 99.6 per week. SALARY: None. HOLIDAYS: None (will be required to remain on stand-by 24 hours a day, seven days a week). OPPORTUNITIES FOR ADVANCEMENT: None (limited transferability of skills acquired on the job). JOB SECURITY: None (trend is toward more layoffs, particularly as employee approaches middle age). Severance pay will depend on the discretion of the employer. FRINGE BENEFITS: Food, clothing, and shelter generally provided, but any additional bonuses will depend on financial standing and good nature of the employer. No health, medical, or accident insurance, no Social Security or pension plan.[1]

On the basis of the value of work on the current labor market, this job, according to the economists at Chase Manhattan Bank, was worth in 1972 a minimum of $257.53 a week.[2] These economists demonstrated that the homemaker's activities can be classified under twelve occupational titles: nursemaid, housekeeper, cook, dishwasher, laundress, food buyer, chauffeur, gardener, maintenance worker, seamstress, dietitian, and practical nurse. The Bank report concludes that if housework were included in calculating the Gross National Product, it would raise the GNP approximately 35 per cent.

Theodore Caplow suggests that housewifery is devalued in our credential-conscious society in part because it is open to all and sundry. The housewife need have no special training; she can be of any age, race, or religion; and there is no standard of performance. The housewife is not respected or dignified in her occupation. To be a housewife is to be infantilized, condescended to, and patronized.[3]

Scott, protesting the unfair treatment of, and attitudes toward, housewives, offers suggestions for abolishing the notion of "woman's work." She argues that husbands and wives should have equal rights to all earned income, regardless of who does the earning. (In forty-two states, a man's salary and his property are considered his own, and his wife has no legal claim to either. A married woman receives only what her husband wishes to give her, out of the goodness of his heart.) Alternatively, the housewife could receive a salary, paid directly by her husband or by his employer. Not only would a salary have practical monetary worth, but it would be a reflection of the housewife's economic value to her family and a boost to her ego.

Most young girls, when they marry, are remarkably ignorant of what being a homemaker involves. Courses in home economics are of dubious value, so most learning is on-the-job training. Furthermore, homemaking is an occupation with so many diversified responsibilities that it is difficult to plan one's time in order to reserve some for oneself. Homemaking also requires little skill and provides few rewards. Most women of only moderate intelligence can perform these tasks mechanically. For most women, there is only slight internal satisfaction in homemaking and no external recognition, such as salary increases or promotion, which other occupations award. Finally, homemaking is a solitary job with little social contact except perhaps at the Laundromat or the supermarket.

When homemaking is a woman's only role, she may have a problem of overdependency on her husband. This may take the form of *social dependency*. Adult women require adult companionship, and this is hard to find during the day for the housewife because of the varied demands on her attention and time. When her husband comes home at night she is likely to want social interaction—someone to talk to. He, on the other hand, has been interacting all day and probably wants peace and quiet in the evening. Thus, when husbands and wives come together at night they have different needs, which can cause marital strain. She wants to interact; he wants to be left alone. This can be very destructive.

Another kind of dependency is *economic*. Nonemployed housewives are traditionally dependent on their husbands for all financial needs. It is not easy for one adult to ask another for everything, even personal expenses. In addition, this kind of economic dependency perpetuates the myth that the male plays the more important role in the marriage and the welfare of the family depends on him.

A third kind of dependency is based on the wife's lack of separate *social status*. Her primary status is that of her husband's wife. Her position in the wider social hierarchy is determined by his. In this sense, the housewife is not a real person, because she is identifiable only through her husband.

The homemaker, then, is engaged in a full-time (in the realest possible sense!) unpaid occupation with few rewards or satisfactions. She has little time that is truly her own and is dependent on her husband for companionship, money, and social position.

The Provider

The typical male role of provider is in counterpoint to the female role of homemaker. Both are task-oriented; both carry the weight of serious responsibility. But the female's orientation is present-directed; the male's is future-directed, especially among middle-class males.

The husband's primary obligation is to provide for his wife

and his children. It is in work that the male in our society is supposed to find his most important source of satisfaction, his selfhood, his identity, just as a woman is supposed to find these things in her home. Thus, the husband must have a job, and the job must be stable and must promise security and advancement.

There is one important class difference in how the role of provider is perceived. In the upper classes, the male is given recognition for the material things he can provide and for the prestige of his occupation. In the lower classes, the stress is on the material things only, and there is little interest in whether he earns the money as a truck driver or as a carpenter.[4] In any social class, the amount of money the husband brings into the home is of great importance and is closely correlated with marital happiness. One study showed that of three crucial factors—education, occupation, and income—income is most highly associated with marital satisfaction, "probably because it has an independent and very concrete impact on a couple's daily life. Other aspects of social status count for relatively little if the family's income is not adequate to its needs."[5]

Because the man's chief social role is his occupation, he is away from his home for the major part of every working day. That he and his wife are separated a good deal of the time is a relatively new development in our society. In earlier times men and women worked on the land or in the small shop together, but now the wife stays at home and the man goes to the office or factory. In short, the male's most important function[6] in relation to his family—that of provider—is performed outside the home.

This dichotomizing of the world is as important for a man as it is for a woman. Generally, the two sides of the man's life are kept distinctly separate. Furthermore, the world of work and the world of home can have very different levels of importance in his mind. The man who strongly identifies with his occupation may give it the major portion of his interest and attention.

> It appears that given a choice between filling his occupational role or his family role, a professional man will choose his occupation. Yet the man is generally expected to put his family roles above all other roles *if* there is a choice. But if it appears necessary for him to pursue his occupational role over his family role for the good of the family, then that is not only socially acceptable but often

socially applauded. . . . We would suggest that often the professional man who says he doesn't want to work late or he doesn't want to make a trip is rationalizing his actions to his family (and possibly himself) by blaming his job.[7]

When a woman marries she is implicitly saying that she thinks her future husband will prosper, so a wife has good reason to be cooperative and to help her husband in his occupational pursuits. Blood and Wolfe devised a typology of the ways in which wives contribute to their husbands' careers. The collaborative wife works in partnership with her husband in a family business, thus directly contributing to his success. The working wife supplements the family income and thereby allows her husband latitude in his work. The supportive wife supplies the background music, so to speak, by being a good listener, entertaining people who can help her husband, and generally bolstering him emotionally. The peripheral wife, usually found in the working class, is barely involved in her husband's job.[8]

The husband's occupation, then, is the primary role in his life, and this primacy has a curious effect on his other major role, that of father. A man's occupation endows him with an aura of importance because the family's social status and well-being are dependent on him, so that the other family members revolve around him as satellites. On the other hand, the attention he devotes to his work diminishes the attention he can give to his family roles, so that the wife makes many of the decisions in the family without consulting him, and the wife and children engage in many activities that exclude him. In one sense, then, the male as provider looms large as a figure of prestige and authority in his home; in another sense, the provider is alienated and apart from his family. It must be difficult indeed to reconcile the two positions.

Parental Roles

Until the past ten or fifteen years, parenthood was viewed as indispensable for self-fulfillment. For a woman, motherhood was regarded as her most rewarding status; for a man, fatherhood was one proof of masculinity.

LeMasters illustrates the changed attitude toward parenthood, mentioning several folk beliefs surrounding it. (A folk belief is one that is widely held and romanticized but is not supported by facts.) Here are some of the myths LeMasters lists: Children are sweet and cute; children will turn out well if they have "good" parents; girls are harder to rear than boys; parents were better in the good old days; modern medicine, psychology, and technology have made childrearing easier; two parents are always better than one; children improve a marriage; all married people should have children; and childless couples are frustrated and unhappy.[9]

According to LeMasters, scientific research has disproved most of these folk beliefs, but they still serve a useful societal purpose. All societies require that the population reproduce itself, and these notions about parenthood powerfully encourage young men and women to assume the important status of parent so that society will continue. Now, however, more realistic ideas about parenthood are becoming prevalent; many young people are apparently recognizing that parents, especially mothers, pay a huge price when they have children. Because they are indeed quite different, the role expectations of the two parents can be examined separately.

THE MOTHER. Alice Rossi[10] notes that motherhood in our society is a full-time job because technology has freed the woman from many household tasks and modern contraception has allowed her to have a smaller family. Mothering one or two children has become central in most married women's lives.

Many women, when they become mothers, focus on this aspect of the wifely role, assigning the homemaker and husband's-companion roles secondary status.[11] Lopata interviewed 299 women and found that they spent almost all of their waking hours with their children. Lopata believes that this is partly because of the child orientation of our society. We tend to focus on our children and to explain many of our actions and decisions in terms of the children. A family moves to the suburbs, a woman leaves her job, mother joins the PTA or a scout organization . . . for the children. American women like to think that they are doing things for their children's good.

Mothers spend so much time with their children for yet another reason. Childrearing is more difficult today. In the past there were unchanging, traditional ways of bringing up children; today we are inundated with imperatives from psychology, sociology, medicine, and so forth. Women spend incredible amounts of time reading, discussing, listening to, and trying to understand the vast number of theories that delineate the problems (some of which mothers never even knew they had!) and the solutions. Current psychological theory states that children do not have fixed personalities at birth. In an earlier time it was believed that very little could change a child's personality, talents, or character, so that mothers were not, as they are today, held responsible for a child's psychological well-being.

Another explanation of the modern stress on motherhood is the heavy responsibility society places on the woman. In more traditional societies fathers, grandparents, and other relatives assumed more active roles. Now the mother is isolated with her children for the major part of the day; if something goes wrong, she is blamed. Lopata expresses it thus:

> Responsibility for the health and welfare, the behavior and ability of the child is basically unshared. The father is usually not held accountable for what happens to the children, because "he is not home much of the time." The former extended kinship group which lived under one roof or quite nearby has dropped away, each member being geographically isolated and able to provide only stopgap help, and this only after a lapse of time and with no sharing of responsibility for the outcome. The community within which the mother is functioning may easily be heterogeneous: indifferent to her child, hostile, or ostentatiously carrying out different child-rearing procedures. She then lacks . . . environmental support for what she does and what she demands of the child and of their relation. She faces nothing but criticism and possible conflict with her offspring as he learns culturally different patterns.[12]

If time is a problem for the full-time housewife, who tends in a mysterious way to satisfy Parkinson's Law—"work expands to fill the available time"—it is an even greater problem after children are born. Of course, mothers use their time in different ways, depending on individual differences in efficiency, amount of help, spacing and number of children, and other factors, but most mothers complain that their work is never done and that they have no time that is exclusively their own.

Biologically a female becomes a mother when she gives birth to a child. The social role of mother is a different story. Like all roles and statuses, it comprises learned behavior, and as females grow up they internalize the patterned behavior with the associated rights and obligations that are attached to the social status of a mother. These statuses, which are familiar to most people, have associated roles that are very well known and generally expected. Everyone "knows" the role of the doctor, and everyone expects certain behaviors from him. The same is true of "mother"—we know and she knows how she is to act.

Most American girls are socialized to want to become mothers, and all but 17 per cent of American women achieve the goal.[13] Probably few realize beforehand just how great a difference the event will make in their lives forever after.

Lopata's subjects pointed out several sets of consequences. One is an identity crisis—a feeling that the birth of a baby, with its attendant constraints, has resulted in a loss of self. Komarovsky[14] noted that this consequence is especially real for women who had careers before becoming mothers, although it is not confined to them. Lopata says the identity crisis is a "multifaceted thing. The care of infants calls for repetitious actions, isolation from interaction and intellectual stimulation, and limitation of occasions to display a wide range of personality behaviors in a variety of social contexts which show the uniqueness of the self."[15]

A second consequence of becoming a mother is a feeling of change in self—an increase in maturity and ability. A mother is an adult, adulthood being itself a new status. Third, Lopata's subjects felt that they were severely tied down by motherhood. Life became limited to the world of infants' needs and demands. Yet most of them accepted this state of affairs and were reassured because they felt it was temporary; they would be released when their children were older. A fourth consequence was simply the addition of work and responsibilities, for which several subjects felt unprepared. This often resulted in a lowered standard of household cleanliness and a diminution of adult social activities.

One of the most important consequences of motherhood is a modification in the role of companion to husband. Georg Simmel was one of the first sociologists to show how the introduction of a third person affects a dyad. He observed that each member of a triad operates as an intermediary between the other two—either uniting or separating them. The mother and child can effectively shut out the father or draw him into their circle, just as the mother and father can shut out or draw in the child. But, Simmel warns, "no matter how close a triad may be, there is always the occasion on which two of the three members regard the third as an intruder."[16]

Even during pregnancy, the wife is likely to become introspective as her body changes and to be less interested in her husband. After the infant's birth, she is frequently frightened by the demands of her new status and even more inclined to exclude her husband. In addition, a baby can be imperious, neither aware of nor willing to concede to the sexual or social needs of the parents.

Lopata concludes that "childrearing, as carried on by the new mother, produces more traditional feminine-masculine role segregation than practically any other social relationship in modern American middle-class life."[17] Furthermore, she found, the birth of the first child causes the greatest discontinuity of personality for American women, unless (as seldom happens) the new mother immediately becomes involved in full-time, outside-the-home activity.

THE FATHER. The father's role is decidedly secondary to the mother's. Most American men consider the paternal role peripheral to the provider role and feel that if they discharge their financial obligations to their children they are "good" fathers. Furthermore, we know less about the paternal role; sociologists do not study fathers anywhere near so frequently as they study mothers.[18] Even when they do look at the role of fathers, they do so indirectly, usually obtaining the information from mothers. Such studies are examples of poor methodology. For instance, in one study of childrearing patterns 379 mothers were interviewed and not one father —as if fathers had nothing to do with childrearing.[19] Another study, which used the word *parent* in the book title, also interviewed mothers only.[20] It is as if the investigators think that fathers are not very important and that "mother" is the equivalent of "parent."

This attitude toward fathers, shared by laymen and social scientists, is in a sense self-generating. We see father as less significant than mother, and, therefore, we treat him that way. In turn, he becomes even less meaningful. Fatherhood is a marginal role because men see themselves as first of all breadwinners. Nevertheless, society holds certain expectations about paternal behavior, and the father is rewarded if he satisfies them and punished if he does not.

Leonard Benson isolated two broad aspects of fatherhood—each containing a group of paternal roles that fulfill needs in all societies. In what he calls the *survival* dimension, the father sustains his child physically; in the *expressive* dimension, the father provides security and pleasure.[21]

The survival dimension can be subdivided into the biological and the social. Biologically, both the society and the family need the father for reproductive purposes. In earlier times, societies encouraged this aspect of the male status, but maintaining the population is hardly a problem any longer. Indeed, in many parts of the world, overpopulation is the problem.

Reproduction is the job of the biological father, who may or may not be the social father, although he almost always is in the United States. There is nothing biological, genetic, or instinctive about the role of social father, which is more complex and difficult to perform than mere paternity. Social fatherhood is a societal invention and must be socially enforced. "Fathers in our society (or any other society) are almost entirely dependent on proper socialization and positive induction into the role of parent if they are to perform this responsibility adequately."[22]

As social father, the male parent is expected—indeed, required by law—to see that the child is physically cared for. It is in this area that the role of breadwinner transcends all else. Frequently mothers today contribute, sometimes equally, to the family purse, but the heaviest responsibility remains the father's.

As the authority figure in the family, the father is also obligated to teach his children proper behavior, values, and attitudes, and to help them internalize these things. Society helps him in this function, because it grants him power to enforce the rules he feels necessary. His physique also helps. He is generally larger, stronger, and heavier than anyone else in the house. He has the deepest, loudest voice. These attributes help him to control his children and to maintain his authority over them.

Benson notes that fathers are also expected to pass on personal qualities and skills that will help their children to survive when they are adult. Children imitate, and fathers are supposed to serve as role models for those traits that the society considers worth imitating, such as honesty, attentiveness to work, and the like.

Of the expressive dimension, Benson writes, "The father's expressive 'work' includes such activities as providing bodily comfort to the children, showing love and respect for them, playing with them, and giving their lives a sense of immediate significance."[23] As was pointed out earlier, the mother is usually considered the most important expressive parent. Nevertheless, most authorities feel that the father's expressions of love and security are very necessary in the child's life, especially after infancy. Fathers encourage young children to enlarge their worlds—to explore, examine, question, test. Fathers may not provide the routine, daily loving acts—that is the job of mothers. But they can show love by offering guidance, by providing encouragement, by acting as confidant.

Sociologists believe that the expressive dimension of the father's role is becoming more important than the survival dimension.[24] It is not that the father is no longer charged with protecting his children but, rather, that there is now more time for a man to show love and more societal acceptance of him in this role. The family has come to be considered a refuge from the cold, impersonal outside world, and the father's expressive role has been enlarged because he is likely to be one of only two adults immediately available to the children. In an agricultural society, there were many more loving adults around; now the child usually has only a mother and a father in the same home.

In summary, one dimension of the paternal role is that of survival. Biologically the father is expected to reproduce; socially he is expected to protect his child physically and prepare him or her for a future status as an adult. The father also serves his child as a role model, teacher, authority figure, supporter, and mediator between the child and the society. The second dimension of the male parental role is expressive. Today more than ever, fathers are expected to be loving, pleasure-giving, warm, comforting figures in their children's lives.

The Husband-Wife Relationship

Many sociologists have noted that the role of wife in relation to that of husband is a reflective one. That is, a wife reflects her husband's social status and his expectations. She accommodates herself to her husband because our society rates the husband's role as the more important one. The life of the family is expected to revolve around his needs, his work, his choice of recreation.* Most wives manage their households according to their husbands' schedules. If the husband comes home from work at 6:00, dinner is served at 6:15. If he dislikes lamb chops, lamb chops are rarely if ever served. If he gets his vacation in July, the family goes away in July. If he prefers the seashore to the mountains, they go to the seashore. Often the couple's friends are the husband's colleagues, or clients, or customers, and, if the husband voices dislike for a couple, it is generally dropped from the list of friends. If a husband prefers blue to green, blue will be the prevailing color in the house and in the wife's wardrobe.

Why do women accept this subordinate position? The Bems[25] posit that Americans subscribe to a "nonconscious ideology" perfectly expressed in the New Testament: "For a man . . . is the image and the glory of God; but the woman is the glory of the man. For the man is not of the woman, but the woman of the man. Neither was the man created for the woman, but the woman for the man."

In spite of the lip-service we pay to equality, the idea that women are basically inferior to men continues to prevail in our society. This can be seen even among radical young people. During the 1968 student rebellion at Columbia University, for example, when militant students from the radical left occupied the

---

* I once heard a middle-aged divorced woman remark that since her divorce she has become a multiathlete. Every time she begins dating a new man she has to take up his sport, so that now she can play golf and tennis, she can ice-skate and swim, and she understands the intricacies of football and baseball.

buildings, the males immediately assigned domestic tasks to the women among them, keeping the decision-making tasks for themselves. The coeds objected, but, as the Bems point out, they were not typical of young women in our society. Most females would have accepted the role into which they were cast by the males.

The Bems' theory was supported by a study conducted by Philip Goldberg.[26] He asked women college students to evaluate a group of professional articles from six fields, three each by men and women. The articles were placed in two sets of booklets with the names of the authors changed so that the same article was written by a "male" in one booklet and by a "female" in another. Goldberg found that, when an article was attributed to a female, it was rated lower than when it was attributed to a male. This finding held whether the field was a "masculine" one, such as law or city planning, or a "feminine" one, such as elementary school education or dietetics. In other words, the women students evaluated male professionals higher than female in every area of endeavor. The Bems commented:

> We repeated this experiment informally in our own classrooms and discovered that male students show the same implicit prejudice against female authors that Goldberg's female students showed. Such is the nature of a nonconscious ideology![27]

A "nonconscious ideology" that supports the notion that males are superior to females is itself based on the idea that biological differences between men and women lead to unalterable psychological differences and differences in talents and abilities. The basic assumption underlying this ideology is that these differences between the sexes and the social inequality that results are inherent because they are rooted in biological differences. Furthermore, the social institutions that structure and support the inequality are just because they follow the "natural" differences. It is proper that the wife's position, life-style, and activities are subordinate to her husband's and revolve around his needs, interests, and wishes.

GENDER ROLES AND OTHER SOCIAL INSTITUTIONS

To this point we have been looking at the relationship between the sexes on a personal level. Most people, as they interact with each other, accept the stereotyped image of how men and women should behave. They do this because they have been well socialized within the family to internalize the prevailing concepts of masculinity and femininity. The family, however, is only one social institution and is related to others, all of which interact with, influence, and change each other. All these institutions play a part in stereotypical gender-role behavior.

Language

Several studies of language patterns indicate that males and females have different speech and writing habits. Adjectives and nouns, for example, are more common in females' language use than in males'; on the other hand, men use more verbs.[28] The sexes also grammatically construct their sentences differently. Men demonstrate a greater interest in movement and action; women a greater involvement with psychological states.[29]

The important point is not, of course, that each sex uses language distinctively. Rather, the differential use of language demonstrates that men and women have different realities, that they think differently, hold different sets of values, and communicate on different levels.

Furthermore, the English language itself reveals a masculine bias. Miller and Swift, who analyzed the language from this point of view,[30] found that words defining behavior as rational, brave, sensible, or intelligent are associated with masculinity, while "feminine" words are temperamental, emotional, inconsistent, or illogical. For example, "sissy," from the word "sister," indicates timidity; "buddy," from "brother," connotes closeness and friendship.

Furthermore, the innumerable generic terms we use when we mean "people"—"man," "mankind," "social man," "average man," and so forth—according to Schneider and Hacker are commonly used in social-science textbooks but rarely by students. The image evoked in students' minds by the term "economic man," for example, is that of a male, not of both men and women,[31] and they continue to think of "man" as the prototypical human being.

The sexism in our language is not to be taken lightly. It permeates our thought and vitally influences the way in which American youngsters develop and learn and use vocabulary. Lynn Sherr,[32] for example, studied the teaching kits widely used in elementary schools and found that vowels are sex-typed as feminine because they are weak and dependent on the masculine consonants. Thus children early internalize the notion that girls (vowels) cannot survive without boys (consonants).

The first dictionary for children that attempted to deal with sexist language, published by the American Heritage Publishing Company,[33] contains approximately thirty-five thousand words commonly used by American children in schoolbooks. As the editors worked on this pioneering task, they discovered, to their astonishment, that, whereas among themselves adults refer to "children," they say "boy" or "girl" when addressing youngsters—thus constantly reminding them of their sex difference. Textbooks refer to males and females in a ratio of 4 to 1. As the numbers of school boys and girls are almost equal, the use of the masculine pronoun is obviously generic—supposedly referring to both sexes. Furthermore, "mother" occurs much more frequently in children's books than "father"; "wife," three times as often as "husband"; sons are referred to as children of a male parent and daughters as children of a female parent. More uncles than aunts are mentioned. "Youth" is defined in some textbooks as "that time between childhood and manhood." One can see that the masculine is considered the more important sex, except in the home—the only place for women.

In addition, it was noted that the different sexes in these books held different sets of values and engaged in different activities. Boys drove fast cars, raced, went to Mars in spaceships. Girls were concerned with *being,* not doing. They were "lovely," "beautiful," had "feminine voices."

As she worked on this nonsexist dictionary, Alma Graham began systematically to note how women and men were labeled. A "gentle" woman was "feminine"; a "gentle" man, "effeminate." A weeping man was "womanish"; a woman in uniform was "mannish." Our language officially takes note of what we consider deviance: the "woman" doctor, the "male" nurse, "feminine" logic (which is really illogic). Then there is the "exclusionary tactic," when the person addressed is automatically considered to be a male. "Dear Sir" is the accepted salutation to business firms. On applications for loans: "Full Name—Wife's Name"; "Employer—Wife's Employer."

The editors decided to equalize the balance in their dictionary. In the examples given, females are presented as active and adventurous and males as occasionally gentle and vulnerable. Examples: "She had *brains*." "She is a woman of political *principles*." "She made a *name* for herself." "She was *determined* to win." "He was striving to attain mastery over his *emotions*." "His resolve began to *waver*." "Tears *welled* up in his eyes." In short, the sex pronouns were used equally, implying the choices both boys and girls could have.

The editors of *The American Heritage School Dictionary* acknowledge that their work is only a beginning. A dictionary is one thing, but it does not begin to reach the number of children textbooks can influence. "As writers and teachers and parents, we have an obligation now to weigh our words, to examine them, and to use them with greater care. Children of both sexes deserve equal treatment, in life and in language, and we should not offer them anything less."[34]

Literature and history books are also sexist. Most of the authors children read are men; the heroes are men; the women are background. Famous women are mentioned only peripherally, if at all, in history books. The role women have played in our national story is minimized or presented in a sex-biased way. In short, the words we use and the way we use them tend to devalue women and overvalue men, so that we perpetuate the sexism in our society every day merely by speaking to each other or by reading the daily newspaper.

Medical Science

Research indicates that medical doctors treat women patients differently from men, tending to patronize them and to minimize their symptoms.[35] In addition, women are less likely than men to be offered physical therapy, because the rate of success is considered to be lower for females.[36]

No medical specialty is more sexist than the mental-health area. With the exception of the feminist therapists, psychiatrists, psychoanalysts, and psychologists define male mental health in more socially acceptable terms than female mental health. Women, to be judged "healthy," must be dependent, submissive, and otherwise "feminine." Men, to be considered "well adjusted," must be self-actuating, high achievers, in control of their lives. When women are successful in the business or professional world, they are "deviant" and may feel obliged to go to considerable lengths to "prove" how feminine they are. They tend to denigrate their professional roles and overstress their "feminine" roles. They are concerned that they should not earn more money or gain higher rank or become more famous than their husbands or lovers.[37] In other words, for women to be considered "healthy" or "normal" according to the mental-health therapists' definition, they must exaggerate characteristics that are either childish or of secondary societal value. Women who are successful in any role other than that of housewife and mother must pretend to be less than they are or accept the stigma attached. "Healthy" men, on the other hand, exhibit the characteristics of adults.

Psychotherapy thus acts as a social-control mechanism to ensure that women stay in their place and behave in stereotypical "feminine" ways. The purpose of therapy for a woman is to learn to accept herself as a "woman," not as a person; to rid herself of all "masculine" traits and ambitions; and to find joy in being a second-class human being.

Inge Broverman and her associates studied seventy-nine mental-health clinicians to test the hypothesis that "clinical judgments about the traits characterizing healthy, mature individuals differ as a function of the sex of the person judged. Furthermore, these differences in clinical judgments are expected to parallel the stereotypic sex-role differences."[38] The investigators conclude:

> The clinicians' concepts of a healthy mature man do not differ significantly from their concepts of a healthy adult. However, the clinicians' concepts of a mature healthy woman do differ significantly from their adult health concepts. . . .
> Acceptance of an adjustment notion of health, then, places women in the conflictual position of having to decide whether to exhibit those positive characteristics considered desirable for men and adults, and thus have their "femininity" questioned; that is, be

deviant in terms of being a woman; or to behave in the prescribed feminine manner, accept second-class adult status, and possibly live a lie to boot.[39]

Law

It would take several volumes to discuss and document all the types of discrimination against women in the law. For example, prostitutes are frequently arrested; their patrons, rarely.[40] Women cannot be prosecuted for rape; however, when a woman claims to have been raped, her word is frequently doubted, and her character often assaulted.[41] Many states do not allow women to sue their husbands for loss of sexual relations or love, on the ground that wives are their husbands' property.[42] Women, once arrested, are treated more paternalistically than men, much in the way juveniles are treated, and thus are more often tried informally by a judge instead of a jury, which can prove detrimental to women[43] because they are being judged only by one male.

Women are more frequently given indeterminate jail sentences than men, on the theory that they are more quickly rehabilitated. Yet this practice often means that women remain in prison longer than men convicted of the same crime.[44] Treatment in jails is also sex-stereotyped. Men are trained for a vocation; women, for low-paying, unskilled work, such as housework.[45] Nagel and Weitzman found that juries with more men on them tend to give larger awards of damages to men than to women. Because most juries contain more men than women, women generally are discriminated against.[46]

The issue of women's surnames is an interesting one. Many married women today are retaining their father's name, with troublesome results that are currently being considered in the courts. Married women have been refused the right to vote under their original names, to receive a driver's license or a passport, to receive a government payroll check (on the ground of "administrative inconvenience"), to run for office, to register a car. All this is in the process of change, so that at the time of this writing it is much easier for women to use their original names than it was as recently as 1972.

The fact is that, according to the English common law, which underlies the American legal system, a woman has the right, but is not compelled, to take her husband's name when she marries. "Any person, including married women, minors and bastards, may adopt whatever name she/he pleases if the name is adopted for an honest and nonfraudulent purpose. A person is not bound to retain the name given her/him at birth but can change her/his name without going through legal proceedings."[47]

The Lucy Stone League, named for the famous suffragist who retained her maiden name when she married Henry Blackwell in 1855, began in the 1920s its fight to help women keep their names. The League was quick to point out that, except in the state of Hawaii, there is no law requiring a woman to assume her husband's name. However, because it is traditional to do so, when a woman attempts to retain her own surname, the reaction is often confusion and anger.

At this writing there is pending in Wisconsin a bill that provides that the marriage certificate allow a choice of surnames for both the wife and the husband. The husband and wife may select either of their names for both spouses; they may elect to retain their own names; they may combine their two names; or they may assume any new name they choose. This bill does not help women who are already married and want to reassume their father's name, but it is a step in the right direction.

I have mentioned only very few of the areas in the law in which women are discriminated against. There is hope for improvement if the Equal Rights Amendment (ERA) is ratified by the states. While the ERA cannot abolish sex discrimination at one stroke, it will go a long way toward preventing government, at least, from abridging the rights of individuals on the basis of sex. Ann Scott, Legislative Vice-President of the National Organization for Women, points out certain legal problems for women that are likely to be resolved by ERA.[48] ERA will probably reduce discrimination against women in colleges and universities in the form of restrictions on enrollment, scholarships, and fellowships. Females will get an equal chance to be accepted and to receive financial assistance.

Scott expects many complex changes in family law. Alimony will be determined by need and the ability to pay, which means that men may be awarded alimony—a rare occurrence today. Child custody will no longer go automatically to the mother.

Women will gain control over their earnings and property; they will retain their maiden names when they marry if they want to do so; and, finally, they will have the same right as men to choose their own legal residence. ERA will make it easier for women to sign mortgages and leases, start businesses, take out loans, and obtain credit—all of which are difficult at present in many states.

Scott, of course, strongly favors the passage of the Equal Rights Amendment:

> By confirming women's equality under the law, by upholding women's right to choose [their] place in society, the Equal Rights Amendment can only enhance the status of traditional women's occupations. For these would become positions accepted by women as equals, not roles imposed on them as inferiors.
>
> Most of all, the ERA will create a moral atmosphere of equality and justice. For the first time in this country's history, women will know that the Constitution applies to them.[49]

Religion

It is interesting to note that in the King James version of the Bible, women are called by three different names. Genesis 2.22 says, "She shall be called 'woman.'" Genesis 3.20: "And Adam called his wife 'Eve.'" And Genesis 5.2: "Male and female created He them and blessed them and called their name 'Adam.'" Thus, from earliest time, there has been confusion about female identity—is she to be known as "woman," "Eve," or only as part of her husband, as "Adam"?

Almost all religions are patriarchal. The Supreme Being is always a male; women are usually not admitted to the clergy; and many religions restrict their participation in religious services. Because religion is important in the lives of many people and because it permeates our lives and affects our attitudes and behaviors, women would like to see the ideals of sexual equality accepted by organized religion so that religion can become more relevant to women's lives.

An organization of Catholic women, St. Joan's International Alliance, has as its primary goal getting women into the priesthood. They feel that, with the possible exception of orthodox Jewish women, Catholic women are the most oppressed of all, not even in control of their households. Some St. Joan's members even favor abortion; others reject the church's stance that women are like children; but they concentrate their attention on getting into the priesthood.

Marriage

In this chapter the personal interaction between men and women and the social forces that structure and perpetuate inequalities in that relationship have been discussed. Change is needed and has probably begun in most institutions. The one institution that could give change a big boost is marriage. Some of the early feminists tried to supply a new perspective on marriage by writing their own egalitarian marriage contracts. Today the practice is growing popular among certain groups of educated women and men. *Ms* magazine[50] recently reprinted one such contract. The highlights of that agreement, between Harriett Mary Cody and Harvey Joseph Sadis, follow:

1. Harriett retains her own name after marriage because the couple feel that the concept of ownership is implied when a woman takes a man's name.
2. Harriett and Harvey agree that each is a strong individual and therefore they cannot view themselves as an inseparable couple. Thus, each is free to pursue relationships, except sexual, independent of the other.
3. Recognizing that they do not need children for fulfillment, Harriett and Harvey agree there is no commitment to have them. They will share the responsibility of birth control and if an unwanted pregnancy should occur, they will obtain an abortion if either party wishes it. Furthermore, if either decides to be sterilized, the other will emotionally and financially support the decision.
4. Harriett and Harvey recognize that their careers may at some point demand separate living quarters; therefore, Harvey waives his right to determine where they shall live.
5. The couple agree to share the responsibility and the tasks of the household.
6. Harvey and Harriett agree that the earnings and property of

each are to remain separate, but they agree to share all living expenses in proportion to their incomes. Harriett also agrees to waive her right to support from Harvey.

7. They also agree that if either should want a divorce at any time, the other shall not contest it or try to seek any financial awards, such as alimony.

If more couples enter into this kind of free marital relationship, the institution of marriage will be strengthened and new options opened up for women and men. The members of our society will then be able to attain new levels of self-actualization and mutual satisfaction with each other and apart from each other. As real adults, they can then work toward changing the social institutions that have hampered us.

NOTES

1. Ann Crittenden Scott, "The Value of Housework," *Ms. Magazine* (July 1972), pp. 56–59.
2. Sylvia Porter, *New York Post* (February 14, 1972); see also Nancy Seifer, "Big Loses in the Hot-Stove League," *New York Times* (April 12, 1974), p. 41.
3. Theodore Caplow, *The Sociology of Work* (New York: McGraw-Hill, 1954), chap. 2.
4. Robert R. Bell, *Marriage and Family Interaction*, 3rd Ed. (Homewood, Ill.: Dorsey Press, 1971), p. 325.
5. Karen S. Renne, "Correlates of Dissatisfaction in Marriage," *Journal of Marriage and the Family* (1970), 32: pp. 1, 61. Other researchers have come to similar conclusions. See Mirra Komarovsky, *Blue Collar Marriage* (New York: Random House, 1962); and Robert O. Blood and Donald M. Wolfe, *Husbands and Wives* (New York: Free Press, 1960).
6. Helena Z. Lopata, "The Secondary Features of a Primary Relationship," *Human Organization* (1965), pp. 118–19; and Leonard Benson, *Fatherhood: A Sociological Perspective* (New York: Random House, 1968), p. 271.
7. Bell, *op. cit.*, p. 328.
8. Blood and Wolfe, *op. cit.*, p. 96.
9. E. E. LeMasters, *Parents in Modern America* (Homewood, Ill.: Dorsey Press, 1970), chap. 2.
10. Alice S. Rossi, "Equality Between the Sexes: An Immodest Proposal," *Daedalus* (Spring 1964), pp. 607–52.
11. Helen Z. Lopata, *Occupation: Housewife* (New York: Oxford University Press, 1971), chap. 4.
12. *Ibid.*, pp. 183–84.
13. *Ibid.*, p. 190.
14. Mirra Komarovsky, *Women in the Modern World* (Boston: Little Brown, 1953).

15. Lopata, *Occupation, op. cit.,* p. 193.
16. *The Sociology of Georg Simmel,* Kurt H. Wolff, ed. and trans. (Glencoe, Ill.: Free Press, 1950), pp. 135–36.
17. Lopata, *Occupation, op. cit.,* p. 200.
18. Leonard D. Eron *et al.,* "Comparison of Data Obtained from Mothers and Fathers on Childrearing Practices and Their Relation to Child Aggression," *Child Development* (1961), 32:457–72; and LeMasters, *op. cit.,* pp. 138–43.
19. Robert R. Sears *et al., Patterns of Child Rearing* (Evanston, Ill.: Row, Paterson, 1957).
20. Daniel R. Miller and Guy E. Swanson, *The Changing American Parent* (New York: John Wiley, 1958).
21. Benson, *op. cit.,* pp. 38–73.
22. LeMasters, *op. cit.,* p. 144.
23. Benson, *op. cit.,* p. 63.
24. Ernest W. Burgess and Harvey J. Locke, *The Family* (New York: American Books, 1953).
25. Sandra L. and Daryl J. Bem, "Training the Woman to Know Her Place: The Power of a Nonconscious Ideology," in D. J. Bem, *Beliefs, Attitudes, and Human Affairs* (Belmont, Calif.: Brooks/Cole, 1970).
26. Philip Goldberg, "Are Women Prejudiced Against Women?" *Transaction* (April 1968), 5:28–30.
27. Sandra L. Bem and Daryl J. Bem, in Eleanor Holmes Norton, *Women's Role in Contemporary Society* (New York: Avon Books, 1972), p. 104.
28. Diana W. Washay, "Sex Differences in Language Style," in *Toward a Sociology of Women,* ed. Constantina Safilios-Rothschild (Lexington, Mass.: Xerox, 1972).
29. Nancy Barron, "Sex-typed Language: The Production of Grammatical Cases," *Acta Sociologia,* 14:1–2 (Winter 1971), pp. 24–42.
30. Casey Miller and Kate Swift, "One Small Step for Genkind," *New York Times Magazine* (April 16, 1972).
31. Joseph W. Schneider and Sally L. Hacker, "Sex Role Imagery and the Use of the Generic 'Man' in Introductory Texts." (Paper read at the ASA meetings, New Orleans, August 1972.)
32. Lynn Sherr, "Teaching Kit to Free Vowels from Chauvinist Consonants," *New York Times* (February 20, 1972).
33. Alma Graham, "The Making of a Nonsexist Dictionary," *Ms. Magazine* (December 1973), pp. 12–16.
34. *Ibid.,* p. 16.
35. Susan Bondurant, "It's All Right, Doc—I'm Only Dying," *Rough Times* (1972), 3:1.
36. Constantina Safilios-Rothschild, *The Sociology and Social Psychology of Disability and Rehabilitation* (New York: Random House, 1970).
37. Margaret M. Poloma, "Role Conflict and the Married Professional Woman," and Neal T. Garland, "The Better Half? The Male in the Dual Profession Family," both in Constantina Safilios-Rothschild, ed., *Toward a Sociology of Women, op. cit.,* pp. 187–215.
38. Inge K. Broverman *et al.,* "Sex-Role Stereotypes and Clinical Judgments of Mental Health," *Journal of Consulting and Clinical Psychology* (1970), 34:1, pp. 1–7.
39. *Ibid.*

40. Pamela Roby and Virginia Kerr, "The Politics of Prostitution," *The Nation* (April 10, 1972), pp. 463–66.
41. Martha L. Weinman, "Q—If You Rape a Woman and Steal Her TV, What Can They Get You For in New York? A—Stealing Her TV," *New York Times Magazine* (January 30, 1972).
42. Stuart Nagel and Lenore J. Weitzman, "Double Standard of American Justice," *Trans-action*, 9:1–2 (March 1972), pp. 18–63.
43. *Ibid.*
44. Leo Kanowitz, *Women and the Law* (Albuquerque: University of New Mexico Press, 1969).
45. "Women in Prisons," *Women's Yellow Pages* (Boston: Women's Collective, 1972), pp. 54–55.
46. Nagel and Weitzman, *op. cit.*
47. Priscilla Ruth MacDougall, "Married Women's Common Law Right to Their Own Surnames," *Women's Rights Law Reporter*, 1:3 (Fall–Winter 1972–73), Newark, N.J., p. 4.
48. Ann Scott, "The Equal Rights Amendment: What's in It for You?" *Ms. Magazine* (July 1972), pp. 82–86.
49. *Ibid.*, p. 86.
50. *Ms* Magazine (June 1973), pp. 63–64, 102–3.

4

Men and Women at Work

Unlike that of the lower animals, man's world is a symbolic one. Man's identity, therefore, is marginal and dependent on his society. That is, selfhood is derived from the configurations of society. It is within the established order of things that the individual must affirm the uniqueness of his personality.[1] Man, socialized within a society, will seek to fulfill himself within society's acceptable institutions.

The Greeks conceived of work as the activity of women and slaves. Work was necessary but without intrinsic gratification; leisure was the only proper activity for free men. This attitude toward work persisted through the Middle Ages and among the Hebrews and early Christians.

The Protestant ethic, by defining work as the highest good (man performing the will of God), transformed it into the only acceptable means of gratification. Work came to be a means of achieving identity, of relating to society.

Here I define work as that activity in which man engages primarily for the purpose of supporting himself. Work is neither "good" nor "bad" but necessary for the maintenance and advancement of the individual and his society. Work is what gives structure to the day and a feeling of personal adequacy. Work is necessary for man's image of himself as a figure of responsibility and respectability.

The reader will note that through these brief introductory remarks the word "man" has been used—not "people" or "human being." This is to highlight the relationship between the male in our society and the activity of work. Women in the modern world have traditionally been outside the institution of work. Women are the housewives.

In spite of the fact that the majority of married women are still primarily housewives, there has been a radical change over the past thirty years in the participation of women in the labor market. The proportion of working wives nearly tripled, from almost 15 per cent in 1940 to almost 43 per cent in 1970. Table 1 illustrates this trend.

Notice also how the proportion of working women with children between six and seventeen years of age doubled, from 26 per cent to 52 per cent; and how that of working women with children of preschool age tripled, from almost 11 per cent to 32 per cent. Robert Blood calls the increase in the number of married women in the labor force "one of the most startling social changes in American history."[2]

The table indicates that women in every marital status are increasingly likely to participate in the labor market. Men, on the other hand, are participating less. In 1947, 86.9 per cent of all men sixteen years of age or older were participating in the labor market. By 1969, the rate had declined to 80.9 per cent. In contrast, 31 per cent of all women over sixteen were employed in 1948, and 42.6 per cent in 1969. Abbott Ferriss points out that the rate of participation for women increased nearly one-half of one percentage point per year and that, if this trend continues, as he assumes it will, 50 per cent of our adult female population will be employed by 1985.[3]

Ferriss believes that this trend is of great importance and can be attributed to several factors: (1) the increase in our overall production rate, which has created a great demand for labor; (2) the increased education of women, which makes them more employable; and (3) the fact that women are becoming less dependent on men, as evidenced by an increase in the proportion of single women and in the percentage of female-headed families.

The basic trend, then, is toward decreased male participation and increased female participation in the labor force. In terms of race, white and black males are following a very similar pattern, but white women are catching up to black women, especially among older groups. In 1947, the differential between white and black females participating in the labor force was approximately 15 per cent; by 1969, it had dropped to about 8 per cent.[4]

TABLE 1
Women in the Labor Force, 1940–70

Marital Status	1940	1944	1948	1952	1955	1958	1960	1970
				Number (millions)				
Single	6.7	7.5	5.9	5.5	5.1	5.4	5.4	7.0
Married, living with husband	4.2	6.2	7.6	9.2	10.4	11.8	12.3	18.4
No children under 18	2.7		4.4	5.0	5.2	5.7	5.7	8.2
Children 6–17 only			1.9	2.5	3.2	3.7	4.1	6.3
Children 0–5			1.2	1.7	2.0	2.4	2.5	4.0
Widowed, divorced, separated	2.9	4.7	3.7	4.1	4.6	4.8	4.9	4.5
All women	13.9	18.5	17.2	18.8	20.1	22.0	22.6	31.5
				Per Cent				
Single	48.1	58.6	51.1	50.0	46.6	45.4	44.1	53.0
Married, living with husband	14.7	21.7	22.0	25.3	27.7	30.2	30.5	42.6
No children under 18	8.6		28.4	30.9	32.7	38.8	34.7	42.4
Children 6–17 only			26.0	31.1	34.7	37.6	39.0	52.0
Children 0–5			10.7	13.9	16.0	18.2	18.6	32.0
Widowed, divorced, separated	35.4	42.0	38.3	38.8	38.5	40.8	40.0	36.2
All women	25.7	35.0	31.0	32.7	33.4	35.0	34.8	42.6

Source: F. Ivan Nye and Feliz M. Berardo, *The Family: Its Structure and Interaction* (New York: Macmillan, 1973, p. 271).

There has always been a correlation between marital status and participation in the labor market. Married men are most likely to be employed (86.5 percent in 1969); single males, next most likely (64.9 per cent in 1969); and divorced, widowed, or separated men, least likely (59.8 per cent in 1969). On the other hand, married women are least likely to be employed (39.5 per cent in 1969); single women, most likely (56.7 per cent in 1969); and widowed, divorced, or separated women are in the middle (40.7 per cent in 1969.)[5] Although participation is increasing for women and decreasing for men, in every category the percentage of working women is still much lower than the percentage of working men.

The primary difference in the work patterns is between women with children and women without children. Those with children have a higher probability of work interruption. With the advent of children, women are likely to curtail, if not discontinue, their work lives. As the children grow older, or when women divorce or are widowed, the tendency is to return to work. Women with children, then, do not exhibit the consistent, continuous work pattern of childless women and men, and, of those who do, the majority are employed part time. Typically, females work full time between the ages of twenty and twenty-three. At this point they either give up work completely or hold part-time jobs. At the age of forty, they return to work. The dramatic change occurs when the children enter school.

What is interesting about this pattern is that it is the younger married women who are most likely to be out of the job market; yet, Nye and Hoffman show, younger women are more successful in combining the roles of homemaker and worker than middle-aged women are. Despite the commonsense notion that the time after the children are grown is most favorable for female employment, the truth is that younger women have the greatest amount of job satisfaction.[6]

The number of children a woman has and their ages are the most significant variables affecting her employment.[7] Childless women and those with children older than six are more likely to be working than any other group of married women. Nonwhite mothers participate more in the labor force than white mothers.[8] Cain believes that children are less likely to deter the lower-class black mother from working, because she must prepare herself for the possibility of becoming the sole earner in the family. How does a woman's working affect the stability of her family? Does a working mother contribute to juvenile delinquency? Is a child's development retarded if his mother is employed? These are some of the questions that have interested sociologists and will be discussed later in this chapter. What is significant is that women are now more active in the labor market, and there are indications that their participation will continue to increase.

SEX-STEREOTYPED OCCUPATIONS

If asked, the reader could probably easily identify which of a list of occupations were "masculine" and which "feminine." Nursing, social work, librarianship, and elementary-school teaching are all "feminine," while the ministry, dentistry, engineering, and science are all "masculine." Occupations are linked to sex roles. Like men and women, occupations are stratified, so that nursing is somehow inferior to doctoring; grade-school teaching is inferior to college teaching. Men occupy the more "important" positions; women, the less important.

One reason for this is that people are placed in occupations according to the imagined characteristics of each sex. Men are thought to be stronger, more intelligent, more aggressive, more devoted to work than women. Therefore, their proper occupations are those that supposedly require such traits—medicine, engineering, the ministry. Women are considered more nurturing, more understanding, kinder, and gentler than men; thus they are the nurses, teachers, librarians. Our society ranks men above women; therefore, their occupations are ranked higher.

Table 2 shows clearly how men and women are differentially employed. It seems to indicate that women are substantially employed as professionals, but they are usually in semiprofessions, such as nursing or social work, as opposed to the learned professions, such as medicine and the law. Women are clerks and secretaries; men are the managers and foremen. Few men are household workers, and almost no women are classified as laborers or farmers.

TABLE 2

YEAR-ROUND FULL-TIME CIVILIAN WORKERS (in millions)

	Male	Female
Professional and technical:		
Self-employed	0.5	0.1
Professional and technical: salaried	5.0	2.3
Managers, officials, proprietors		
(nonfarm)	6.1	0.9
Sales workers	2.0	1.7
Craftsmen, foremen	7.7	0.4
Clerical	2.7	5.8
Operatives	7.2	2.3
Service (except household)	2.1	2.0
Laborers	1.8	0.2
Farmers and farm managers	1.5	0.2
Farm laborers	0.5	0.1
Private household workers	0.05	0.3

SOURCE: Abbott L. Ferriss, *Indicators of Trends in the Status of American Women* (New York: Russell Sage Foundation, 1971), Series HO18–HO79 and Census, "Income in 1968 of Families and Persons in the United States," Current Population Reports, Consumer Income, Series P-60, No. 66. Washington, D.C.: U.S. Department of Commerce.

Valerie Oppenheimer found that, as occupations come to be sex-defined as feminine, women prepare themselves to enter those pursuits, so that the stereotypes are self-perpetuating.[9] Edward Gross constructed an index to measure occupational sexual segregation and found that between 1900 and 1960 there was almost no change. Sex-linked occupations tend to remain segregated.[10] Women have difficulty entering "masculine" fields, and their best chance is to find employment in fields that are new or suddenly growing, where there is less tradition and more need for workers.

There is no question that sex is widely used as a basis for discrimination. Women are clearly concentrated in the least prestigious occupations, and the two familiar explanations are that (1) women are not trained and (2) women are not committed to their jobs, because they are concerned primarily with their homes and children.

The first reason is simply untrue. When the educational levels of men and women are compared in relation to the requirements of their jobs, the findings indicate that women are in general overqualified.[11]

The second reason is a self-fulfilling prophecy. If the alternative is a menial or boring job, women will surely choose to stay at home and be full-time wives and mothers. Research shows that, when women are offered interesting jobs, they are as devoted to them as men are.[12]

Randall Collins claims that a more reasonable explanation for the concentration of women at the bottom of the employment totem pole is that women are in the subordinate class in our system of sexual stratification.

> The principle of this system is that women take orders from men but do not give orders to them; hence only men can give orders to other men, and women can give orders only to other women. . . . Women's subordinate position at work may be viewed as a continuation of their subordinate position in the home. . . . [T]he female role in the home continues to center around that of domestic servant. The married woman has primary responsibility for cooking, dishwashing, laundering, housecleaning, and child care—occupational roles that are classified as low-prestige service positions.[13]

Not only are occupations sex-typed, but so are subspecialties within occupations. This can be seen most clearly in the professions (discussed on pages 109–24). In medicine, for example, women tend to become pediatricians, gynecologists, and psychiatrists. Female lawyers generally enter family-connected areas, such as trusts, or specialize in domestic relations. The same is true in white-collar occupations, where women are the secretaries and the assistants while men are the managers.

We know, then, that men and women are distributed unequally through the occupations. Some occupations reject women almost completely; others accept them reluctantly and in limited numbers; still others encourage women to enter because they are desperately needed. There are also occupations, such as nursing, in which women dominate—not because they keep men out, but because men are unwilling to enter, because of some felt stigma. Table 3 shows how women are distributed in the twenty-five occupations in which they are predominantly employed. Notice

TABLE 3

THE TWENTY-FIVE LARGEST OCCUPATIONS OF WOMEN, 1960

Occupation	Number of Women Employed	Percentage of Total in Occupation
Secretaries	1,423,352	97%
Saleswomen, salesclerks (retail)	1,397,364	54
Private household workers	1,162,683	96
Elementary-school teachers	860,413	86
Bookkeepers	764,054	84
Waitresses	714,827	87
Professional nurses	567,884	98
Sewers and stitchers (mfg.)	534,258	94
Typists	496,735	95
Cashiers	367,954	78
Cooks (not private households)	361,772	64
Telephone operators	341,797	96
Private babysitters	319,735	98
Institutional attendants	288,268	74
Laundry and dry-cleaning operatives	277,396	72
Assemblers	270,769	44
Apparel and accessory operatives	270,619	75
Hairdressers and cosmetologists	267,050	89
Packers and wrappers	262,935	60
Stenographers	258,554	96
Secondary-school teachers	243,452	47
Office-machine operators	227,849	74
Checkers, examiners, inspectors	215,066	45
Practical nurses	197,115	96
Kitchen workers (not household)	179,796	59

SOURCE: U.S. Department of Commerce, *Bureau of the Census: 1960 Census of Population; Women's Bureau* (1966), p. 92.

how almost all of the listed jobs are in the lower echelons of the occupational hierarchy.

Changes in the status of women can be traced in the labor force. In 1890, for example, women could enter only three occupations—domestic service, factory work, or teaching—and only one was even somewhat "respectable." "Ladies" did not work. Most employed females came from lower-class families, had no more than a sixth-grade education, and worked because it was financially imperative that they do so. Working women, who were largely unskilled, filled menial jobs and were treated poorly because they could easily be replaced. Working conditions were abysmal; job security, infinitesimal.

Society did not approve of the working woman. For one thing, women were thought to be physically inferior to men, and work was considered harmful to them. Furthermore, a working woman, especially if she had actually chosen to work, was thought to be trying to compete with men. These attitudes persist today to some degree, but change has been occurring over a long period of time. What factors account for this attitudinal change?

One factor is the need of many women to find work outside the home in order to contribute to the family finances. On the farm or in the small town, the woman made a direct contribution to the household, and there was no need for her to earn money. But the United States today is an urban society, and a woman's monetary contribution is often of far greater importance to her family than any other kind of contribution she can make.

A second factor is industrial growth, paralleling the growth of cities, which created a demand for manpower that could not be satisfied by males alone. The gradual shift to automation meant that the physical strength factory work once required was no longer needed, and women could be employed as readily as men.

The growth of unions during the 1930s and 1940s was a third factor, making factory work more attractive for women. Women now work shorter hours under safer and more sanitary conditions with more job security. Some of these changes encouraged females to enter the labor market by making it easier to discharge the obligations of both work and home. Related to this is the development of labor-saving devices, shortening the hours needed for housework.

Finally, female participation in the labor market increased as a result of the new stress on education for women, which made the traditional roles of wife and mother less attractive and less satisfying. College stimulates intellectual interests, and many college-educated women are not content to devote their lives exclusively to home and children.

The chart on page 92 illustrates the changing situation. It is clear that the proportion of mothers who are employed has been steadily rising since 1948.

LABOR-FORCE PARTICIPATION RATES OF MOTHERS,
BY AGE OF CHILDREN, SELECTED YEARS, 1948–70

Per Cent

Year	0	20	40	60

1970 ———————————— 52%
------------------ 32%
1967 ——————————— 49%
---------------- 29%
1964 —————————— 46%
------------- 25%
1960 ————————— 43%
----------- 20%
1956 ———————— 40%
--------- 18%
1950 —————— 33%
------- 14%
1948 ————— 31%
------- 13%

———————————————   With children six to seventeen years only
- - - - - - - - - - - - - - - -   With children under six, but may have older
children also

SOURCE: U.S. Department of Labor, Women's Bureau, *Bulletin 296*, p. 4,
from U.S. Department of Labor, Bureau of Labor Statistics; U.S. Department
of Commerce, Bureau of the Census (*Law Journal*), 1:3, p. 17.

INCOME

Income is associated with educational level, occupation, length
of experience, region of the country, age, and race. It is also very
much associated with sex. Although there is no question that income varies by sex when all other factors are held constant, it is
difficult to determine the extent of the difference. Among several
reasons, two stand out: Women are usually employed only inter-
mittently and part time, and they are typically employed in low-
salaried occupations. Therefore, any comparison has limitations and
must be examined with caution. Nevertheless, according to Herbert
Stein, former chairman of the President's Council of Economic
Advisers, pure discrimination accounts for a differential of between 10 per cent and 20 per cent in the earnings of men and
women. Furthermore, Stein predicts that the disparity between

male and female unemployment rates will widen as more women enter the labor market.[14]

Women are more likely to be without any income than men are, although the percentage of incomeless women is declining while the percentage of incomeless males has remained constant. For example, from 1956 to 1968, the percentage of white women with no income dropped thirteen points. The median annual income for everyone has increased since 1956; however, although black males have improved *vis-à-vis* white males, there has been no improvement for white females as compared to white males.[15] The increase for males has been 34 per cent, compared to only 23 per cent for females. In 1956, the difference between males' and females' median earnings was $2,097; by 1968 this differential had increased to $3,207.[16] Women's income status compared to men's has obviously declined.

Table 4 shows that in each occupation women consistently earn less than men. This can be seen most clearly in the last column,

TABLE 4

NUMBER AND MEDIAN EARNINGS OF YEAR-ROUND
FULL-TIME CIVILIAN WORKERS, BY OCCUPATION AND SEX,
AND FEMALE-MALE RATIO OF EARNINGS, 1968

Occupation	Median Earnings		Female-Male Ratio (×100) of Earnings
	Male	Female	
All occupations	$ 7,664	$4,457	58
Professional, technical			
Self-employed	17,358	—	—
Salaried	10,243	6,634	65
Managers, officials, proprietors			
(nonfarm)	9,794	5,101	52
Sales workers	8,292	3,388	41
Craftsmen, foremen	7,958	4,315	54
Clerical workers	7,324	4,778	65
Operatives	6,773	3,956	59
Service workers (not household)	5,898	3,159	53
Laborers	5,606	3,490	62
Farmers, farm managers	3,353	—	—
Farm laborers	2,870	—	—
Private household workers	—	1,464	—

SOURCE: Adapted from Ferriss, p. 143.

which shows the ratio of females' median annual income to that of males. For example, the total median earnings for women is $4,457, which is 58 per cent of the median earnings for men.

American income tax laws also discriminate against women, especially working wives. In effect, our income-tax provisions favor the position of housewife, often to the extent of discouraging women from working outside the home at all.

An example of favoritism toward the nonworking wife is the joint income tax. This system rewards the married head of household by requiring him to pay less tax than a single man provided that one member of the dyad does not work. One earner shares his income with the spouse; two earners save nothing. "The effect of the joint return provisions is to say you get a reward if you marry and take one spouse off the job market. And of course, that spouse, because of job discrimination and therefore lesser earning potential, will almost invariably be the wife."[17]

Columbia Law School professor George Cooper suggests changes in the tax laws to make them fair to working women. First, the benefits that accrue to married couples with only one wage earner, almost always the husband, should be eliminated. Such couples are being subsidized by single workers, frequently women, and by husbands and wives who both work. The joint-return benefits, in other words, should be abolished. Second, in order to encourage female employment, Cooper suggests that women should be permitted to deduct the cost of childcare and household-cleaning services regardless of how much money they earn. Third, a working wife should pay a lower Social Security tax than her husband because she derives lower benefits than he does.[18]

Cooper does not believe that his three proposed changes will totally relieve women's working problems. However, they will go a long way toward alleviating the situation. It does seem remarkable, when one considers that women constitute over half of the population, that our income-tax laws discriminate so heavily against them.

The Social Security system also discriminates against women in several ways. For example, everyone, male or female, who earns up to $12,600 pays 5.85 per cent of his or her salary into Social Security, the maximum payment being $1,472. This means that the higher-paid workers, mostly men, pay a lower percentage of their salaries into the fund. In a dual-working family, if both spouses are paying the maximum, they are depositing $2,944 per year. The nonworking wife, of course, deposits nothing.[19] What happens to these funds upon retirement or death?

The single working woman is almost always in the lowest income bracket, and her benefits will therefore also be lowest, even though she had paid in the highest percentage of her earnings. Even when she receives the maximum, it amounts to only two-thirds of a married man's benefits. The nonworking wife qualifies for benefits from her husband's account when he dies only if the couple has been married at least twenty years and then not until she is sixty years old. (There are exceptions when there are children under twenty-two enrolled in school.) And if she takes the benefits at age sixty, they will be lower than what she would receive if she waited until she is sixty-five. The working wife, although she has deposited her own 5.85 per cent into Social Security, is eligible upon her husband's death for half of either his benefits or hers, whichever are highest, but not both. Because men's benefits are almost always higher (men generally earn more), in most cases the widowed working woman never receives any money from her own account!

Clearly, reforms are needed. A bill pending in the House at this writing provides for benefits to nonworking wives when their husbands retire, and reduces from twenty to five the number of years the couple must have been married for the wife to receive her deceased husband's benefits. Another bill in the House would permit a married couple to combine its earnings records and earn higher joint benefits upon retirement. These are vital first steps toward greater equality under the Social Security system. More is obviously needed.

In summary, many factors determine female employment. The most significant are whether or not a woman has children and how old they are. The trend is clearly in the direction of greater employment of females, including mothers of children under six years of age.

It has also been noted that occupations are sex-stereotyped and therefore take on gender characteristics.

Finally, it was pointed out that in all occupations women are overrepresented in the lower echelons and are paid lower salaries than men even when they do the same work. In addition, income-tax laws discriminate against women.

BLUE- AND WHITE-COLLAR FEMALE WORKERS

Blue-Collar Women

Most working women are concentrated in white-collar occupations. Furthermore, most research on working women is concerned with professional women. Thus, little has been reported about the 17.6 per cent of all employed women who are in blue-collar jobs,[20] primarily as domestics, factory workers, and waitresses.

The "culture of poverty"[21] describes a way of life for people who are semiskilled or unskilled, marginally employed or chronically unemployed, without hope of improvement in their lifestyle. Such people live in rural farm areas in the South or in the slums of our cities. Many of them are welfare recipients for a major portion of their lives, sometimes into the third or fourth generation. They have no security of any kind, either economic or emotional. Life is lived today because tomorrow is unknowable and unplannable but will probably be worse. Luck, not self-determination, is the hope of the people. Without skills, education, power, family, friends, or marketable talents, there is only fatalism.

The world of the very poor, especially the very poor woman, is circumscribed by the neighborhood. The young girl, often father-less, comes to rely on her mother as the only dependable figure in a chaotic, bewildering, constantly dangerous world. Her image of her mother does not change when she marries. The young wife turns to her mother for help, advice, even food when necessary. The husband-wife relationship is likely to be a tenuous one, and the wife is not surprised to be abandoned. She has always known that men tend to be here today and gone tomorrow. It is the security and emotional support of her female relatives that she trusts and relies on. The husband's position is always that of an outsider.[22]

Lower-class women work because they must work. Either they are heads of households with dependent children or their husbands are employed in temporary jobs with very low wages. Those who are employed work at dull, menial, meaningless, degrading jobs from which they derive no satisfaction. Often, however, they are unemployed. The unemployment rate is always higher for women than for men, especially in the full-time labor force, in the youngest age group (sixteen to twenty-four) and in the oldest group (over sixty-five), and on the lowest rungs of the occupational ladder.[23]

All that has been said applies doubly to poor black women. Indeed, poverty and unemployment are associated more directly with race than with sex.[24] Blacks of both sexes always have higher unemployment rates than whites. The black female today can be found at every occupational level, but she is most likely to be employed in the lowest-paid jobs with the least prestige, and she is still more likely to be unemployed.[25]

Housework is one of the major occupations of lower-class black women. The state Department of Labor estimates that there are sixty-three thousand household workers in New York State alone, most of them female and black. Such workers are completely without protection, overworked, and underpaid. Workmen's Compensation protects the domestic, but only if she works forty-four hours per week for one employer. She is specifically excluded from the minimum-wage laws. She cannot claim unemployment insurance, and she is guaranteed no vacation, pension, or hospital benefits.

The problem, says Stanley Saxenberg, lies in the public's attitude toward household servants. Domestics are stigmatized, viewed as inferior. He claims that the solution lies in an amending state law to include these workers and provide them with adequate workmen's compensation and disability and unemployment insurance. There must be legislation covering wages and hours and an avenue through which complaints can be channeled.[26]

A waitress testified before the New York City Commission on Human Rights:

> There were five of us, all attractive, who testified at the wage hearing before the Labor Department. None of us had received a salary from the . . . restaurant where we worked. Naturally, we received no Social Security benefits and no sick leave. Nor did we have health insurance, severance pay, vacation time or holidays. . . . We worked nine, nine and a half hours daily under incredibly unpleasant conditions. No smoking. No coffee. No talking. No sit-

ting down, ever. Twenty minutes for dinner. And constant harassment from Sam and his managers. All of this for about $100 a week in good times and no wages. Only tips.[27]

This is the testimony of one waitress. Thousands of others can say at least as much. Most women are discriminated against in the labor market, but those in the most menial occupations are treated only slightly better than slaves.

White-Collar Women

Of all working women, 59 per cent are in white-collar occupations;[28] that is, they are secretaries, bookkeepers, stenographers, or saleswomen. This discussion is limited to middle-class, married women with children, whose husbands earn salaries that would permit their wives to stay at home. The group is increasing in size. In 1940, only 30 per cent of employed women were married; in 1967, 58 per cent were married.[29]

Women are no longer automatically relegated to the roles of homemaker and mother. They can now choose to combine those roles with that of employee. Catherine Arnott's study of working wives underscores the fact that "freedom of role choice is replacing the old norm of predetermined roles for married women. Educated wives and mothers are asserting their desire to maximize life rewards in roles chosen, rather than assigned."[30]

Several investigators have tried to explain the changes in the work patterns of middle-class women. One reason for the changes is a response to the change in our labor market. More workers are needed, and there are simply not enough men to fill all the jobs that need filling. Related to this is the fact that, because of our labor-saving devices, women no longer need to spend as much time as was once necessary to do housework.[31] Another reason is that the extra income provides luxuries—vacations, cars, clothes—not otherwise obtainable by the average middle-class family in today's inflated economy.

The most important explanation is that there has been a change in our social value system, which now somewhat justifies and even encourages female employment. We now have more nearly equal opportunity in education and job placement.[32] Many women are coming to recognize and admit that the social roles of wife and mother are not enough for them. The emphasis in our society on personal fulfillment helps to motivate individual women to enter the work force.[33]

Nevertheless, many married women, especially mothers, continue to face opposition to their working outside the home. The working wife must overcome the force of tradition, which says that a woman's place is in the home, that if she works she will jeopardize her marriage and become "masculine" and aggressive, while her husband will be thought of as an inadequate "provider," his masculinity will be challenged, and her children will be left in the care of "strangers" and may become delinquent.

Furthermore, many other women hold negative attitudes toward working women because they are violating tradition and bringing into question the *non*working woman's behavior. Many women, perhaps most, do not want the equal responsibility that equal opportunity involves. They prefer the passive role; they enjoy the reflective glory of husband and children; they like being taken care of and passing up decision-making.

These are the overt motives for objection. There may, of course, be covert motives. The nonworking wife may lack the requisite courage to enter the work world. She may fear that she lacks the necessary drive or talent. She may secretly wish to work but feels it is too late. In any event, the nonworking wife scorns her working sister and serves as an example for those men who wish to point her out as a "normal" woman, not a frustrated, discontented female.

Marion Sobol[34] postulates that three conditions are necessary for married women to enter the labor force. There must be *enabling conditions*, which means that a woman's life situation must permit her to work—if, for example, she can afford a housekeeper, her children are grown, or a good daycare center is available. *Facilitating conditions* are those that make the woman a desirable employee—for example, education or experience. The *precipitating conditions* are those that make a woman want to work—for example, financial problems, a desire to "kill" time, a wish to meet new people. Apparently, all three kinds of conditions must be present to explain a middle-class woman's presence in the labor force. In short, she must be ready, willing, and able.

Employers, usually men, often hesitate to hire married women, especially mothers, ostensibly on the grounds that they would be depriving children of a mother's care and depriving some man with a family to support of a job. Incidentally, economist Paul A. Samuelson says that "an end to job discrimination against women would not, in most cases, take anything away from men."[35] In fact, if women were treated equally in the labor force, Samuelson believes, there would be greater purchasing power throughout the economy, to everyone's benefit.

Many male employers also believe that they must contend with real problems when they hire women—for example, that females have higher turnover rates than males, that they are more prone to accidents on the job, and that their absenteeism rate is higher. These assumptions on the part of male employers affect women's success in the marketplace, and it is therefore necessary to see how true they are.

The turnover rate for women apparently *is* higher than the rate for men. During the 1950s the rehiring rate for women was 15 per cent greater than that for men, and the total turnover rate was approximately 55 per cent higher.[36] This means that an employer cannot be certain that his female help will stay on the job as long as his male help.

Women's turnover rates are influenced most by personal variables; men's, by economic ones. For example, a woman's age is an important consideration. Younger women, who leave to marry and have children, have the highest turnover rate. The lowest is for women between forty-five and sixty whose children either are in school or have left home.

Women's higher turnover rates, then, justify employers' caution about hiring women. However, there is some evidence that their turnover rate is declining,[37] perhaps because of more household labor-saving devices, greater desire for full-time employment, greater social pressure to maintain a high standard of living, more bureaucratic understanding of special female problems (such as children's illnesses), and the increase in the number of older, more stable women in the market, who lower the turnover rate.

Lewis predicts that, if the trend continues, the turnover problem will become unimportant, although he feels female employment will never be so stable as male because the sexes are differently motivated to work.[38] However, he says, there are employer advantages to a high turnover rate in that women are always available for short-term employment during peak seasons and women can be paid less because they do not remain on one job long enough to be in higher-salaried positions.

The belief that females have more industrial accidents is another employer worry and one that, according to Lewis, is totally without foundation. Females in fact have a much lower accident rate than males,[39] probably because they are not usually hired to fill dangerous jobs. It may also be that women have been socialized to be more cautious in their physical movements, and women, because their turnover rate is higher, may not know their jobs so well as men and therefore may be less likely to take risks.

Employer concern about absenteeism is also partially unfounded. Women are absent from work about twice as many times during a year as men are, but they are absent for shorter periods of time. The result is almost no difference in the actual number of days men and women are away from work.

It appears that female absenteeism is related to the number of dependents rather than to age or marital status.[40] When a child is ill and one parent must remain home, it is almost invariably the wife who accepts this responsibility, because she is unlikely to take her job so seriously as her husband does his. Women generally rate their home responsibilities as more important than their work responsibilities[41]—or maybe society does it for them. In any event, in a conflict between the two obligations, women choose the home.

In short, male employers' fears regarding female employees are largely unfounded. Women have far fewer industrial accidents than men; they are absent from work no more often (in number of days); and, although their turnover rate is higher at the present time, there seems to be a definite downward trend.

Not only do women generally earn less than men, but on an income-tax return the married woman's income actually represents less profit than her husband's because it may put the family into a higher tax bracket. There are, in addition, other costs. Hiring household help and paying for baby-sitting services cut into her earnings. She may need to use an outside laundry service and more prepared foods; she may require a more extensive wardrobe. It has been estimated that women pay out 25 per cent to 50 per cent of what they earn in order to meet the expenses of working.

Frances Feldman reports that the income contributed to the family by the wife is used either for luxuries or for savings. Among lower-middle-class families, the wife's income rapidly becomes necessary.[42] Margaret Carroll believes that women work toward a specific end—a new car, a house, an extended trip. Furthermore, Carroll reports, a woman is satisfied to know she *can* work if necessary, so her employment potential becomes a security blanket even when she is unemployed.[43]

Middle-class women generally say that they are working either because the money they earn is required for family necessities or in order to have "extras." According to Lois Hoffman, financial reward is the motive most often offered.[44] Lewis, however, believes that financial need has been overemphasized as a motive for working, especially for middle- and upper-class wives. Instead, he posits psychological satisfaction as the chief reason. Lewis feels that women defend their working on economic grounds because they are afraid that society will not understand more personal motives.[45]

Two studies support Lewis's theory. Dornbusch and Heer[46] found from an examination of census data that there was no correlation between the employment of wives and economic necessity. Orden and Bradburn studied almost two thousand couples and found that more than half the wives who worked did so because they wanted to, not because of financial need.[47]

What kind of woman decides to go to work when there is no pressing financial need and she does not have a commitment to a professional career? There is some evidence that women who are employed are more intelligent than those who are not. However, the positive correlation between employment rates and IQ is not high.[48] It also seems that the employment rate for women varies according to the region of the country in which they live. One reason for this involves industrial development and the opportunity to obtain a job; another is a difference in regional traditions. The employment rate for married women is lowest in the Northeast and highest in the South and West. In addition, urban women are twice as likely to be employed as rural women.[49]

Although once again the research is scanty, there is some evidence that men and women have different reasons for choosing their occupations. However, we are not sure of their precise reasons. White-collar women do not usually have any special training, so their choice of job frequently depends less on any specific interest in a field and more on what is available at the time. Furthermore, most women must restrict their choice to "feminine" occupations, and they seek employment that will not commit them to extensive commuting.

Apparently, women are less concerned than men are about long-term advantages in a job, such as retirement benefits, pension plans, or chances for advancement. Instead, they are more likely to be interested in the immediate working conditions, such as attractive surroundings and pleasant colleagues. Women tend to shy away from jobs demanding long-term commitment or extensive preparation. Parrish's study revealed that 95 per cent of all employed women held short-term jobs with little skill required or long-term jobs requiring only a moderate amount of skill. Parrish feels this is because there are many low-skill jobs available that married women find attractive, and because married women prefer to avoid the training necessary for highly skilled jobs.[50]

Another poorly researched question is female job satisfaction. Women seem to be more likely than men to leave their jobs for reasons besides personal dissatisfaction, such as pressure from a spouse, the birth of a child, or a husband's transfer to another city. Women generally find less satisfaction in their work than men, and they are quicker to leave if dissatisfied. Satisfactory employment for women seems to be correlated more with interpersonal variables (the people they work with, for example, or the working surroundings) and less with achievement; the opposite is true for men.[51]

After World War II it became clear that in spite of the propaganda urging women to leave the job market to the returning veterans and go home to the suburbs and have babies, women were going to continue to work. At this point, many social problems were laid at the door of the working mother. The working mother was blamed, for example, for increasing juvenile delinquency and for an increasing divorce rate.

It is not difficult to understand the social factors that give rise to this attitude. When a woman goes to work she does alter the patterns of her family life. Change of any kind always meets resistance. But it is necessary to look carefully to see if the working mother is guilty as charged. First, what are the effects of mothers' working on children?

Several studies argue that children's school performance is not related to mothers' employment. Nye found that the children of working women actually performed somewhat better in school than the children of nonworking women, although the differences were not significant.[52] Nye and Gold, in two separate studies, found that in middle-class families there is a slightly higher proportion of juvenile delinquency among the sons of working women.[53] It should be stressed that all differences found, between mother's employment and school performance and between mother's employment and juvenile delinquency, are very small and that the findings cannot be considered conclusive by any means.

A controversy that has engaged social scientists for a very long time concerns the infant's need for continual contact with one maternal figure. Those who favor the "maternal deprivation" theory, principally John Bowlby,[54] hold that the working mother does irreparable harm to the infant's personality by leaving him in the care of others. Research has not supported this hypothesis at all. No difference has been found in mental health between the children of working and of nonworking mothers. Nye and Berardo put this position succinctly:

> The authors believe that it matters little who or how many people care for a child, provided it is given affection, stimulation, exercise, and adequate food and clothing. Of course if this is true, it still might follow that mothers are more likely to provide for those needs than are other women. The *quality* of the care of the child, whether by its mother or by someone else, appears to be the crucial variable.[55]

Another question that has interested investigators is the effect of working on maternal attitudes. Nye found that employed mothers wanted to have more children than they did have, were less nervous and irritable with their children than nonemployed mothers, and were, in general, happier in their maternal roles.[56] Hoffman found that there is a direct correlation between a woman's job satisfaction and her attitude toward her children. If her job satisfaction is high, her pleasure in her children is likely to be high.[57] Alice Propper's study suggests that although there was more friction between adolescent children and their working mothers than between adolescents and nonworking mothers, there was no difference in the amount of help the parents gave the children with school and personal problems or in the amount of interest in the children the mothers showed and that ties between them were equally close.[58]

In short, most research indicates that working at a job that gives her satisfaction enhances a mother's relationship with her children. The job seems to act as a safety valve, permitting the mother to release frustration that might otherwise build up if all her activities were confined to the home.[59]

Almost all the research shows that when the mother is employed full time, the members of her family, especially the adolescent children, are likely to have household responsibilities.[60] Elizabeth Douvan also found that daughters of working mothers were more likely to have part-time jobs than those of nonworking mothers. Propper reported the same thing and added that the household chores did not deprive the youngsters of leisure-time activities.

In summary, the children of working mothers do not seem to be very different from children whose mothers stay home with them. Infants do not suffer from being cared for by more than one "mother." There are no deleterious effects on schoolwork. These children are not loved less by their mothers, nor do their mothers take less interest in them. There may be a slightly higher incidence of juvenile delinquency. When mothers work full time, children are more likely to have household responsibilities which do not interfere with their outside activities. In general, then, contrary to commonly held notions, the children of working mothers are as well off as the children of unemployed mothers, if not better off.

Social scientists have centered a great deal of interest on the effect of the wife's employment on marital stability. The problems are threefold: the husband's ego may be threatened; the husband may lose his authority position; or the wife may neglect her household roles.

The research does not support the hypothesis that a working wife threatens her husband's self-image. Nye's study[61] reported that 89 per cent of the husbands in the sample approved of their wives' working. Some husbands of nonworking wives even expressed the wish that their wives would go to work. Nye feels that husbands are not threatened because most women have jobs that are lower in status than their own and earn lower salaries. Furthermore, Nye thinks that if the wife did earn a very large salary, this would compensate for any feelings of insecurity the husband might experience.

In another study,[62] the same investigator found a correlation between a husband's disapproval of his wife's working and marital maladjustment. Leland Axelson found a generally higher level of marital happiness among husbands of nonworking wives.[63] Wise and Carter reported that the husband's attitude was the most influential factor determining the working wife's self-attitude,[64] and his attitude depended on how strongly she was committed to her work and how successful she was.

Orden and Bradburn[65] also looked into the question of husbandly attitudes from a slightly different perspective. They found that marital adjustment was highest when the wife had a choice. If she worked out of necessity or if she stayed home because of her husband's insistence, she was less likely to be happily married. This is a significant piece of evidence. The question does not turn on whether or not a wife works but, rather, on whether or not she does whatever she does because she wants to. If she has free choice, her marital happiness is likely to be greater than if she is forced into one role or another.

Arnott's study showed that marriages in the United States are not threatened by female employment. In fact, there is an increase in the number of men who are urging their wives to work. Arnott concludes that the institution of marriage is actually strengthened when married women go to work out of choice, with their husband's approval, and with a real sense of commitment.[66]

Edna Rostow pointed out: "For a woman to perform in two worlds, as men do, her marriage must countenance her dual goals and support her in seeking them."[67]

All this is not to say that conflict is reduced when a wife works. Indeed, research shows more frequent conflict in marriages with working wives.[68] Several hypotheses are available to explain this fact. Nye says that conflict between spouses may lead to the wife's employment, rather than the other way around.[69] David Heer feels that employed women and their husbands are probably more dominant personalities than unemployed women and their husbands, and when two dominant people are married to each other conflict is inevitable.[70] Heer offers a second hypothesis. He believes that wives who are financially dependent on their husbands are less likely to oppose them than working wives. He thinks the feelings of conflict may be the same in both types of marriages, but the independent wife is freer to express herself.[71]

Clifford Kirkpatrick offers yet another and more subtle explanation. He says that changes in social status (nonworking to working) bring confusion, conflict, and frustration. Each spouse attempts to retain old privileges while acquiring new ones and to get rid of old obligations while avoiding now ones. For example, a working wife may try to keep her earnings to herself and at the same time get her husband to share household tasks. Husbands, on the other hand, will try to share wives' salaries and avoid taking on household jobs.[72]

All these hypotheses are attractive explanations of the increased conflict in families when both spouses are employed, but there has been as yet insufficient evidence to support any one of them. Probably all are somewhat true, and there may be others in addition.

Another common research question concerns the effect of female employment on the divorce rate. Although clearly a large percentage of working mothers are divorced, they probably work because they need the salary. Nye's study does not address the question directly, but from his data we can infer that it is more likely that divorced women go to work than that working women get divorced.[73] The increased conflict, then, does not necessarily imply a higher divorce rate. Nye found that working women may report more conflict and less happiness, but they do not report less marital satisfaction. He points out that the working wife is compensated for the conflict by greater financial security, more authority in her family, more money, and more enjoyable relationships outside her marriage.[74]

Carl Ridley studied the relationship between job satisfaction, job involvement, and marital adjustment. He found, contrary to many others, that males do not separate the two areas of their life—home and work—and that there is therefore a significant positive relationship between job satisfaction and marital satisfaction for men. If a husband is happy at work, he is likely to be happy at home. For working wives the matter is more complex. There is a positive relationship between job and home satisfaction only when the job is important to the woman. If the work is unimportant, it does not have an effect on marital adjustment. In short, when the work role is salient to them, women are like men in the impact their work has on their home life. When the work role is low in salience, work satisfaction does not influence the home.[75]

An old argument against female employment was that women lacked the physical and emotional strength to fulfill the dual roles of homemaker and worker. Nye and Berardo contend that women in poor health are unlikely to attempt both roles in the first place; and if they do become ill, they are likely to quit. In fact, research indicates that employed women are physically healthier than unemployed women. The findings suggest that the notion that employment is harmful to women's health is nonsense.[76]

The same is true for mental health. Sheila Feld found that working women are more self-accepting, although they continue to express some doubts about their adequacy as mothers and some feelings of guilt and anxiety. Nevertheless, Feld reports that these mothers exhibit fewer psychosomatic symptoms than nonworking mothers.[77] The evidence is sparse, but it strongly suggests that working women are neither more nor less likely than nonworking women to suffer from emotional problems.

The essential question is whether or not working increases a married woman's satisfaction with life. The question is nearly impossible to answer because of the thousand and one variables that would have to be accounted for. Nye made one attempt to cope with the problem when he asked 2,000 mothers to rate their satisfaction with seven aspects of their lives: income, home and furnishings, recreation, work, community, relationship with children, and relationship with husband. There was no difference between working and nonworking women in their ratings in respect to income, home and furnishings, recreation, and work. Working women were less satisfied with their relationships with their husbands, but they rated their relationships with their children and their liking for their community higher than unemployed women. Employed women therefore had higher over-all satisfaction scores than unemployed women. Nye is careful to explain that the employed women might have been more satisfied with their lives under any circumstances, for whatever reason, but he believes that working enhances their lives.[78]

All the evidence indicates that middle-class women will be increasingly represented in the labor force. In the past, a female's horizon was limited to two acceptable roles: wife and mother. Today she can opt to combine these with the role of worker. Whether the married middle-class woman stays at home or goes to work is almost irrelevant. What counts is that she has the freedom to decide for herself what she wants to do with her life.

PROFESSIONAL WOMEN

Sociologists agree that occupations can be placed on a continuum from the least professional to the most. Actually, the most highly professional occupations tend to serve as the ideal to which all other occupations aspire. This implies that occupations can change their status over time, so that an occupation may become more professionalized as it acquires the characteristics associated with professions.

What, then, defines a profession? Ernest Greenwood[79] includes college professors, lawyers, medical doctors, dentists, clergymen, and engineers, among others, in his list of professionals. The literature, he claims, shows that social scientists agree on five characteristics of professions that are lacking in nonprofessions: systematic body of theory, authority, community sanction, ethical codes, and a culture. But, he cautions, the difference is quantitative rather than qualitative, because these attributes can be found in nonprofessions and in semiprofessions to lesser degrees.

By a *systematic body of theory* Greenwood means that the skills used by the professional in his work derive from, and are supported by systematic and orderly theories. There are, for example, sociological theories, legal theories, and medical theories; but there are no theories for bricklaying or secretarial work or plumbing. Professionals spend years learning the theories related to their work; they are not trained on the job.

The professional's education permits him to acquire theoretical knowledge beyond the ken of the laymen. Thus he attains *professional authority*. The nonprofessional has customers who may or may not accept his advice, but the professional has clients who depend on him to make any decisions necessary. The client surrenders his prerogatives; the customer does not.

This authority or influence extends into the community; the professional has *the sanction of the community*. That is, the society grants the profession the right to control its own training centers; to decide who can enter the profession; to license practitioners; to set standards. The community grants privilege also. The professional may elicit otherwise confidential information and need never reveal it to others. The profession may not be judged by community outsiders, only by its own members. No one may usurp these privileges and powers who is not recognized by the professional group. Thus, the doctor must earn his medical degree; but anyone can declare himself a carpenter.

These special rights granted to a profession by the society allow the profession to become a monopoly. However, the profession is expected to protect the society against the abuses of a monopoly by regulating its members. Thus, professionals subscribe to a self-imposed *code of ethics*. Among other things, fees are regulated; so are attitudes toward clients. Knowledge acquired by one practitioner is to be shared with others. Professions, in short, set up both formal and informal standards of behavior to which members are expected to adhere. If they fail to do so, punishment may be meted out, even to ostracism.

Finally, the professional gets his social identity from his occupation, and thus professions tend to develop *subcultures* of their own. People in the same professions tend to spend time together, to intermarry, to live near each other, to belong to the same clubs and organizations, to share political views. Often they have symbols, such as clothing, cars, residential areas, vacation places. They have their heroes, folklore, even slang.

Most important, Greenwood points out that the concept of career applies only to professions. Doctors and lawyers have careers; electricians and truck drivers do not. This implies that a professional career is more than a job; it is a life-style, an end in itself. Doctrine has it that the profession offers intrinsic values— i.e., curing the sick, teaching the young—that are above and beyond the monetary rewards. To be a professional, one immerses oneself in one's work. There is no distinction between working and leisure hours. Work is life.

There is no profession in which women are not represented. The problem, however, is that women are grossly underrepresented in all professions in relation to their proportion in the population, and there has been little increase in the ratio during this century. "Women who have chosen careers in the elite professions are as deviant (in comparison with most American women) in 1968 as they were in 1898, although the notion of a woman doctor or lawyer is not as bizarre today as it was then."[80] Table 5 illustrates Epstein's contention.

Women are underrepresented in the learned professions. They

TABLE 5

WOMEN IN SELECTED PROFESSIONAL OCCUPATIONS, 1900–1960
(as percentage of all workers)

Occupation	1900	1910	1920	1930	1940	1950	1960
Lawyers	—	1.0	1.4	2.1	2.4	3.5	3.5
College presidents, professors, instructors	—	19.0	30.0	32.0	27.0	23.0	19.0
Clergy	4.4	1.0	2.6	4.3	2.2	8.5	5.8
Doctors	—	6.0	5.0	4.0	4.6	6.1	6.8
Engineers	—	—	—	—	0.3	1.2	0.8
Dentists	—	3.1	3.2	1.8	1.5	2.7	2.1
Scientists	—	—	—	—	—	11.4	9.9
Biologists	—	—	—	—	—	27.0	28.0
Chemists	—	—	—	—	—	10.0	8.6
Mathematicians	—	—	—	—	—	38.0	26.4
Physicists	—	—	—	—	—	6.5	4.2
Nurses	94.0	93.0	96.0	98.0	98.0	98.0	97.0
Social workers	—	52.0	62.0	68.0	67.0	66.0	57.0
Librarians	—	79.0	88.0	91.0	89.0	89.0	85.0

SOURCE: U.S. Bureau of the Census, *Census of Population*, 1960, Vol. I, Table 202, pp. 528–33; 1900–1950 statistics from U.S. Department of Labor, *Changes in Women's Occupations*, 1940–50, Women's Bureau Bulletin No. 253, 1954, p. 57.

represented 12 per cent of all professionals in 1900 and only 10 per cent in 1970; they earned 40 per cent of all bachelor's degrees in 1940 and in 1960, but only 35 per cent of the master's degrees in 1960 compared to 40 per cent in 1940, and only 12 per cent of the doctoral degrees in 1960 compared to 15 per cent in 1940. Athena Theodore attempted to account for these statistics.

Theodore writes that men and women are differentially represented in occupations because of our deeply rooted cultural values, which prescribe the proper "masculine" and "feminine" role behaviors.[81] The masculine role is primarily based in the occupational structure, and it is from his work that the male derives his status. Although the male confers social status on his wife, the feminine role is based in the home, and it is as wife and mother that the female is expected to derive her basic gratification. Thus, even for the professional woman, marriage is the primary goal. Furthermore, says Theodore, the female role is by definition inferior to the male, a view that is held by both men and women. Thus, no matter how well trained or highly educated a woman is, she is almost always evaluated on her physical attributes first, not her intellectual capabilities. She is a sex object. Taken together, these factors discourage women from seeking careers in the higher professions.

The crucial period of life in which these notions are formed and developed is during early childhood socialization. Girls and boys learn the meaning of their gender and the behaviors appropriate to it. Boys learn that they must eventually become providers; girls learn that they must become wives and mothers. Boys learn that to be masculine means to be aggressive, bold, acquisitive, and forceful. Girls learn that to be feminine means to be reticent, nurturing, and gentle. Such notions influence youngsters' self-images and their ambitions. Boys and girls then select occupations that will reflect these acceptable characteristics. It is not so much that females lack equal educational opportunities or that hiring practices favor men, although both of these are true to some extent; rather, women are underrepresented in the higher professions because of the cultural values accepted by both sexes. Even when a female does enter a "masculine" occupation, she is supposed to rank her work below her home responsibilities.

These values produce conflict for women. On the one hand we

have the factors that inhibit women from work; on the other, we have an educational system that encourages career aspiration. In addition, because marriage is so prominent a goal, career decisions are often deferred until the marital decision is made. "In the face of institutional and status inconsistencies, the costs to personality structure, although not easily isolated, are high. Unclear role expectations and uncertainty about the future affect the self-concepts and achievement needs of young females."[82]

Matina Horner studied what she called the "motive to avoid success" as a "psychological barrier to achievement in women" and beautifully illustrated the conflicts of which Theodore speaks. Horner shows that when young, ambitious women are faced with a choice between developing their abilities and their feminine image, they will choose to behave in ways that reflect their internalized gender-role images. Horner argues that "the motive to avoid success is a *latent*, stable personality disposition, acquired early in life in conjunction with sex."[83]

Support for Horner's theory comes from the work of Money, Hampson, and Hampson,[84] who studied hermaphrodites, unusual people who are born with one external set of sexual apparatus but with the sex chromatin patterns, gonads, hormones, or internal reproductive structures of the other sex. These investigators found that when the difference in sex status is discovered in these individuals, even if the discovery occurs in childhood, the pattern of behavior is set and cannot be altered. In short, if a child is brought up as a boy because he has external male sex organs and if it is found later that "he" is really female, nothing can be done to change his psychosexual orientation because the sex status has been reinforced constantly since birth. Theodore and Horner agree that the most important impediment to advancement for women in the learned professions is the gender training children receive in early childhood, which is irreversible.[85] Most girls therefore cannot resolve the conflict that arises when their "masculine" ambitions threaten to shake the image they need of themselves as "feminine."

Earlier it was noted briefly that occupations are sex-typed. Nowhere is this practice more extensive or more obvious than in the professions and semiprofessions. Law, engineering, medicine, the clergy, and dentistry are examples of clearly "masculine" occupations. Nursing, librarianship, and social work are just as clearly "feminine." These occupations are stratified, and male occupations are ranked higher and are more professionalized. Today, women comprise about two-thirds of all semiprofessionals and one-tenth of all professionals. Both males and females are stigmatized for entering opposite-sex occupations. The woman engineer is a rarity; we raise our eyebrows at male nurses.

The semiprofessions—social work and nursing, for example—are dominated by women and may have the aforementioned characteristics of the professions, but they differ in degree. They often have only a minimal body of theoretical knowledge, they have less autonomy, the community restricts some of their right to regulate themselves, they have weaker codes of ethics, and their sense of being a subculture is less strong and pervasive.

In recent years, however, males have been found in greater numbers in the semiprofessions, except for nursing. What is interesting is that when men are found in the semiprofessions, they have taken over the authority positions. They are the head librarians, the principals in the grade schools, the supervisors in the social-welfare agencies.

The increased participation of men in the semiprofessions is partly because of the increased demand for workers in these areas and the concomitant low supply of females. It is partly the result of a general rise in prestige in these occupations—that is, higher pay—which makes them more attractive to men. More important, it seems that women encourage men to enter "their" professions because they prefer males in positions of authority and because they think that the presence of males raises the prestige of the occupation. Semiprofessions therefore are climbing up the occupational ladder, but largely because there are now more males in them.

These changes have not occurred in the learned professions. Women have hardly penetrated or altered these fields. Even in the newer professions, such as science, the old patterns obtain. "No doubt men and women have been granted the right to equality, in general terms, as a vague human right. However, for women the translation of that ideal into practice has been imperfect and unenthusiastic."[86]

Men and women, then, are segregated in the professions. They are also segregated *within* the professions. Female lawyers are generally in such family-related areas as trust and estate law or domestic relations. Female physicians are usually in pediatrics, public health, or psychiatry. This segregation within professions is as confining to women as the segregation from professions because it continues and reinforces the dominance-subordination pattern in the general society.

The evidence seems to indicate that most professional women marry men in the higher social classes; therefore they do not work for financial reasons.[87] Unlike her nonprofessional female counterpart and like her professional male counterpart, the professional woman works for the intrinsic satisfactions. One study of 200 women faculty members showed that they were as satisfied with their careers as their male colleagues were, although the reasons for their satisfactions differed. Women stressed human relations while men were concerned with material rewards, opportunities to do creative work, and independence.[88]

A committee formed by the American Sociological Association to report on the status of women in this profession disclosed that some progress had been made by women between 1968 and 1972.[89] For example, 33 per cent of the 8,095 graduate students in sociology in 1968–69 were women, compared to 36 per cent of 5,882 students in 1971–72. The committee expected to find these women underrepresented in elite universities, either because the schools would be reluctant to admit them or because they would be shy about applying. They were wrong. Women were almost equal in number to men at the top schools, which shows, according to the Committee, how ambitious women sociologists are. Furthermore, they found that women were receiving 37.5 per cent of the total financial support, such as assistantships and fellowships, slightly more than the female proportion in the student body. This indicates that there is currently reverse discrimination. That is, women are being encouraged and recruited over men by universities. It may be that there is a less admirable way to evaluate the fact that women get more of their just share of financial support money. It may be that male professors prefer women as assistants because women perform more readily in the subordinate role and are therefore more willing than men students to take orders, do scut work, and give attention to detail.

Perhaps women get the assistantships because they really are better assistants—it is their "natural" role.

After graduation, however, women sociologists fare much less
well. In 1968–69, when women represented 33 per cent of the
graduate student body, they represented only 15 per cent of the
3,353 sociologists who were teaching or doing research in academic settings. The situation was even worse in 1972, when
women were 36 per cent of the students but only 12 per cent of
the faculty members. Apparently "there is substantial leakage
between graduate school and faculty appointment—and the discrepancy is continuing."[90] When women are represented on facul-
ties, they cluster in the lower ranking positions: the proportion of
women in full-time nonladder positions is almost three times as
high as the proportion of men. Table 6 shows this clearly.

TABLE 6

FACULTY MEMBERS, ALL GRADUATE DEPARTMENTS,
1970, 1971, 1972, BY SEX AND RANK

Rank	1970		1971		1972	
	Total Faculty	Women	Total Faculty	Women	Total Faculty	Women
Full professor	900	4%	1,079	4%	1,035	5%
Associate professor	672	10	744	11	686	12
Assistant professor	996	13	1,163	12	1,115	16
Lecturer	76	12	114	21	106	30
Instructor	212	16	106	29	84	29
Total	2,946	9%	3,249	10%	3,026	12%

SOURCE: Helen MacGill Hughes (ed.), *The Status of Women in Sociology*,
Washington, D.C.: The American Sociological Association, 1973, p. 11.

Furthermore, when females do hold full or associate professor-
ships, they are usually in less prestigious schools, as Table 7 indicates.

Women also tend to dominate in the part-time appointments.
In 1971–72, 40 per cent of the women faculty members, compared to 23 per cent of the men, were part-time lecturers and in-
structors. Finally, although teaching graduate students is most

TABLE 7

FACULTY MEMBERS, 1970, 1971, 1972,
BY SEX AND QUALITY OF DEPARTMENT

	Distinguished		Strong		Good		Adequate		Unranked	
Year	Total Faculty	Women	Total Faculty	Women	Total Faculty	Women	Total Faculty	Women	Total Faculty	Women
1970	186	5%	379	5%	179	7%	366	7%	2,136	11%
1971	218	5	395	8	176	9	349	7	2,111	12
1972	202	5	339	11	154	12	380	10	1,951	13

SOURCE: Hughes.

desirable, women teach twice as many undergraduate classes as their male colleagues.

The committee blamed the college administrations for the continuing inequality in sociology departments. Chairpersons are more than willing to hire women. Fifty-eight per cent said they were making special efforts to recruit women, and 25 per cent said they had no trouble placing their women graduate students. Yet in spite of these efforts on the part of chairpeople to place and hire women, their situation is barely improved, primarily because the universities continue their outdated rules against nepotism.

The committee felt that although women suffer in respect to appointments and promotions, the greatest problem is the unequal salary structure. In 1967–1968 the median salary for women sociologists was $9,300 as against $11,000 for men. Table 8 shows

TABLE 8

SALARY DIFFERENTIALS BETWEEN MEN AND WOMEN,
1967–68, BY ACADEMIC RANK

Academic Rank	Salary Differential
Professor	$1,100
Associate	600
Assistant	400
Instructor	400
All sociologists	$1,700

SOURCE: Adapted from Hughes, p. 15.

the salary differential between men and women at different academic levels.

Finally, women sociologists have poor visibility in their own professional organizations and on editorial boards, councils, and committees. They constituted only 15 per cent of the active members of the American Sociological Association in 1972. Until Alice Rossi took office as president in 1972, there had only been one other woman president in the Association's 66-year history. Between 1967 and 1972, only 112 women, or 12 per cent of all the authors, had articles in the three major journals.

Ann Davis[91] attempted to discover why academic women in general and women sociologists in particular drop out of academia more than men; why they have been thought of as poor risks; and whether or not there is really sexual discrimination in universities. Davis interviewed four male sociologists and one male anthropologist in depth in order to learn their *subjective* opinions of their female colleagues. The subjects agreed that women are in an inferior position in sociology, that they are rarely hired by prestige schools, and that they do not write as much as male sociologists. The professors believed these conditions were due to cultural pressures that require a woman to denigrate her career in favor of her husband, home, and children. They also felt that discrimination against women did exist in sociology departments and that men perpetuated myths about women's lack of scholarly productivity to protect themselves. Davis concludes:

> We continue to be faced with the facts that good intellectual ability among women is being wasted as a social and national resource and that lack of clarity about the female role may be productive of personal unhappiness.[92]

Davis's remark applies as well to women physicians as it does to women sociologists. As in sociology and other professions, the number of women in medicine is increasing. In 1960, for example, 600 women were accepted into medical schools—7 per cent of all applicants. In 1968, however, women comprised 9.7 per cent of all applicants admitted. Nevertheless, as Table 5 (page 111) shows, in 1960 only 6.8 per cent of all medical doctors in the United States were female.

Some studies[93] reveal that the lay public does not fully accept the woman physician and, when offered a choice, will select a male doctor. Furthermore, the female physician is not fully accepted by her male colleagues.

Kosa and Coker[94] outlined three areas of role conflict for women doctors: (1) the professional role restricts the female role; (2) the female role restricts the professional role; and (3) female doctors have difficulty taking on the professional obligations that are incompatible with the female obligations. The researchers believe that women doctors cope with these conflicts by choosing medical specialties that will be least incompatible with their female role. To test their hypothesis, they interviewed 525 public health doctors. They selected male and female subjects who were matched on religion, socioeconomic status, medical education, age, and other variables. They noted that even though our cultural norms encourage marriage, especially for females, professional training generally counters this norm. Fewer of their subjects were married than one would expect to find in the general population (37 per cent of the males and only 18 per cent of the females). These data suggest that the professional role is more compatible with the "normal" male role than with the "normal" female role. Thus, though both defer marriage, females do so even more than males.

Gender role restricts women throughout their medical careers. On the average, women work for a shorter time than men; they are more likely to be in part-time positions; and they stay in one job for a shorter period of time. More important, women physicians are much less likely to be in private practice. Seventy-three per cent of Kosa and Coker's female subjects worked in salaried jobs compared to only 56 per cent of the male subjects. These authors believe that women enter salaried jobs because they are reluctant to assume the entrepreneurship aspect of a medical career. They define entrepreneurship as independent work, money as a primary reward for work, a willingness to work, and competitiveness. Women avoid entrepreneurship because it is, according to our social values, a male "trait," and female doctors find it conflicts with their female image.

Income differentials are apparently as great in the medical profession as in other occupations. In public health, for example, one of every five men earns over $15,000, compared to only one in every twenty-two women. In the first position after leaving public health, men average $17,672, compared to only $14,676 for women.[95]

Women profess, however, to be less interested in money, more interested in patients and new problems. Women also express a preference for shorter working hours, a dislike of competitiveness, and a disinterest in independence. It is probable that women have no innate preference for these things but are socialized to prefer them.

The principal question Kosa and Coker asked was how women manage these conflicts. The answer is in choice of medical specialty. Women overwhelmingly select one of three fields: pediatrics, psychiatry, and public health. Eighty per cent of the female doctors were in these three areas, compared to only 36 per cent of the male doctors.

Men and women, then, are segregated into subspecialties according to sex within the medical profession. This is in part because certain areas allow women to correlate their two life roles —professional and feminine. The study concentrates on public health doctors, and the authors felt the women entered this field because they could expect a fixed income, freedom from entrepreneurship, regular work hours, and a controllable work load—all factors that create ease in adapting the work role to the feminine role. Thus, it is not public health *per se* that attracts women, but the facets of it that make for compatibility with their feminine obligations.

The study just described was conducted in 1965 and six years later, Kosa re-examined the subject of women physicians.[96] He felt that social changes had occurred which would affect female doctors; therefore, he interviewed twenty female residents in large metropolitan hospitals. He found that twelve of the subjects were children of doctors and all came from families in high social strata. Money had never been a problem in the subjects' lives and it was not important in their careers. All wished to avoid entrepreneurial positions or competition with male doctors. All the female residents believed that only exceptional women should enter medicine because it required great commitment, self-confidence, and energy. They agreed that marriage and a medical career were not incompatible, and families would have to be carefully planned. Most of the subjects felt there were no formal restrictions on women doctors, but that there were informal ones.

The 1971 study confirmed most of the author's 1965 findings, but the later subjects believed that many social innovations, such as the civil rights movement and women's liberation, were having an effect on women in medicine. It was becoming easier to enter medical school; there were more salaried positions available; the restrictions placed on the professional role by the feminine role were being lifted; there was more public and colleague acceptance; and women were entering more diversified specialties.

Kosa concluded that American women are making progress in the medical profession, albeit their progress is snail-like and still very far behind countries like Russia, Israel, Germany, Italy, and England.* He notes that there are pressures that encourage women doctors, but counterpressures militating against them. He predicts, then, that change will occur, but it will be slow, so he does not expect that more than 10 per cent of our doctors will be female in the near future or that women will take positions of leadership within the medical profession itself.

In 1960 women comprised only 3.5 per cent of all the lawyers in the United States,[97] but by 1974 the percentage had risen to 16.[98] This is still a low percentage, of course, and much can be laid at the door of outright discrimination. Erwin O. Smigel, in his study of Wall Street lawyers, says:

> Women are discriminated against to a greater degree than Jews. . . . Not until 1950 did Harvard Law School begin to accept women students. There were almost no female lawyers in the Wall Street firms until World War II brought about a shortage of male attorneys. . . . While most large law offices now do have some women in their organization, very few become partners.[99]

The easiest way to document discrimination is to look at income differentials. James J. White writes:

> On the basis of the available figures and analysis one can conclude with near certainty that the income differential between men

---

* *The Fuller Utilization of the Woman Physician*, Washington, D.C.: Women's Bureau, U.S. Department of Labor, January 1968, shows that one of four doctors are women in the Philippines, Finland, and Israel, one of five in Germany and Italy, one in six in Sweden and England, compared to one in fourteen in the United States.

and women was not caused by any of the following factors: (1) the fact that women were employed only part time; (2) a lack of experience on the part of the women lawyers; (3) lower class rank and less law review participation by the women; (4) a difference in schools attended; or (5) different types of employers. In addition . . . the income difference was not caused by (1) response bias among the members of the sample; (2) differences between general type of work performed by the men and women; or (3) differences in the type of jobs sought.[100]

White substantiates his charge against the law profession. Of the sixty-three placement directors and deans he interviewed, only four believed there was "insignificant" discrimination against women law graduates. Table 9 shows the responses of women lawyers to the question: "Do you believe that you have been the object of discrimination because of your sex by your present, former, or any potential employer from whom you sought a job?"

TABLE 9

BELIEFS OF FEMALES CONCERNING DISCRIMINATION

Degree	Per Cent of Females (N = 1,148)
Certainly discriminated against	38.2
Almost certainly	9.6
Probably	17.6
Probably not	15.8
Certainly not	18.8

SOURCE: Adapted from White, p. 1085.

White then wondered if the discrimination against women was actually functional for the law firms. Did excluding women produce an economic gain for the firm? Do women have intellectual or psychological defects that make them inferior lawyers? If so, White says, the discrimination is defensible. But when he compared lawyers on four pertinent variables—intelligence, emotional suitability, probable length of service, and ability to inspire confidence in clients—White found that men and women were equally represented on Law Review and that there was no difference between the sexes in class standings. Emotional suitability was more difficult to measure; however, White determined that women are not, contrary to popular opinion, reluctant to argue in court nor did they avoid criminal cases. Furthermore, when asked why they had become lawyers, most had the same motivations as men—to make money and to get ahead. As to probable length of service, the data did show that women change jobs and leave the profession more frequently than men, but the differences are small. At the end of seven years, for example, 14.5 per cent of the men and 11.1 per cent of the women were still in their first jobs. Finally, White's data indicate that women lawyers see fewer clients than men; however, that doesn't mean they cannot inspire client confidence. It is possible the firms lack confidence and send fewer clients to their women associates.

White concedes that his study does not conclusively resolve the question of whether or not discrimination against women in law firms is functional. However, he feels it does explode some of the myths about women lawyers. Therefore, he concludes that the "enormous differential between the males and females is attributable to nonfunctional discrimination."[101]

In a study of fifty female attorneys, Cynthia Epstein found that there are different role expectations and norms for women than for men lawyers. "In addition, expectations regarding appropriate female sex-role behavior often were in conflict with norms governing occupational-role behavior."[102] Very often there is ambivalence, confusion, even hostility. The result is that women lawyers often opt for part-time or low-level jobs in their efforts to reduce the conflict. Epstein brands this a "successful control process." By undercutting the motivation of women lawyers to engage their talents at the highest levels, it maintains the cohesion of the collegial group; makes for ease of social intercourse in the *male* legal community; and reduces competition by closing higher level opportunities to women."[103]

The situation for women lawyers, however, seems promising. For the past two years, according to a survey by the American Bar Association, there has been a sharp rise in the number of female law students. As of October 1973, of the 106,102 law students, 16,760 were women, an increase of almost 38 per cent over 1972.[104]

All three groups of professional women described here—sociologists, physicians, and lawyers—are poorly represented numerically in their occupations. All of them suffer discrimination, especially financial. Within every profession there are sex-segregated subspecialties. Women do not occupy positions of power in their fields. The expectations and norms surrounding women professionals are different from those that apply to men, creating conflict and ambiguity and often leading to limited careers and personal unhappiness.

THE DUAL-CAREER FAMILY

There are two major studies on the dual-career family, one by Lynda Lytle Holmstrom[105] and the other by Margaret Poloma and T. Neal Garland.[106] In addition, several sociologists have done work in the area and several others have written on the subject. The notion of a "dual-professional" family is a startlingly new one. Families traditionally contain only one "serious" worker —the male. When both spouses are professionally engaged, the structure of the relationship must change. What changes occur? How successfully are they handled? Such couples are "deviant" in our present society, but there is no doubt that their numbers will continue to increase; therefore, it is important to learn about them.

Holmstrom points out that there are three main barriers that dual-career families face: the rigid structure of the professions, the isolation of the small modern family, and the equation of masculinity with superiority.

Professions require that those involved be very much involved. That is, full time means more than from nine to five; it means a complete emotional commitment, with all else subordinate. It also means a willingness to be mobile, to move from one geographic location to another. Often one member of such a family is offered an opportunity hundreds of miles from the other. Then they must decide which career is to be sacrificed or whether to sacrifice neither but instead give up at least part of their personal life together. This is one constant problem described by Holmstrom: the demands always put on the professional and the possibility of conflicting demands in the two-career family.

The second difficulty is the isolation of the nuclear family. Little help can be expected from relatives and friends. Servants and daycare centers are only problematical in our society. Childrearing becomes a major drawback because in the dual-career family the task almost automatically falls to the female partner.

The third area—the "natural" superiority of men—permeates the two aforementioned problems because our society gives men the right to the career. Families should move when the man is offered a new opportunity; women should take care of the home and children.

Holmstrom studied twenty dual-professional couples to find out how they resolved the problems outlined. The couple sample contained a wife with a Ph.D., between twenty-five and thirty-five years of age, involved in a full-time career, and associated with a professional institution. For comparative purposes, the researcher also interviewed seven couples in which the wife had a limited career.

Holmstrom found that professional women married later than nonprofessionals and were less oriented toward marriage. Furthermore, although they placed a high value on having children, they had smaller families than the average and they waited longer to have them. These couples faced the mobility question by considering both the husband's and wife's careers; but when a sacrifice had to be made, it was typically the wife who made it.

One important area to explore was the home. Was the division of labor along sexual lines? Since career wives cannot devote their full time to housework, how do they manage? For one thing, professional wives entertain less than traditional wives, and when they do, they either employ professional help or take guests out to dinner. Second, professional wives get more help in household tasks than traditional wives, either from paid employees or from their husbands. The tasks are still allocated somewhat along sex lines—wives cooked, men did the heavy work. But there seems to be a great deal of interchangeability based on fairness, availability, and skill. In other words, professional couples share more of the household chores than traditional couples, although the men regard their share as "helping," and they do so along pragmatic lines.

The problem of childrearing was less easily resolved. Generally they used one of three methods: the husband shared the child-rearing responsibilities, they hired help, or the wife modified her professional life. Ideologically, these couples subscribed to the notion that it is good for both the mother and the child to have someone else care for the child at least part of the time.

Holmstrom addressed herself to the important question of competition. Popular mythology has it that when two people work, a feeling of competitiveness will develop that can be destructive to the marital relationship.* Holmstrom did find this a problem for five of the couples. Competitiveness did not seem to be related to the fields the man and woman were in but, rather, to masculine, subjective feelings of lack of self-assurance and feelings of threat and inadequacy.

Almost all of the twenty professional couples in the sample reported they were helpful to each other's careers and were able to discuss each other's work without animosity. In addition, not one of the husbands held a negative view of his wife's career, and almost all were actively supportive. These men were willing to change their life-styles, help extensively with home and child care, move if necessary, do almost anything within reason to further their wives' careers. This kind of attitude is very important because the professional women stressed the need for their husbands' support. They felt that they could not succeed either as professionals or as wives without it. Holmstrom feels that "for the two-career family to become an effective reality, both partners have to desire it and make this a basic assumption in their lives."[107]

Holmstrom concludes from her study that professional women, in terms of personal relationships, are relatively better off than nonprofessionals. Nevertheless, relative to men, they are less well off and there is still a great deal of inequality. The husband's career is still considered more important; the wife still does more accommodating and still makes the most sacrifices. Holmstrom suggests that, if sexual equality is really to be achieved, we must, for one thing, make occupational demands more flexible. Both

---

* Talcott Parsons expresses this theory. He believes that the solidarity of the family is threatened when both members of the marital dyad are engaged in full-time careers. "The Kinship System of the Contemporary United States," *Essays in Sociological Theory* (New York: Free Press, 1954), p. 192.

men and women should be able to pursue part-time careers without penalty, and the criteria now used to evaluate professional achievement must be amended. Second, the norm that children must be constantly attended by their mothers must be altered to allow fathers and daycare centers greater participation without stigma. Both these problems are rooted in the "nonconscious ideology" (see Chapter 3) that men are innately superior to women. This ideology needs changing. The rest will follow.

Poloma and Garland came to very similar conclusions on the structure and functions of the dual-career families, after studying fifty-three professional couples. These authors acknowledge that discrimination in the job market and in the home certainly impede female professional careers, but they claim that underlying this discrimination are certain assumptions about the family and the woman's role in it. These assumptions include the notions that marriage is the most important event in a woman's life and being a wife and mother are the major statuses. Accepting these ideas, professional women come to "tolerate domestication."[108] According to Poloma and Garland's study, professional women do not seek full equality. The idea of the egalitarian family is really a myth. Only one of the fifty-three couples was truly egalitarian, which Poloma and Garland consider an essential family form if the woman is to have the full freedom necessary to advance her career. In this one family, both spouses shared, not helped in, all household tasks. Both were equally responsible for cooking, cleaning, laundry, childcare, and economic needs.

The distaff side of the other couples, however, did not feel discriminated against. They were willing to tolerate domestication so they could have both a career and a family. Poloma and Garland blame several factors for this female acceptance of second-placehood, but they give a large share of it to socialization. Women have been socialized to accept the responsibility for household chores and childcare chores, and undoing one's early training is no easy task. Thus, even if we were to make changes in the social structure as Holmstrom suggests, career women would retain this acceptance of the traditional role. However most of the women these authors studied were satisfied with their lives and, to paraphrase W. I. Thomas, "if they defined their situation as happy, they were happy in consequence."

To summarize, most researchers who have investigated married career women found that while there is an increase in the number of women with careers, they retain their traditional roles in the family and view of themselves. While the husbands of career women may "help" more than men with nonworking wives, there is no real role reversal.[109]

Furthermore, the evidence suggests that women are not really interested in relinquishing or truly sharing their household responsibilities,[110] largely because they have been socialized to seek their identity in these roles. Women prefer to add an additional status, not substitute the housekeeper status for the professional one. Even college girls retain this traditional stance. Shirley Angrist reported that one-half of the college subjects she interviewed said they would want to work only if their husbands did not earn enough money.[111] Both men and women appear, from almost all available research, to accept the fact that the home and children are the primary responsibilities of the female. A career does not lessen this responsibility, albeit the career woman will get more help from her husband. Thus, no matter how well-educated or respected professionally, the career woman does not have the freedom to pursue her occupational goals that her husband has.

A female professor, testifying at the New York City Commission on Human Rights, summed it all up:

> I could manage a husband and a household and still go to teach a class—I suspect just that made the male members of the department look at me as though I were a talking dog, as though I had a really remarkable quality. And I always felt, particularly on the part of one department chairman, a kind of resentment, because after all, the bald fact was that I was doing twice as much as he was. I was a pretty good professor. I was also a good housewife, mother, cook, and runner of errands and all the other things. And I suspect in that way women like me must have represented a kind of threat.[112]

Notes

1. Georges Friedmann, *The Anatomy of Work* (New York: Crowell-Collier, 1961); Erich Fromm, *Escape from Freedom* (New York: Avon Books, 1941); Karen Horney, "The Neurotic Personality of Our Time,"

reprinted in J. A. C. Brown, *Freud and the Post-Freudians* (Baltimore: Penguin Books, 1961); Patrick Mullahy, *Oedipus: Myth and Complex* (New York: Grove Press, 1948); and David Reisman and Warner J. Bloomberg, "Work and Leisure: Fusion or Polarity?" in *Research in Industrial and Human Relations*, eds. C. M. Arensberg *et al.* (New York: Harper & Bros., 1957).

2. Robert O. Blood, Jr., "Long-Range Causes and Consequences of the Employment of Married Women," *Journal of Marriage and the Family* (1965), 27:43–47.

3. Abbott L. Ferriss, *Indicators of Trends in the Status of American Women* (New York: Russell Sage Foundation, 1971), pp. 85–87.

4. *Ibid.*, pp. 91–95.

5. Malcolm S. Cohen, "Married Women in the Labor Force: An Analysis of Participation Rates," *Monthly Labor Review* (1969), 92:31–35.

6. F. Ivan Nye and Lois Wladis Hoffman, *The Employed Mother in America* (Chicago: Rand McNally, 1963), pp. 327–29.

7. Cohen, *op. cit.*

8. Glen S. Cain, *Married Women in the Labor Force* (Chicago: University of Chicago Press, 1966).

9. Valerie Kincaide Oppenheimer, *The Female Labor Force in the United States: Demographic and Economic Factors Governing Its Growth and Changing Composition* (Berkeley, Calif.: Institute of International Studies, University of California, 1970).

10. Edward Gross, "*Plus ça change* . . . ? The Sexual Structure of Occupations Over Time," *Social Problems*, 16 (1968), pp. 198–208.

11. Ivar Berg, *Education and Jobs: The Great Training Robbery* (New York: Praeger, 1970), pp. 38–60.

12. Cynthia Fuchs Epstein, *Woman's Place* (Berkeley: University of California Press, 1970), p. 73.

13. Randall Collins, "A Conflict Theory of Sexual Stratification," *Social Problems*, 19:1 (1971), pp. 5–6.

14. *New York Times* (July 11, 1973), p. 16.

15. Ferriss, *op. cit.*, p. 138.

16. *Ibid.*, p. 140.

17. George Cooper, "Women and Employment Benefits," in Eleanor Holmes Norton, *Women's Role in Contemporary Society* (New York: Avon Books, 1972), p. 381.

18. *Ibid.*, pp. 384–86.

19. " 'Social Security'—A Gross Misnomer, Especially for Women," *Prime Time*, 2:1 (January 1974), pp. 11, 13, 14.

20. Ferriss, *op. cit.*, p. 107.

21. Oscar Lewis, *Five Families: Mexican Case Studies in the Culture of Poverty* (New York: Basic Books, 1959).

22. Gail Putney Fullerton, *Survival in Marriage* (New York: Holt, Rinehart, and Winston, 1972), chap. 8.

23. Ferriss, *op. cit.*, chap. 8.

24. *Ibid.*, p. 122.

25. *Ibid.*, p. 126.

26. Norton, *Women's Role*, *op. cit.*, pp. 392–98.

27. *Ibid.*, pp. 399–400.

28. Ferriss, *op. cit.*, p. 107.

29. U.S. Department of Labor, Women's Bureau, *1969 Handbook on Women Workers* (Washington, D.C.).
30. Catherine C. Arnott, "Married Women and the Pursuit of Profit: An Exchange Theory Perspective," *Journal of Marriage and the Family*, 34:1 (1972), pp. 22–30.
31. Esther Peterson, "Working Women," in *The Woman in America*, ed. Robert Lifton (Boston: Beacon Press, 1964), p. 148.
32. *Ibid.*, p. 164.
33. Edwin C. Lewis, *Developing Woman's Potential* (Ames: Iowa State University Press, 1968), p. 237.
34. Marion G. Sobol, "Commitment to Work," in Nye and Hoffman, *op. cit.*
35. *New York Times* (July 11, 1973), p. 16.
36. Edwin Lewis, *op. cit.*, p. 130.
37. *Ibid.*, pp. 130–31.
38. *Ibid.*, p. 131.
39. *Ibid.*, p. 132.
40. *Ibid.*, p. 131.
41. Margaret M. Poloma and T. Neal Garland, "The Myth of the Egalitarian Family: Familial Roles and the Professionally Employed Wife," in *The Professional Woman*, ed. Athena Theodore (Cambridge, Mass.: Schenkman, 1971), pp. 741–61.
42. Frances Feldman, "Supplementary Income Earned by Married Women," in National Manpower Council, *Work in the Lives of Married Women* (New York: Columbia University Press, 1958), pp. 93–115.
43. Margaret Carroll, "The Working Wife and Her Family's Economic Position," *Monthly Labor Review* (1962), 85:366–74.
44. Lois Hoffman, "The Decision to Work," in Nye and Hoffman, *op. cit.*, pp. 18–39.
45. Edwin Lewis, *op. cit.*, pp. 125–26.
46. Sanford M. Dornbusch and David M. Heer, "The Evaluation of Work by Females, 1940–1950," *American Journal of Sociology* (1957), 63: 27–29.
47. Susan Orden and Norman Bradburn, "Working Wives and Marriage Happiness," *American Journal of Sociology* (1969), 74:392–407.
48. Edwin Lewis, *op. cit.*, p. 126.
49. *Ibid.*, p. 127.
50. J. B. Parrish, "Professional Womanpower as a National Resource," *Quarterly Review of Economic Business* (1961), 1:54–63.
51. Edwin Lewis, *op. cit.*, p. 129.
52. Nye and Hoffman, *op. cit.*, chap. 10.
53. *Ibid.*; and M. A. Gold, *A Social Psychology of Delinquent Boys* (Ann Arbor, Mich.: Institute for Social Research, 1961).
54. John Bowlby, *Child Care and the Growth of Love* (Geneva: World Health Organization, 1952).
55. F. Ivan Nye and Felix M. Berardo, *The Family: Its Structure and Interaction* (New York: Macmillan Co., 1973), p. 282.
56. Nye and Hoffman, *op. cit.*, chap. 24.
57. *Ibid.*, chap. 6.
58. Alice Marcella Propper, "The Relationship of Maternal Employment to Adolescent Roles, Activities, and Parental Relationships," *Journal of Marriage and the Family*, 34:3 (1972), pp. 417–21.

59. Horace Gray, "The Trapped Housewife," *Marriage and Family Living* (1962), 24:179–89.
60. Elizabeth Douvan, "Employment and the Adolescent," in Nye and Hoffman, *op. cit.*, chap. 11; Lois Hoffman, *ibid.*, chap. 19; and Propper, *ibid.*
61. Nye and Hoffman, *op. cit.*, chap. 10.
62. F. Ivan Nye, "Maternal Employment and Marital Interactions," *Social Forces* (1961), 40:113–19.
63. Leland Axelson, "The Marital Adjustment and Marital Role Definitions of Working and Non-Working Wives," *Marriage and Family Living* (1963), 25:189–95.
64. Genevieve M. Wise and Don C. Carter, "A Definition of the Role of Homemaker by Two Generations of Women," *Journal of Marriage and the Family* (1965), 27:531–32.
65. Orden and Bradburn, *op. cit.*
66. Catherine C. Arnott, "Husbands' Attitude and Wives' Commitment to Employment," *Journal of Marriage and the Family*, 34:4 (1972), pp. 673–84.
67. Edna Rostow, "Conflict and Accommodation," in *The Woman in America*, ed. Robert Lifton, *op. cit.*, p. 224.
68. Nye and Hoffman, *op. cit.*, chaps. 15, 19, 20.
69. *Ibid.*, chap. 19.
70. David M. Heer, "Dominance and the Working Wife," in Nye and Hoffman, *op. cit.*, chap. 18.
71. *Ibid.*
72. Clifford Kirkpatrick, *The Family as Process and Institution*, 2d ed. (New York: Ronald Press, 1963), pp. 126–48.
73. Nye and Hoffman, *op. cit.*, chap. 10.
74. Nye and Berardo, *op. cit.*, p. 288.
75. Carl A. Ridley, "Exploring the Impact of Work Satisfaction and Involvement on Marital Interaction When Both Partners Are Employed," *Journal of Marriage and the Family*, 35:2 (1973), pp. 229–37.
76. Nye and Berardo, *op. cit.*, p. 289.
77. Sheila Feld, "Feelings of Adjustment," in Nye and Hoffman, *op. cit.*, chap. 24.
78. Nye and Berardo, *op. cit.*, p. 290.
79. Ernest Greenwood, "Attributes of a Profession," in *Man, Work, and Society*, eds. Sigmund Nosow and William H. Form (New York: Basic Books, 1962), pp. 206–18.
80. Cynthia Fuchs Epstein, *Woman's Place*, *op. cit.*, p. 6.
81. Athena Theodore, ed., *The Professional Woman*, *op. cit.*, chap. 1.
82. *Ibid.*, p. 11.
83. Matina Horner, "The Motive to Avoid Success and Changing Aspirations of College Women," in Bardwick, *Readings*, p. 16.
84. J. Money, J. L. Hampson, and J. G. Hampson, "An Examination of Some Basic Concepts: The Evidence of Human Hermaphroditism," *Bulletin of the Johns Hopkins Hospital*, 97 (1955), pp. 301–19. See also J. Money, "Sex Hormones and Other Variables in Human Eroticism," in *Sex and Internal Secretions*, vol. 2, ed. W. C. Young (Baltimore: Williams and Wilkins, 1961).
85. Money, Hampson, and Hampson, *op. cit.*
86. Cynthia Fuchs Epstein, *Woman's Place*, *op. cit.*, p. 6.
87. Theodore, *op. cit.*, p. 12.

88. Ruth Eckert and John E. Stecklein, "Academic Women," *Liberal Education* (1959), 45:390–97.
89. Helen MacGill Hughes, ed., *The Status of Women in Sociology* (Washington, D.C.: The American Sociological Association, 1973). Other investigators in this area support the report of the Committee. See also Ann E. Davis, "Women as a Minority Group in Higher Academics," *American Sociologist*, 4:2 (1969), pp. 95–99: Eckert and Stecklein, *op. cit.*; Patricia Albjerg, "Women in Academe," *Science*, 169:3952 (1970), pp. 1284–90; and Jessie Bernard, "My Four Revolutions: An Autobiographical History of the ASA," *American Journal of Sociology*, 78:4 (1973), pp. 773–91.
90. Hughes, *op. cit.*
91. Ann Davis, *Women as a Minority, op. cit.*
92. *Ibid.*, p. 99.
93. Josephine J. Williams, "Patients and Prejudice: Lay Attitudes Toward Women Physicians," *American Journal of Sociology* (1964), 51:282–87; and Carla A. Pullum, "Women, Medicine, and Misconceptions," *Journal of the American Medical Women's Association* (1963), 18:565.
94. John Kosa and Robert E. Coker, Jr., "The Female Physician in Public Health: Conflict and Reconciliation of the Sex and Professional Roles," *Sociology and Social Research*, 49.3 (1965), pp. 294–305.
95. *Ibid.*, p. 99.
96. John Kosa, "Women in Medicine in a Changing World," in Theodore, *op. cit.*, pp. 709–19.
97. *United States Bureau of the Census of 1963*, vol. 1, p. 528.
98. *New York Law Journal* (January 15, 1974), pp. 1, 4.
99. Erwin O. Smigel, *The Wall Street Lawyer*, 2d ed., (Bloomington: Indiana University Press, 1969), p. 46.
100. James J. White, "Women in the Law," *Michigan Law Review*, 65:6 (1967), p. 1084.
101. *Ibid.*, p. 1093.
102. Cynthia F. Epstein, "Women Lawyers and Their Professions: Inconsistency of Social Controls and Their Consequences for Professional Performance." (Paper presented at the 64th annual meeting of the American Sociological Association, San Francisco, September 1969).
103. *Ibid.*
104. *New York Law Journal, op. cit.*
105. Lynda Lytle Holmstrom, *The Two-Career Family* (Cambridge, Mass.: Schenkman, 1972).
106. Poloma and Garland, "The Myth of the Egalitarian Family," *op. cit.*, and T. Neal Garland, "The Better Half? The Male in the Dual Professional Family," both in Theodore, *The Professional Woman, op. cit.*
107. Holmstrom, *op. cit.*, p. 142.
108. Pierre L. Van den Berghe, "The Two Roles of Women," *American Sociologist* (1970), 5:375–76.
109. Robert O. Blood, Jr., and Donald M. Wolfe, *Husbands and Wives, op. cit.*
110. Constantina Safilios-Rothschild, "Marital Expectations and Marital Experience: Why Such a Discrepancy?" (paper read at the ICOFA meetings in Rennes, France, April 3–7, 1969); Ralph Turner, "Some Aspects of Women's Ambition," *American Journal of Sociology* (1964), 70:

271–85; and John E. Tropman, "The Married Professional Social Worker," *Journal of Marriage and the Family* (1968), 30:661–65.
111. Shirley S. Angrist, "Changes in Women's Work Aspirations During College (Or Work Does Not Equal Career)." (Paper read at Ohio Valley Sociological Society, Akron, Ohio, May 1970.)
112. Ruth Waxman, in Norton, *Women's Role, op. cit.*, p. 701.

5

Class and Race Differences in Gender Roles

*HELEN MAYER HACKER** *

Social-Class Differences

It has often been asserted that women's liberation makes no appeal to blue-collar women because it is irrelevant to their problems. The argument continues that such women are not seeking a broadening or redefinition of the traditional feminine role but, rather, an opportunity to fulfill the middle-class version of that role. Further, they do not wish to encroach upon formerly masculine prerogatives but lament the deficiencies of their husbands and lovers in enacting the middle-class masculine role. They would like their men to be better providers, to assume more responsible leadership in the family, to take greater interest in the development of the children, and to offer more companionship to their wives, including romantic attentions. If the blue-collar wife works —and she is more likely to do so than her white-collar counterpart —it is thought that she is only waiting for the day when her husband's earnings are sufficient to permit her return to full-time homemaking.

This is the portrait fostered by the mass media. For example, in a recent episode of the popular television series "Maude," the maid, Florida, the linchpin of the family, almost provokes a nervous breakdown in Maude when she announces that her hus-

* This chapter and Chapter 6 will appear, in slightly revised form, in a forthcoming textbook by Helen M. Hacker to be published by Harper & Row and tentatively entitled *American Gender Roles: Present and Possible.*

band's promotion has made it possible for her to quit her job and lavish her ministrations on her own house and family. Her complaint is mostly against the class system, not the sex-caste system.

Her male consort is also seen as wishing not to change the traditional norms of masculinity but, on the contrary, to acquire the financial wherewithal to play the patriarch. He may pretend to long for the days before the prison gates of marriage and family closed upon him, but in fact he accepts the roles of husband and father as indicators of his status as an adult male. Courtship and early wedded bliss represent only a brief interruption of his emotionally more satisfying relationships with male buddies, hanging out at the corner or local bar in periods of unemployment or with the work gang on the job. Women are tolerated and placated when necessary to ensure sexual satisfaction and regular home-cooked meals. The chief responsibility for childrearing properly belongs to them. In later years the man's interests are more car than carnal. Such is the stereotype of the working-class man.

The burden of this section is to correct and refine this brief sketch and to assess current changes and possible future directions. For these purposes reference must be made to empirical studies. First, though, it may be helpful to discuss the concept of social class as a modulator of American cultural values.

Although most Americans give lip service to the idea that all men and women are created equal, in fact they recognize that the commodities of power, property, and prestige are not distributed equally in this society. There is a long history of sociological analysis and research concerning the stratification system in the United States, including such vexing questions as whether we have a continuous gradient of prestige or a specific number of discrete social classes—and, if the latter, how many, whether membership in a social class is determined objectively by such factors as occupation, education, and income or subjectively by a person's feeling of identification with one class or another, how much mobility occurs from one class to another, whether or not there is more or less movement today than in the past, and to what extent a person's behavior and social values can be explained in terms of the class to which, by some objective criterion, he belongs or the class to which he aspires.

Without entering fully into these controversial areas, we shall assume for the purpose of this discussion that there are distinctive styles of life that are common to broad groups in the American population, resulting from a combination of the level of living made possible by their economic resources, their social interaction with similarly situated people, and their value orientations or beliefs about what is and what should be. Our interest here is to delineate the differential assumptions about the nature of men and women, role expectations for husband and wife and other relationships between the sexes, and actual behaviors that can be attributed to differences in the life situations of the various classes.

Following Joseph Kahl,[1] we shall isolate five classes as displaying sufficiently meaningful clusters of related variables to warrant being considered approximations of a far more complex reality. Their designations and their distribution in the population are as follows:

Upper class	1%
Upper middle class	9
Lower middle class	40
Working class	40
Lower class	10

The Upper Class

To belong to the upper class one must have possessed money long enough for it to be purified of all sordid origins, a creditable family tree of several generations, manners that seem inborn rather than bred—all three summed up in Kahl's term "graceful living." On their pinnacle of power, pelf, and prestige, upper-class people have the social security, despite their reverence for the past, to be individualists and indulge their idiosyncrasies. As dilettantes they may dabble in the arts or even in radical politics. One might expect them to show considerable latitude in man-woman relationships and to work out their own variations on the theme of gender roles.

The fact is, however, that the measures required to maintain upper-class status from one generation to the next impose certain limitations on individual freedom. First, since the family is the basic unit of the stratification system, family loyalty and solidarity are important. Minor pecadillos may be covered up, but public scandal must be avoided. Ancestral portraits frown down upon the young to remind them of the glorious family tradition and to keep them in line. It has been said of the upper-class woman that her name should appear in the newspapers only three times during her life—when she is born, when she marries, and when she dies. The patriarchal extended family helps to preserve the impermeability of the upper class against social climbers. Control over the financial welfare of the family is usually vested in its oldest living male member or his widow. It is only by virtue of their superior longevity that women attain a matriarchal position.

Continuity of the family name is important and leads to the greater significance of sons, who are expected to follow in their fathers' occupational footsteps. Unless her family is more illustrious than that of her husband, the wife loses her identity in the marital merger and minimizes the traditions of her family while extolling those of his. According to Baltzell,[2] upper-class men prefer to marry women who have no serious career interests.

The most crucial line of defense in protecting upper-class status is parental control over mate selection. Marriages serve to consolidate and augment family fortunes. Although the claims of romantic love are not disallowed, the pool of eligible partners is coterminous with the boundaries of the upper class. The young usually conform to class endogamy (the custom of marriage within one's own social class) because of their economic dependence upon the family and the significant rewards at stake. The emphasis on not marrying beneath one's station (hypogamy) works a greater hardship on young women than on young men. First, the operation of the "Brahmin syndrome" permits men more freedom in marrying down, since the wife can acquire the status of her husband. With some prospective mates thus drained off, the upper-class woman has a more difficult time than the man in finding a suitable marital partner. She suffers greater sanctions in marrying outside her class and may have to choose celibacy as the cost of maintaining her social standing. In addition, the double standard of sex morality offers men an escape valve denied to women. Men are free to have liaisons with women of lower status, provided that they do not eventuate in marriage.

Also hampering the upper-class girl's marital chances is the premium placed on grace and beauty. As already noted, it is less feasible for her to offset physical unattractiveness with wealth and position in marrying outside her class. Further, sex-segregated educational institutions (more common in this than in other classes) and her lesser freedom of movement outside her own circle diminish her opportunities for meeting men. In fact, the function of the debut for upper-class girls is to identify eligible mates. The poet Amy Lowell has written movingly of the suffering she experienced in her invidious self-comparisons to other girls.[3] In her "stiff, brocaded gown" she protested the patterns of the upper class. Eleanor Roosevelt provides another example of the vulnerability of even upper-class girls to this traditional form of feminine self-depreciation.

With its orientation to the past, the upper class has been viewed as a citadel of conservatism. Some observers, however, note cracks in the armor. As more and more upper-class girls go to college, increasingly coeducational, and even graduate school, they are acquiring the intellectual substance to break the family mold and present nonpedigreed but interesting young men to their parents as prospective sons-in-law.[4]

Traditionally, the roles of husband and wife in the upper class were clearly separated. The wife acted as hostess and companion for her husband but had little involvement in his business life. She aided him in the proper use of money—that is, in the cultivation of culture rather than in conspicuous consumption. She was instrumental in expressing the humanistic values of the upper class and supervised social activities. Although she was not engaged in paid employment, she might involve herself in community activities, an outlet for creative energy that is increasingly cut off as professionals pre-empt the previously volunteer civic and charitable functions. Although the upper-class husband has greater marital power than husbands in other classes, his wife enjoys equality on social occasions. She, of course, must put up with his infidelities, since divorce is truly a court of last resort. On the other hand, spacious living quarters and ample funds enable her, if she so wishes, to manage her own extramarital affairs discreetly.

The upper-class wife knows no "viciousness in the kitchen." Her homemaking role is purely ceremonial. Nor need the care of children tie her down, since these are reared by parental surrogates. She is free to travel with her husband or on her own. That flamboyant possibilities are open to the defiant upper-class wife by her freedom from either financial worry or domestic drudgery is illustrated in the life of V. Sackville-West, who took off for France or Italy when it pleased her and did not find it at all necessary to join her husband, Harold Nicolson, in the various capitals to which he was posted by the Foreign Service.[5]

Although it is not specifically designated as an upper-class phenomenon, Kirkpatrick's characterization of the companion role in marriage sums up social expectations for the upper-class wife:

> The privileges pertaining to this role include pleasures shared with the husband, a more romantic emotional response, admiration, funds adequate for dress and recreation, leisure for social and educational activity, and chivalrous attentions. On the other hand, it implies as obligations, the preservation of beauty under the penalty of marital insecurity, the rendering of ego and erotic satisfaction to the husband, the cultivation of social contacts advantageous to him, the maintenance of intellectual alertness, and the responsibility for exorcising the demon of boredom.[6]

While upper-class life imposes strains upon men as well as women, such men constitute the most privileged group in American society, with the greatest opportunities for validating feelings of self-worth. Their business and professional activities release them from the tedium of measuring out their lives with coffee spoons. Upper-class women, despite their social and financial security, share the ascribed status of all women and indeed, may experience most poignantly the problems of identity and self-actualization, especially as social change shrinks and invalidates their traditional roles in the family and community.

The Upper Middle Class

As already noted, the complexity and fluidity of American society are such that researchers rarely agree on the number and relative sizes of social classes or on the proper assignment of a family to one class or another. The objective complex of occupation-income-education generally serves as a rough indicator, but discrepancies among these variables, as well as outlooks on life that do not conform to those of the bulk of families with similar objective characteristics, produce status inconsistencies that interfere with any neat categorization of people. The reader may have noticed, for example, that in the discussion of the upper class, explicit attention was *not* given to those self-made men (and occasionally women) who lacked the qualification of ancestry and inherited wealth but nevertheless had climbed from middle-class origins to positions of power and influence on a par with those of the "old elite," had embraced their social values, and aspired to social intimacy with them, if not for themselves, at least for their children, through marriage.

When we turn our attention to executives and their wives, it is a moot question whether they should be placed in the upper class or the upper middle class. Since they seem to be more concerned with "career" and "getting ahead" than with "graceful living," their assignment to the upper echelons of the middle class seems appropriate.

The wife of an executive[7] is primarily an appendage of her husband's job. Management's problem, according to one executive, is how "to deliberately plan and create a favorable, constructive attitude on the part of the wife that will liberate her husband's total energies for the job." The good executive wife (1) is highly adaptable, (2) is highly gregarious, and (3) realizes that her husband belongs to the corporation. It goes without saying that she runs her home and children so efficiently that her briefcase-toting husband steps over his threshold at night into an atmosphere of sweet tranquillity. He finds a wife ready to listen, to serve without resentment as a "sounding board," a "refueling station," a "wailing wall"—in effect as a stabilizer who rests and rejuvenates him for the next day's battle. Needless to say, she never complains if her husband comes home late or is transferred to another city so that she must move away from her friends, family, and children's school, nor does she meddle in her husband's business affairs or volunteer advice. She is agreeable to all her husband's business associates and their wives, but not too friendly, because one never knows when upward or downward mobility might introduce embarrassment into the relationship. What thanks does she get for her self-abnegation? Material comforts, a round of social activities, leisure for recreation—and the possibility that her husband may outgrow her or tire of her.

Regardless of the special pressures placed on corporate wives, if one wanted to pinpoint the segment of American society that has the greatest material and psychological freedom to work out its own life-styles, it would probably be the upper middle class. John F. Cuber and Peggy B. Harroff demonstrate the variety of marital relationships found in this group.[8] Of particular significance is their documentation that important man-woman relationships are not confined to marriage, nor are they necessarily sexual.

In contrast to the upper class, the upper-middle-class nuclear family is less embedded in the extended family. Husband and wife are more dependent upon each other for companionship and mutual self-development. The wife as well as the husband may seek satisfaction in professional work. Or, if the wife is not interested in success-careerism, she finds a more complete expression of the traditional feminine role of mother and homemaker, since she is less likely to have full-time, live-in servants. Despite the common interests that she and her husband may be expected to have or develop on the basis of their higher education and income, the upper-middle-class wife and mother is the person most prone to the ravages of role conflict in our society.

This assertion receives support from a nationwide survey of some 2,000 American women conducted by the author.[9] Almost one-fourth of those questioned said that they looked at life as housewives do; a similar number of housewives looked at life as working wives do. We shall call these two groups of women "the deviant 25 per cent." These groups were found to have many social characteristics in common. They were better educated, had higher incomes, were more likely to have husbands in the professional and clerical-sales occupational categories—in short, to be higher in the social scale—than the wives whose outlook conformed to their actual status.

The fact that housewives of higher social status may identify with working wives is not surprising, but how can we explain the tendency of a similarly situated group of working wives to identify with housewives? The reasons given by the deviant 25 per cent for their cross-identification may clarify this issue and also point to a basic conflict of modern women, which we shall discuss later. Over half the working wives who identified with their nonworking sisters did so on homemaking grounds. A smaller group said they were good mothers. Thus, by implication, they suggest that being a good homemaker and a good mother is not typical of working wives. Others of them said that the job did not represent their primary interest. A few reported that they were busy in the home. Only 5 per cent referred to psychological aspects of the housewifely role, including being one's own boss and having leisure and contentment. Thus, their reasons for identifying with the housewife were largely altruistic. They wanted to see themselves as fulfilling the wife's traditional role. They coveted not self-oriented wifely satisfactions, but the psychological gratifications of filling a socially approved role.

How about the housewives who identified with working wives? Over half of them did so protesting that they were indeed active outside the home, had outside interests and a broad viewpoint. By implication, they suggested that these traits are not typical of housewives. Over a fourth said they identified with working wives because they understood the problems of working wives and had recent work experience. And, indeed, housewives who had worked in the past were more likely to cross-identify. A lesser number revealed their negative image of the housewife by saying that they—presumably in comparison to other housewives—were not idle nor trivial, nor were they absorbed in household routine. Others attributed to themselves feelings of independence and concern about personal grooming, which they believed to be typical of the working wife. It is also interesting to note that a few housewives identified with the working wife because they considered themselves rushed and overworked, thereby implying that the working wife works harder than the housewife and that her lot is not a happy one.

In comparing the ways in which housewives and working wives cross-identify, we can see the main conflict of modern women and the cross-pressures to which they are subject. Girls and boys alike are educated to develop their individual capacities and to participate in the life and work of the society. Both are imbued with achievement goals, but this is done in a direct manner for boys, in ambiguous ways for girls. That is, there is no question in a boy's mind that he will work, that in order to be a man he must work. There is no conflict about the goal of occupational success for him. But work does not help a girl to become a woman. She becomes a woman when she marries and has children. However, masculine values—or American values—are dominant in our society, especially those values involving money and work. So women want a share in them too, and men, while expecting women to display the behaviors and attributes of the traditional, nurturing feminine role, accord more prestige to the woman who also realizes some of the traditional masculine (or American) values of education and achievement.

Talcott Parsons sees this dilemma of modern women as a conflict between the values of a particularistic and of a universalistic orientation to life, and has indicated the serious obstacles that confront women in the implementation of universalistic goals. "Broadly, married women in our society are not in direct competition for occupational status and its primary reward symbols with men of their own class."[10] His theoretical background for this statement is summarized by Robin Williams: "If women were to compete for jobs on an equal basis with men, drastic changes would be necessary in the family system, or in the occupational structure, or in both."[11]

To the extent that such changes have not occurred, women have resolved the conflict by making claim to the *performance* of the particularistic role and the *attributes* of the universalistic role. Housewives feel more secure and successful in the former endeavor and working wives in the latter. In bolstering their own feelings of realizing the new, composite feminine role, each group reacts defensively by denigrating the other and compensating for their own perceived deficiencies. The housewife, secure in the homemaking component of the feminine role, wants to be valued as a person with an emotional and intellectual life of her own. The working wife, confident of her interest and attractiveness as a person, wants to be adjudged a good wife and mother.

Thus, the entry of women into the labor market has affected the conception of the feminine role held by all female definers, whether they are currently working or not. All women want recognition as wives and mothers and something more. This something more is not work for its own sake or occupational achievement as such but, rather, the direct monetary rewards of work and the indirect personality gains of feeling enriched by a life and interests beyond the home. The behavioral components of the traditional feminine role do not seem to have changed in what is considered mandatory, although paid employment outside the home is permitted under certain conditions. However, personal attributes have been added to the feminine role and are rapidly becoming mandatory. In the present transitional stage of our society, both working and nonworking wives experience doubts and frustrations in their attempts to fulfill their concept of the new feminine role.

The concept of upper middle class covers a wide range of incomes. Some families and individuals are more successful than others in bringing their aspirations within their grasp. Since their work ethic and stress on getting ahead represent the dominant value orientation in America, it does not seem necessary to elaborate on the gender roles of those middle-class professionals, technicians, civil servants, and business persons whose incomes are more modest than those of the top executives. In a sense they have been the focus of all the other chapters in this book. Instead, we turn now to the common men and women who make up the lower middle class, admitting that the dividing line between upper and lower is very imprecise.

The Lower Middle Class

The lower middle class has expanded to almost half the nation's population. Within this class of the "common man" are the skilled, semiskilled, and lower white-collar workers, including salesmen, secretaries, foremen, public school teachers, ministers, and most civil service employees. The paid employment of the wife often serves to lift families into the level of living associated with this class. Perhaps a third are descendants of the "old" immigration from northern and western Europe. Although "respectability" has been identified as the dominant motif in the outlook of this segment of the population, upward mobility strivings are not absent, and especially are projected on the children, who are increasingly attending college. The lower middle class is also joining the upper middle class in the exodus to the suburbs. Still, the major fear of this group is sinking in the social scale, and they feel especially vulnerable to the threats of economic depression or inflation.

The husband is clearly the head of the house, and, even if the wife works, she caters to his wishes. She regards her employment as an extension of her homemaking role, as "helping out" rather than as independent career. The home is her domain, and she typically makes most household purchases. Nevertheless, joint activity between husband and wife and sharing of obligations are highest in this stratum. The husband has more time to participate in household tasks than his upper-middle-class confrère, nor is he restricted from doing so by a rigid working-class definition of the masculine role. A breakdown of traditional role segregation is also fostered by the physical and social distance of the nuclear family from the extended kin group, although ties remain close and exchanges of visits frequent.

Although empirical evidence is lacking, one might surmise that women's satisfaction with their gender role is highest in this class. The husband is sufficiently successful in his "instrumental activities" to call forth "expressive" rewards from his wife. The educational discrepancy between husband and wife legitimizes her acceptance of a slightly subordinate or "junior partner" status. They share a home-centered social and recreational life. Her ascriptive status as wife and mother contains enough content and esteem to release her from striving for success in a career and to make her the pivot of family life. She has leisure for hobbies and humanistic pursuits. In contrast to the nonemployed upper-class woman, she has less need for motherhood to provide a *raison d'être*, and thus is less likely to feel unneeded when her children assert their independence.[12] Homemaking and shared activities with her husband continue as stabilizing influences.

The Working Class

The difficulties in demarcating the social classes below the upper class are compounded when we consider the variety of subcultures encompassed in the working class. The boundary line between working class and middle class is blurred and can no longer be dichotomized in blue-collar versus white-collar terms—not only because many skilled blue-collar workers earn more than clerical and sales employees, but also because, and partly as a consequence, they have become "middle-classified" in their outlook and patterns of behavior. The force of ethnic tradition is more of a differentiating factor in the working class than in the middle class because the former are closer to their European or Asian roots. While many researchers acknowledge a distinction between the working class and the lower class, they tend to use these terms interchangeably, and often self-consciously so, in their reports of findings, thus complicating the problem of making generalizations about either class. The distinction at the lowest level is usually couched in terms of the stability of employment rather than the kind of work. Thus, depending on his ability or his motivation to hold a steady job, an unskilled manual worker might be classified as either working class or lower class. In practice, the lower class is viewed as composed of a "hard core" of old-stock Americans who, for a variety of imputed reasons, including a generational repetition of the "culture of poverty" and biological inferiority, have remained at the bottom of the social heap, plus such "disadvantaged" groups as blacks, Puerto Ricans, "native" Americans (Indians), and Mexican Americans, who, in addition to cultural deprivation, are subject to prejudice and discrimination.[13]

Further complications are introduced by social mobility—that is, some families display inconsistencies in their level of living and social values because they are in the process of moving up or down the social ladder. These are among the factors that account for conflicting findings in regard to populations labeled "working class." Nevertheless, we attempt to sketch the portrait of gender roles in the white urban working class.

Perhaps the masses of data on working-class family life and, by implication, gender roles can be organized according to the division suggested by Arthur B. Shostak, who sees the forces of social change operating unevenly to separate "modern" from "traditional" families.[14] In the traditional type, nominally headed by "the poorest paid, least educated, least mobile blue-collar husbands and fathers," a clear segregation of gender roles obtains. Although both sexes subscribe to an ideology of patriarchy and male dominance, the husband-father's actual power in the family is circumscribed by his lack of success and esteem in his occupational role as well as by his noninvolvement in domestic affairs, which stems from the threat to stereotyped conceptions of masculinity that such participation would produce.[15] He sees his role as strictly limited to that of economic provider and considers his obligations adequately discharged when he brings home his paycheck. Herbert Gans quotes one Italian-American housewife as saying, "When my husband comes home with the pay, I can't ask him to help in the house." Gans does not believe that the husband consciously rejects sharing the responsibilities of homemaking and childrearing, except in emergency situations; it is simply foreign to his experience.[16]

In practice, the stable working-class family may be said to operate according to matriarchal norms, although the wife makes every effort to maintain the fiction that the husband is the head of the house. She, however, is the one who commonly handles the household finances—even to the extent of buying life insurance for her husband—rears the children, whom the husband regards as belonging to her, deals with shopkeepers, manages relations with neighbors, keeps in touch with the extended family, and acts as mediator between father and children.

The clear separation of marital roles is conducive to the isolation of the marriage partners and the lack of closeness and communication between them. While husband and wife may have been brought together initially by physical attraction and romantic love, they rarely expect continued friendship. Their whole previous life experience contributes to the lack of communication between them. First there is the model supplied by their own parents; the mother was the pivotal and the father the peripheral figure in the home. Second, the differences in the upbringing of working-class boys and girls lead to social distance. Not only are girls early absorbed as mother's helpers and boys dissuaded from any interests or activities labeled feminine, but both sexes come to rely on same-sex gangs and cliques for friendship, moral support, and validations of self-worth. Family and community frown on intersex dyadic relations that are not specifically erotic, in the case of males, and do not contain the potentiality of marriage, in the case of females. Male-female interaction tends to occur at dances or other public places which young men and women come to and return from in groups, in contrast to the middle-class pattern of the boy's calling for the girl at her home.

Definitions of future gender roles are instilled early in the working class. Girls may entertain romantic dreams of being glorified by Hollywood or marrying a Prince Charming who comes riding on a gigantic charge account, but realistically they expect to work at mundane jobs after marriage because their earnings will be needed to help out. They also know that their jobs must be tailored not only to their own qualifications but also to the demands of home chores. Although their aspirations, like those of middle-class girls, include the wish to be doctors, teachers, and other professionals, only one-fourth really expect to obtain the jobs they would like to have, and most of the others see marriage as the chief obstacle.

A second and no less potent obstacle to one's goals is lack of education, mentioned more than twice as often by blue-collar girls than by the daughters of professionals and managers. Perhaps the position of secretary, the most frequently chosen occupation, represents the real summit of their ambition.[17] Such a realistic adaptation is foreshadowed in the discrepancy between the expressed desire of working-class mothers for their children to have a college education and the practical steps they take toward this goal.[18]

It is significant to note that more blue-collar girls than women of any other social-class origin believe that most women would like to have a job in addition to a home and children. Many blue-collar boys, however, believe that girls should not work unless it is absolutely necessary.[19] A further sex difference is revealed in the anticipated job satisfaction. Blue-collar girls emphasize the chance to help others in contrast to the boys' wish for high pay.[20] This orientation appears to be functional in dealing with the frustrations that might otherwise arise from differential treatment in regard to pay, promotion, and other job perquisites and serves also to protect the wife from competition with her husband.

Those blue-collar girls who are bent on achievement have to contend with a cultural environment that is even more hostile to careers for women than the middle-class milieu. The majority choose high school courses that will prepare them for bearable short-term jobs prior to early marriage, to which they can return if need be.

Many are preoccupied with the romantic notions of male-female relations purveyed by the movies and pulp magazines. Courtship represents the high point of their lives, during which sexual relations are often accepted in the hope of moving men toward marriage. It should be observed that class differences in sexuality are far fewer among females than among males.[21] For adolescent males, sexual success is directed primarily at an audience of male peers and is used to prove masculinity, rather than to learn how to develop long-term emotional relations with girls. The reverse is true for girls. This conflict of interest between the sexes, which is especially marked in the working class and is fostered by sex segregation, sets the stage for lack of rapport in marriage.

Blue-collar young people are further hampered by stereotyped conceptions of the opposite sex. "Men tend to think of women as timid, emotional, and inferior; women are apt to view men as arrogant, insensitive, and childish."[22] The wife's wish for appreciation, response, and counsel from her husband is countered by his desire to be left alone except for satisfaction of his physical and sexual needs. The wife dare not press too hard lest he leave her. Enduring emotional deprivation, economic limitations, insecurity, narrow horizons, and feelings of self-deprecation, the working-class wife has been characterized as the most deprived of all women.[23] She tries to compensate for the shortcomings of the wifely role by investing in her role as mother, seeking from her children the gratifications denied her by her husband. She also turns to female family members and neighbors for comfort and relief from her husband's deficiencies in companionability and the dullness of life. The husband, too, finds it easier to talk to his male kin and work associates about his interests and problems.

Rainwater and his associates[24] describe the pervasive anxiety and feelings of helplessness endemic to this role. On the one hand, life is experienced as unrewarding, dull, routine, and lacking in deep fulfillment; on the other, it is subject to sudden deprivations and unhappy turns of fate. Two major aims are imputed to the working-class wife—searching for a stable world, and trying to add brightness to life. She tries to improve her situation by making herself and her surroundings as attractive as she can.

Nathan Hurvitz has constructed an ideal type of modern working-class marriage:

A summary of the role relationships between working-class spouses may best be seen in the interaction of a hypothetical couple. Here, then, are Jim and Mary Bluecollar as each begins his [*sic!*] day and reflects on his experiences of the day before.

Jim Bluecollar, wearing a bright sport shirt, drove to work in his 1960 Buick. Driving along the Freeway, no one would know what he did; other drivers might even think that he was a project engineer. Jim worried about his job. He wondered whether the rumors about the cancellation of the job he was working on were true, and whether there really were machines that could replace forty guys like him. Guys like him were a dime a dozen. If he only had something people really needed, then he wouldn't be scared all the time; he'd be a different person altogether. The auto—he bought the auto when he was working overtime and now there wasn't any more overtime. He was also paying on the bedroom furniture Mary insisted on buying for the kids. The kids made Jim mad last night. They had on a stupid kids' show and when he came home tired and switched the TV to a program about fishing, they started to yell. And Mary hollered at him! He tried to explain to her that she was always sticking up for the kids, that she babied them too much, but she kept busy in the kitchen. He tried to watch the kids' show, but the kids climbed on him. So he went out to mow the lawn just to get away. He came back in when Mary called him for supper. While they were eating, the kids raised hell and he yelled at them some more—even though he didn't want to. After dinner Mary got the kids off to bed, so he lay down on the sofa and fell asleep. When he got up, Mary was in her bedclothes. She had showered and looked relaxed and pretty. He tried to kiss her, but she turned away. When he asked her what was wrong, she started to tell him off about the kids—that he didn't play with them, that he always yelled at them. He tried to explain that he played with them and tried to toughen them up, but she complained that he was too rough—that he'd hurt them. But she was the one who was making sissies out of them. He saw he wasn't getting any place, so he tried to get Mary off this kick. He tried to touch her, and although she let him, she didn't respond. He thought he got his message through to her and prepared for bed. When he came out of the bathroom, he heard the TV. He asked Mary to come to bed with him but she refused—she said there was a movie on she just had to see. Not again! He'd be damned if he'd get her that dishwasher. Let her ask him! If they didn't argue about the kids, it was about money—and then she held out on him. Damn! But maybe things would be different tonight. . . .

While her husband was driving to work, Mary Bluecollar cleaned up after breakfast. She always prepared breakfast for him—that's the way her mother did for her father. This morning she wanted to explain she was sorry she didn't come to bed with him as she knew he wanted. But she couldn't tell him because he was mad, and she couldn't cajole him out of his mad because the kids were around. There wasn't the chance. There was never a chance to tell him how she felt. But why did he always complain about the kids? Who was he to talk? He wasn't such a big success to tell her how to raise the kids. If they grew up his way, they'd end up in the shop like him. He treated the kids like grownups, like he came first. It was true, he worked hard. But if he had gone on in school or taken that class they offered him, he'd have a better job now. So he had no one to blame but himself. He wanted to do what was right, but sometimes he did such foolish things. Why did he have to get such an expensive car. To baby it all the time? Like that gadget for the motorbike he was building for the kids—and they were years too young to use it. They should save their money, build up a reserve, put some aside for the kids' schooling—he wanted it that way. And why did he always expect her to have sex with him just because he wanted it? He hardly spoke a dozen civil words to her and then he wanted to go to bed with her. Were all men like that? But he really felt bad when she turned him down. And he wanted her to enjoy sex, too—and sometimes she did. Sometimes she didn't believe he wanted her—why should he want her? She wasn't that pretty, nor that smart, nor sexy. She liked him. They could make a good family together. He really liked the kids, but he didn't know how to show it. He didn't know how to show her he liked her, if he did. She didn't want to turn him down, but it kept him in line. He knew she wanted him to save money for the kids' school. She wanted him to go to church, too. When he'd open the kids' account or when he'd come to church with her, they'd have a party. But was that all he needed her for—to keep his house and to go to bed with him? Damn! But maybe tonight things would be different.

Maybe they would and maybe they wouldn't.[25]

A more modern style of life is emerging in the working class, particularly when the husband—and, even more important, the wife—has graduated from high school or the family has moved to the suburbs. Two factors may be said to contribute to a new definition of gender roles among such members of the working class. First, "the occupational success, greater earning power, and heightened self-esteem that frequently accompany educational attainment play a large part, as do also the improved powers of personal reasoning and the improved ability to communicate that hopefully go along with a high school or junior college diploma."[26]

Secondly, the marital pair is removed from the ethnic traditions and highly connected networks of the parental generation. In her study of twenty London families, Elizabeth Bott[27] found support for the hypothesis that the degree of segregation in the role relationships of husband and wife varies directly with the connectedness of the family's social network. Long-established working-class areas were characterized by a considerable overlap of social role—that is, the same person might be simultaneously friend, neighbor, and colleague. A rigid division of the roles of husband and wife was facilitated by the distinctive networks of the husband and wife. The wife turned to relatives and neighbors for some of the domestic help and emotional support that would otherwise be sorely missed in her husband. He, in turn, had his friends. When either social or geographical mobility removes the married pair from the previous pattern of relationships with outsiders, not only is the couple thrown more upon its own resources, which leads to greater mutuality and more flexibility in marital roles, but it is also exposed to the influence of family patterns in its new community or social stratum. Bennett Berger, on the other hand, did not find a large change in auto workers who moved to suburbia, but it may be because they moved as a group rather than as individual families. Furthermore, they did not participate in formal associations or make close friends among their neighbors.[28]

In regard to the role of the wife, Handel and Rainwater sum up the difference between the traditional and the modern pattern as follows:

In the traditional working-class family, the wife thinks of herself in terms of what she does *for* her family. Her self-conception as a wife and mother centers around those situations in which she is separated from the other family members—cooking, doing the laundry, cleaning house. The traditional wife considers the kitchen the most important room in her house.

The modern working-class wife thinks of herself in terms of what she does *with* her family. Her self-conception is broadened from that of servant of the family's needs to that of sharer in family affairs. She considers the living room the most important room in her home, because that is the room in which the family relaxes together.[29]

In the modern working-class marriage, then, the balance of power is not weighted so heavily on the husband's side. There is more sharing of responsibility and a deeper emotional involvement. Wives are more likely to work outside the home, which not only alleviates their boredom and provides camaraderie with other working women but also enables them to enter into a new universe of discourse with their husbands. Both spouses collaborate in the home-improvement projects and plans for the children's future made possible by extra income. Especially in the early years of marriage, husband and wife try to listen to each other and talk out rather than avoid conflicts. This effort, however, may prove too exhausting as the partners age, as suggested by Komarovsky's data,[30] although its abandonment may represent a throwback to early socialization rather than disillusionment and may not necessarily hold true for the younger generation.

Sex relations are more satisfying, especially for the wife, in the modern blue-collar family. For both spouses, sexuality may serve as a welcome retreat from the exigencies of daily life, but the wife's new control of fertility and overthrow of old inhibitory attitudes plus the courage to communicate her preferences to her husband enhance the value of sexuality for her. On the liability side, the integration of sex with over-all marital satisfaction introduces a new note of jeopardy in this area.

Although the modern style involves more risk-taking than the traditional model and affords less insulation from conflict in the form of social distance and separate networks, not to mention membership in conflicting interest groups, it holds the potentiality for richer returns.

Further change in working-class gender roles, especially masculine, may be expected to come from female pressure. A harbinger of this trend may be seen in New York City, where consciousness-raising groups have been formed by a number of middle-aged women whose husbands are blue-collar union men or white-collar employees of the city government.[31] The feminist movement, the women say, has encouraged them in the belief that they need not follow "the traditional path laid out by their mothers and grandmothers." At first their most salient problem appeared to be what they regarded as premature retirement as a sex object and persuading their husbands to express affection even without sexual performance. Later the discussions centered on the need to work outside the home and preparing their daughters for jobs with a future. The interconnectedness of the two problems was highlighted by the experiences of one working woman whose earnings permitted her husband to reduce his taxi-driving hours and go to bed with her more often. Many voiced plans of entering college programs. Although not completely convinced that Judy O'Grady and the colonel's lady are sisters under the skin, the dozen women in this group agree with the women's liberation movement on a variety of specific issues—"daycare centers, equal pay for equal work, the right to abortion and contraceptive information, the need to educate young girls to think of themselves as individuals in their own right instead of viewing themselves as only future wives and mothers." These women are trying to implement some of these ideas in their neighborhood.

With worries about fertility overcome, with flattering attention from men at their places of work, with new feelings of financial independence, with new ideas absorbed from the mass media, working wives of working-class husbands are beginning to demand the same kind of comfortable home atmosphere that is available to their spouses and relief from the double burden of household and job.[32]

The working-class male has had a deservedly poor reputation in all his family roles: husband, lover, father, and son. Komarovsky's study revealed that working-class wives view their marital relationships as devoid of genuine sharing, appreciation, and love. Rainwater's research showed that sex in blue-collar marriage is unimaginative, mechanical, and limited, lacking in sentiment, romance, and generosity. Shostak found an enormous generation gap between the conservative, patriotic, crewcut father and his long-haired, politically disillusioned son. Shostak also found that in addition to failing as fathers, middle-aged blue-collar males are generally threatened by the image of their own elderly parents and thus do not perform adequately in their role as sons.

According to Shostak, the picture may be changing, and the blue-collar man may not be ready to adjust to it as yet. Women have been able to use new, safe contraceptives to free themselves from the tyranny of endless pregnancy and childcare. Television has taught them to expect more companionship, emotional support, affectionate attention, and sexual satisfaction. Sons, now attending college, are seeking more meaningful relationships with their fathers, searching for communication and sensitivity. Elderly parents, also influenced by the media, are expecting more filial attention in the form of letters, phone calls, and visits. In short, the working-class man is being asked to redefine himself. Whether or not he will be able or willing to do so remains a moot question.

The Lower Class[33]

Persons in the lower class are those who live at or below the poverty level throughout their lives.[34] This definition would exclude young people on their way up, elderly persons trying to cope on reduced incomes, and possibly farm families whose cash income is supplemented by their own produce. Most of them are white.

Perhaps reflecting an androcentric bias, some sociologists have divided this group into "stable" and "disorganized" families, according to whether a functioning husband-father is present or not.[35] In stable families the father tries, often against great odds, to enact a patriarchal role, but he may have to resort to physical coercion rather than rely on financial resources to implement his power. His job is likely to be menial, low-paid, and perhaps subject to seasonal layoffs. When his wife and grown children bring home their own paychecks, his authority is further undermined.

In disorganized families the husband-father may be incapacitated by alcoholism, mental illness, or other demoralization; or he may have escaped the field, either temporarily or permanently.

(More rarely the wife is the "disabled" partner.) His default creates the mother-centered family, in which the strongest bond is that between mother and daughter—a situation movingly portrayed, albeit in an Irish setting, in Sean O'Casey's play *Juno and the Paycock*.

Despite the obeisance paid to the concept of male superiority by both sexes and the nonparticipation of men in household tasks, both sexes "act out" in masculine ways in interpersonal relationships, displaying aggression in word and deed. (In the same manner, upper-class men and women adhere to "feminine" norms in their low-keyed interactions.)

Whether the survival tactics adopted by this declassed group have produced a set of values at variance with middle-class norms (called by Oscar Lewis "the culture of poverty")[36] or whether the handicaps experienced anew by each generation call forth in them similar responses[37] is a matter of controversy. But whether it is cause or result, some sociologists argue that a stable family life is a precondition for rising out of poverty.[38]

Even acculturation to the values of the stable working class as a more realistic intermediate goal may present seemingly insuperable obstacles to lower-class youth. Their personal experiences and observations of parents and peers and their stigmatization by the authority figures with whom they come into contact as immoral, irresponsible, and unproductive lead them to discount "getting ahead" in favor of "getting by" and "getting kicks." Apathy toward the serious concerns of the higher strata, such as work and education, is balanced by a hedonistic interest in the here-and-now and a search for excitement. Only luck—holding the winning number or catching on as a pop singer or becoming a boxing champion —may rescue them from the ranks of the depressed. Such avenues to fortune are even narrower for girls. Dancing, action-packed movies, sports, and sexual adventures may camouflage lives of noisy desperation, but underclasslings are spared the competitive strivings of the rat race and keeping up with the Joneses as well as the conflicts of career versus family, since emotional investment in either may be minimal.

Marriage occurs at a young age, as do maximum earnings, and is often a hit-or-miss affair. Young people drift together with little conscious choice, or the girl's pregnancy may hasten their legal union. And marriage may be cursed with more children than are desired because *machismo* and lack of empathy between husband and wife prevent effective practice of birth control.[39]

It is the mother-centered family, above all, that sets off the lower class from the working class. In taking on the dual role of nurturer and economic provider, working-class women are not expressing any ideology of feminine equality, since superiority is still ascribed to the man. They are simply coping with the realities of slum existence. Mutual dependency among female kin represents survival tactics in the slum world, where men come and go. In the ethnic and rural traditions of present-day slum dwellers, woman's province had been the home, supplemented by farm chores or minor employment, and this role was easily transferred to the city. The male's dominance, however, which had been founded in his role as principal economic provider and task leader of the family, lost its underpinnings when technological change and a new environment rendered his old skills obsolete and the perpetuation of previous habit patterns, coupled with lack of opportunity for acquiring new skills, made him a marginal participant in both his family and the economy. Although she would prefer a stable, caring husband and breadwinner, the lower-class woman often finds a consensual union with a man preferable to supporting a husband in addition to her children. In the lower class, solidarity among women often becomes the mainstay against the vicissitudes of life and the unreliability of men.

Summary

The locus of change in American gender roles appears to be the middle class. It is in this segment of our society that the wife is striving to become a full partner in marriage, sharing with her husband the responsibility both for maintaining the home and caring for the children and for striving for success in a career. Higher education, changes in the climate of opinion, and improvements in the opportunity structure for women, fostered by the feminist movement and the "feminization" of occupations to discount the importance of physical strength, conduce to an ideology of egalitarianism and a more relaxed definition of gender roles on the part of both sexes.

Patriarchal traditions persist in both the upper and the lower classes, although there are countervailing forces. In the upper class the importance attached to continuity of family lineage and men's effective monopoly of positions of power and prestige, coupled with the privileged position of the wife, reduce the pressure for redefinition of roles. Those women who tire of the endless round of social activities have the money and leisure to participate in a variety of community and cultural causes. This American elite has always in each generation produced a sprinkling of rebels who turned their backs on family and fortune, although in the past it has been observed that the bohemians of one generation became the philistines of the next. Still, the decline of "society" and the spread of the achievement orientation to women may cause more upper-class women to break ranks and join their upper-middle-class sisters in demanding more scope for their creative energies.

It has already been noted that lower-class and working-class people on the move are beginning to emulate middle-class patterns of consumption and marital relations. The breakdown of rigid gender-role separations seems functional for enhancing the productivity of the nation and its consequence of higher levels of living for individuals and families.

Masculine leadership and responsibility in the lowest stratum of our society exist more in the nostalgic past or the hoped-for future than in the present reality of the underclass. Men have little beyond their ascriptive status as superior males and their physical strength to implement male dominance. Women's struggle for survival has taught them not to rely on men. For all strata in our society, efforts are directed toward changing men to accommodate the needs and wishes of women. Whether this means a relinquishment of privileges or an easing of burdens depends partly on social rank and partly on the personal outlook of the men themselves.

GENDER ROLES IN BLACK SOCIETY

Any discussion of black sex roles is charged with controversy. There is disagreement on the historical facts of the Afro-American family as well as its contemporary nature. In the triangle formed by family organization, discriminatory social institutions, and individual disadvantage, different analysts direct their attention to different sides. The ordering of the chain of causation becomes a political issue, for the social policies one advocates may flow from one's assessment of black history and current experience. Indeed, the temptation is great to evaluate statements about black sex and family roles more in accordance with their implications for social action, race pride, and white guilt than in terms of their validity. Further, many statements are denied in one breath and explained away in the next. Thus, one might conclude from some recent articles that there is no black matriarchy, but matriarchy is just as good as, if not better than, patriarchy; or that the black man is not impotent, but whites castrated him.

Complicating the problem of a dispassionate analysis of black sex roles is the fact that black society is more complex, more richly varied even than the larger white society. Typologies that seek to separate class from ethnic factors in identifying meaningful strands in black society—as, for example, Jessie Bernard's division of black families into the "acculturated" and the "externally adapted"[40]— are subject to criticism as biased and false to the facts. Despite these difficulties, let me attempt to present the main points of controversy, beginning with the historical background.

The story of the Afro-American family can be divided into four parts: (1) the structure of the family in Africa; (2) black family relationships during the slavery period in the United States; (3) changes wrought after emancipation during the so-called Reconstruction period; and (4) family life and sex roles in urban centers, both North and South, in the twentieth century. The issue in regard to these four stages is twofold: (1) what are the facts, and (2) to what extent may later periods be accounted for by preceding ones?

There is little disagreement concerning the kind of family organization that prevailed in the part of West Africa from which most Afro-Americans come. Among the Yoruba of Nigeria and the Dahomeans it was a closely knit, polygynous system in which each nuclear family was linked to a larger kinship grouping. Each wife had her own hut in the compound of her husband and took turns with his other wives in living with him until she conceived.

Then she returned to her own hut and dropped out of the routine of visits to her husband until the child was weaned. The familial group might include the oldest male, his unmarried children, his married sons with their wives and children, and his brothers. The males were tied to one another by strong bonds of mutual obligation. Women, though, had high economic status, deriving from their role as sellers of goods in the market.

Authorities differ on whether the African heritage exerted any influence on family relationships during slavery. E. Franklin Frazier[41] is the protagonist of the view that African social organization was wiped out by slavery, since the enslaved people were moved around as individual chattels without any regard for family ties or tribal groupings. Melville J. Herskovits,[42] on the other hand, has argued that survivals of African customs fitted in with and contributed to the family characteristics that were fostered by slavery, including female dominance, common-law marriage, and illegitimacy. In his view, the closer ties between mother and children than between either husband and wife or father and children are a predictable result of polygyny because the children of any one wife must share the father with the children of all the other wives, whereas they need share their mother only with her other children. In addition, the rotation of wives under African polygyny in particular and the suspension of wifely visits to the husband until the child was weaned intensified this effect.

The practical upshot of these two views, however, is much the same. Both agree that the African heritage did not contribute to a stabilization of family relationships in the white, middle-class patriarchal pattern. A third approach, put forward by Bert N. Adams on the basis of his reading of Andrew Billingsley, is that although family and lineage stability may have been disrupted by the transportation of Africans to America as slaves, "the basic humanity and mutual concern which were functions of the African heritage"[43] survived as a source of strength in the period of social confusion following emancipation.

Nor is the slavery period free from scholarly dispute. The dominant view is that slavery and the plantation system provided small opportunity for the institutionalization of the role of husband and father as head of the family, responsible for its support.

If not in African culture, then at least in slavery began the tradition of strong, responsible women and detached, footloose men. The only attributes of the white masculine role that the slave master permitted the black male were physical strength and sexual prowess. Opportunity to play the traditional white feminine role, albeit a lower-class one, was, however, afforded the black woman, except that she was dependent upon and at the mercy of her white master. Chastity was not expected of the black woman. If the black man was emasculated, then the black woman was raped.

Admittedly, this oversimplified picture does not do justice to the complexities arising from variations in the status of Negroes even under slavery—whether they were field servants or house servants, freedmen or slaves, favored illegitimate offspring of white masters or wholly slave-parented, skilled artisans or field hands. Nevertheless, it can fairly be said that any strong family ties developed by Negroes represented a drawing upon their own resources, either from African culture or from an adaptive struggle against dehumanizing conditions.

Opinion, however, is divided concerning the stability of black family life under slavery. Stanley Elkins[44] argues that slavery acted like a vast concentration camp, forcing perpetual childhood upon the slaves, while Bert Adams asserts that "the weakness of family ties under slavery has been overdrawn."[45] But most chroniclers of the Negro family appear to equate weak or loose family ties with matriarchy and strong family ties with patriarchy.

With regard to the slavery period, then, the two questions for further research and analysis are: (1) how prevalent was matriarchy, and (2) in regard to what goals is matriarchy less desirable than patriarchy? In answer to the first question, Frazier says:

As a rule, the Negro woman as wife or mother was the mistress of her cabin, and, save for the interference of master or overseer, her wishes in regard to mating and family matters were paramount. Neither economic necessity nor tradition had instilled in her the spirit of subordination to masculine authority. Emancipation only tended to confirm in many cases the spirit of self-sufficiency which slavery had taught.[46]

But there seems some ambiguity in the term *matriarchy* when no power is exerted over men. It is not the converse of patriarchy, in which men boss women as well as children. Thus the term *matricentric* or *matrifocal* is used to describe the family that is mother-supported as a consequence of the absence or default of the father or fathers. In fact, it might make more sense to view the mother-headed family as polyandrous (one woman with several husbands) rather than polygynous (one man with several wives). Frazier continues:

When emancipation came, many Negro mothers had to depend upon their own efforts for the support of themselves and their children. Their ranks were swelled by other women who, in seeking sex gratification outside of marriage, found themselves in a similar situation. Without the assistance of a husband or the father of their children, these women were forced to return to the plow or the white man's kitchen in order to make a livelihood for their families. From that time to the present day, . . . each generation of women, following in the footsteps of their mothers, has borne a large share of the support of the younger generation. Today (1948) in the rural sections of the South, especially on the remnants of the old plantations, one finds households where old grandmothers rule their daughters and grandchildren with matriarchal authority. Sometimes their authority dates from the days following emancipation when, in wandering about the country, they "found" their first child.[47]

The ambiguous nature of the so-called black matriarchy is well expressed by Patricia Robinson:

Those black women who worked in the big house and the fields acted not as a dominant factor over the black male but as his protector and savior. Her primary strategy was to allow herself to be used sexually, often to save the life of the black male. She could speak out to the master and to the white boss if she pleased him with good food, good sex, good care of his children, a role which the master's own woman was seldom allowed to pursue . . . a vocal link between the white man and the black man, the black woman often forced opinions and bargained successfully for whatever pitiful reforms were possible under slavery.[48]

Although statistics are lacking for the slavery period, the evidence suggests that the maternal family was the dominant form among the slaves. Exception must be made, however, for male craftsmen and skilled mechanics, who often assumed the conventional role of husband and father, and for free Negroes, who, over a period of several generations, acquired the economic means to build up patriarchal traditions. In the New World setting male dominance implied an institutionalization of the family, whereas in its absence the family was based more upon human impulses and individual wishes than upon law and the mores.

The disorder and confusion generated by the Civil War and emancipation had contradictory effects on the Negro family. In some cases weak ties were broken, but many freedmen went in search of relatives and spouses from whom they had been separated by sale during slavery. When conditions became more settled, the effects of opposing forces could still be observed. On the one hand, patriarchal stability was fostered by the contracts Negro men signed with whites as either tenant farmers or purchasers of farms and by the mutual dependence and economic cooperation between man and woman in the struggle to make a living. On the other hand, the establishment of the color caste system in the South isolated Negroes and threw them back upon the cultural heritage of slavery and female dominance. Nevertheless, increasing economic opportunities, and especially land and home ownership, brought about a social differentiation of the Negro population in which a stable and conventional family life became a mark of high status.

Then, in the twentieth century the drift of rural Negroes to Southern cities and later the mass migrations to Northern cities put a strain on the informal family arrangements that had represented an adequate adjustment to conditions of life in the rural South. In the new urban environment, illegitimacy, paternal desertion, and lack of supervision of children have become defined as social problems.

It is not our purpose here to enter into the politics of controversy engendered by the Moynihan Report,[49] which so dramatically called attention to the "tangle of pathology" of black, lower-class families. Moynihan attributed the continuance of black unemployment and low income to family role deviancy which fails to produce in children, especially males, the kind of personality structure that leads to economic success. Many members of the black community became incensed by the implication that social effort should be directed to normalize the black family rather than to combat white racism. At the same time they accepted the main point of the thesis in making the pivot of the black movement the economic advantage of the black man.

The concept of the "black family" is even more perilous in the twentieth century than in preceding periods. Few generalizations can hold across such differentiating factors as region, rural versus urban residence, income, religious and other value differences, and family composition. Unfortunately, available statistics do not always isolate these intertwined factors. The best one can do is try to match black and white families in such a manner that race is the only objective difference between them. Even when this step is consciously attempted, the black family has been seen as being in many ways the mirror image of the white.

First, the stereotype postulates the black family as matriarchal rather than patriarchal, in that it is more likely to be headed by a female or, if the husband is present, to have a more powerful wife, to have more of the income supplied by the wife either directly through her earnings or by virtue of welfare payments to her, and to entertain a more positive image of the working wife.

Second, it is held that blacks place less emphasis on marriage, as evidenced in higher rates of illegitimacy and the black woman's valuing motherhood above wifehood, the lower rate of marriage for lower-class black males than for lower-class white males, and greater marital instability of blacks at all income levels.

Third, blacks are considered to have less puritanical attitudes, as revealed in their single standard of sex morality, their greater emphasis on interpersonal relationships than on institutional obligations, and the male's more ready acceptance of the economic exploitation of women.

Let us now try to examine the evidence in regard to each of these three characteristics.

Matriarchy

In 1971, 29 per cent of black families were headed by a female as compared to 9 per cent of white families. Much of this difference however, can be attributed to the greater proportion of black families who live under the poverty line. In 1972, for families with incomes under $4,275, 67 per cent of black and 32 per cent of white are female-headed, a difference of 35 per cent.[50] This comparison, it must be noted, suggests that family composition has a greater impact on white poverty than on black, despite frequent arguments to the contrary.[51]

When it comes to assessing the power of the black wife in intact families, the problem of a valid indicator arises. Decision-making has been the most frequently employed criterion, but it may well represent greatness thrust upon one partner in accordance with the conscious preference rather than the mere default of the other. In their 1960 study, Blood and Wolfe[52] found that the wives were dominant in decision-making in almost half their sample and the husbands in less than a fifth. Among white families, a little more than a fourth could be called male-dominant and a fifth female-dominant. Blood and Wolfe interpret these results, however, as representing greater deprivation for Negro wives, who get less cooperation and sharing of experiences from their husbands.[53] It is Robert Staples's[54] opinion, though, that few decisions are made by the wife in opposition to her husband's wishes, and that he willingly defers to her in certain areas where she may have superior knowledge. This kind of argument would seem to apply equally well to whites, so that in effect the greater "matriarchality" of blacks is explainable in terms of the greater likelihood that the black wife will possess resources superior to those of her husband and/or his greater reluctance or inability to participate in the decision-making process. Whatever the explanation, the supposed facts are themselves open to question, since in a reanalysis of three existing surveys on this problem, Hyman and Reed discovered little difference in female influence between white and black families.[55]

Nor can it be said that the black wife makes a substantially larger contribution to family income than her white peer. In 1966 only 12 per cent of nonwhite working wives, as compared to approximately 10 per cent of white, earned half or more of the family income. Half of the nonwhite wives contributed only a fourth, again similar to whites. Whether black or white, women are less likely than men to work full-time during the entire year or to earn as much.[56]

Still, by virtue of cultural values or the unequal employment opportunities for black men, a more positive imagery surrounds the black working wife than the white working wife enjoys. The 1959 survey by the author, mentioned above, showed that Negro women and men, in contrast to whites, viewed the working wife as a good wife, a loving mother, efficient in household tasks, better liked by men, and a good citizen.[57] This favorable portrait of the working wife cannot be accounted for in terms of the disproportionate representation of Negroes at lower income levels, since (1) white views did not vary according to socio-economic status and (2) a direct comparison between low-income blacks and whites upheld the original difference. Further, a study conducted by Leland J. Axelson also revealed differences between white and Negro males in their perceptions of the working wife, though more indecisiveness was found among the blacks.[58]

Less Emphasis on Marriage

Oscar Wilde once quipped that marriage was such an important institution that no family should be without it. Whether they subscribe to this middle-class norm or not, "disadvantaged groups" experience difficulties in fulfilling the traditional obligations of marriage. The black man in particular continues to experience economic deprivation and discrimination. Low wages and irregular employment patterns lead to a negative self-image and general defeatism. He may shirk family responsibilities because providing economic and emotional support to a woman and children seems beyond his resources.

Similarly, the black lower-class woman does not look to the black man for financial and social security. Instead, she attaches more importance to her maternal than to her marital role. Even a child born out of wedlock signifies the achievement of an adult feminine status and the fulfillment of her function as a woman. In some cases the husband-father may even be seen as a threat to the maternal role, if he squanders rather than supplies family resources. The lower-class black woman views the black man more as a lover than as a husband or father. Black wives express themselves as more satisfied with sex but less with love than white wives.

Statistical data comparing proportion married by age, sex, and race are not available at this time, but some indirect evidence of a lower propensity to marry on the part of blacks can be cited. Jessie Bernard points to a "downward trend in the proportion of nonwhite infants born in wedlock,"[59] which she takes as indicative of nonconformity to the institutional norms of marriage. She also discusses a study which reports only 58 per cent of sixteen- and seventeen-year-old Negro boys saying that they "would like to get married some day."[60] Elliot Liebow explains why most of the street-corner men he studied had tried marriage and found it wanting. These men were often able to establish a more spontaneous and pleasant relationship with the children of the women with whom they were living than with their own children, with whom their obligations far outdistanced their performance.[61]

Corroboration is also found in Reynold Farley's analysis of demographic data.[62] Unfortunately, he makes no comparisons with whites, but he does show that since 1940 black divorce and desertion rates have increased, while widowhood has decreased. He links changes in the distribution of marital statuses among blacks and the age of marriage to changes in their economic status.

Although 84 per cent of the sixteen- and seventeen-year-old Negro girls in the study mentioned above said they would like to get married someday, this is probably a lower figure than would be found among whites.

Less Puritanical Attitudes

Accompanying the greater power and independence of women, the relative absence of stigma on children born to unmarried women, and the lesser importance attached to marriage is the prevalence of a single and permissive standard of sexual morality. Among lower-class blacks what's sauce for the gander tends to be sauce for the goose. Female virginity at marriage is hardly expected or desired, nor are black women expected to trade sexual exclusivity for social security. Rather, male-female relationships are based more on mutual gratification than on institutional obligations.

Black Culture Versus Accommodation

To the extent that the foregoing characterization of differences between black and white familial attitudes and behaviors is valid, the question arises: Do these attitudes and behaviors of blacks represent a realistic accommodation to present circumstances, which can be expected to change as mainstream opportunities become open to blacks, or are they self-consciously valued outlooks which blacks will seek to preserve as part of their ethnic distinctiveness?

A provisional answer to this question may emerge from a glance at higher-income blacks and Black Muslims. In a study of black families "above the lower class or underclass," John Scanzoni reports that they are adopting the family forms of the dominant society and contends that the conjugal family, in which the husband fulfills his chief role obligations as provider in exchange for the wife's tendering of expressive rewards, is not distinctively white but adaptive to a "modern, individualistic, achievement-oriented, acquisitive society." He, as well as others, believes the evidence indicates that even lower-class blacks share this aspiration as prerequisite to their participation in the "American dream," and that their present way of life is more *faute de mieux* than positive affirmation of deviant values. Scanzoni states further: "It is not a coincidence, for example, that the Black Muslims, once they adopted a work ethic virtually indistinguishable from that of the dominant society, have likewise evolved an identical family form."[63] He feels that any differences between white and black family patterns reflect only differential access to the economic rewards of the total society.

Indeed, many investigators have found differences between black and white families at the same social-class level. Richard Udry, for example, presents 1960 Census data showing that "nonwhite marital instability for males exceeds white even when education, income, and occupation are controlled, and, in fact increases with income."[64] To explain the persistence of divergencies between whites and blacks of similar socio-economic status, one can invoke history or contemporary "ghettoization." Whether or not a viable and distinctive Afro-American culture will continue to obtain after the handicap of past discrimination has been erased and blacks are enabled to compete on an equal footing with whites may be too far in the future to be worth more than idle speculation at the present time.

Needless to say, relationships between black men and women are influenced by the environing white society. Fundamental changes in the family and the economy, in dominant materialist values, enroll the support of relatively few blacks, but their current survival tactics may receive ideological support when they converge with the efforts of counterculture youth, liberationist women, and leftists concerned with the "quality" of life. At this moment in history, though, the majority of blacks are concerned primarily with obtaining a proportionate share of the rewards of an affluent society without having to abandon life-styles that they find congenial. They are interested in structural and cultural changes in the larger society only to the extent that such changes improve their own position within it.

Black Women's Reference Groups

It is in the light of the black struggle that the issue of black power versus women's liberation—or, better, radical redefinitions of gender roles—must be examined. An advanced industrial, pluralistic society, such as our own, contains many crisscrossing and often conflicting interests. What complicates the situation is the fact of multiple memberships. The conflicts are among groups, and each one of us wears many hats. What is in one's interest as a worker, for example, may run counter to one's interest as a consumer. In fact, a major reason why certain reforms may not be enacted is that they expose individuals to cross-pressures stemming from their various roles. It is possible, of course, that one role will dominate the others, and the question can be asked concerning a person's *primary* identification from among his group memberships. What will he or she say first in answer to the question, "Who are you?" Man or woman, white or black, middle class or poor?

Previous research indicates that minority-group membership is more salient than dominant-group, whether this be as problem or as pride. Thus, a white, middle-class man might give none of these attributes as his first response but possibly his occupation. A black middle-class man might say, "I am black." A black lower-class man might say either "I am black" or "I am a worker." A white middle-class woman would be most likely to say, "I am a woman"; a white lower-class woman, "I am working class." More problematic are the responses of a black woman, whether middle or lower class. At the present time race-consciousness would probably triumph over sex- or class-consciousness.

Need there be conflicts among these memberships—sex versus class, class versus race, race versus sex? Movements professing the interests of each of these minority groups have claimed that they will free the others. Marxist revolutionary movements say a socialist society will free woman from her social and economic dependence upon man and overcome the barrier between black and white fostered by the divide-and-conquer strategy of the capitalist class. When all must be workers, all, regardless of sex or race, will share according to their needs in the bounty of an unfettered production. Black power, by putting an end to discrimination against blacks, will secure the position of middle-class blacks, unchain lower-class black men from poverty, and thereby provide the black woman with a confident and responsible male partner. Further, the white man will be relieved of his burden of guilt; the white woman may step down from her pedestal; and the productivity of the whole society may be enhanced by the development of black talent. The woman's movement will benefit black and lower-class white women through the economic upgrading of all women, giving them control of their own bodies in sex and reproduction and transferring the burdens of homemaking and childcare either by redistribution of tasks in the home or by collectivized services.

Not only does each of these three movements, based on class, race, or sex membership, claim to emancipate the other two, but it also attributes competing allegiances to false consciousness. Thus, in appealing to poor women, feminists say that socialism will not necessarily free women, or at least has not done so in Marxist countries. Nor will black power terminate discrimination against women. Black nationalists say that male-female relationships in the black community have been distorted by whites, and that women's liberation, if not a direct attempt to co-opt black women away from the black struggle, is at best irrelevant to the primary interest of the black women in economic opportunity for the black man. Socialists say that although capitalists have set whites against blacks, only working-class solidarity can end the oppression of blacks, while black nationalism that does not over-throw capitalism perpetuates their exploitation by a white ruling class and its black upper-class allies.

In taking these positions they are implying that it is necessary for each minority group to organize around its own oppression in order to counter the resistance of the dominant group, which may stand to lose both materially and psychologically. The situation from the standpoint of the poor black woman is one of triple jeopardy. In acceding to her demands as a woman, men, both black and white, will lose their monopoly of scarce resources, exemption from domestic responsibilities, dominance in dyadic relations, sexual privileges, one-sided services, deference from women, and feelings of superiority. In granting her full equality as a black, whites, both male and female, have the number of their competitors increased and suffer a prestige loss. In lifting her out of poverty, middle-class people, both white and black, lose a source of cheap labor and may have to pay higher taxes, in addi-tion to having competition increased and prestige diminished.

To put it another way, does the poor, black woman have most to gain from joining forces with poor whites, middle-class women, or black men? It is not just a question of priorities, because of the conflicting interests of the beneficiaries of these movements. Thus, black liberation and women's liberation make black men and white women competitors for the same jobs. (A black writer, for example, complains to the *New York Times* that black postal car-riers have been displaced by hippie-type white college girls, who have an easy educational advantage.) As for socialist and revo-lutionary parties, there have been instances when immediate black interests were jettisoned or exploited for propaganda pur-poses; of labor unions that used black support without due re-ward, but there would seem to be less conflict between working-class movements than between women's liberation and black liberation, with its male-dominant overtones.

Let us restrict ourselves, then, to the issues of sex and race, and see what arguments can be marshaled in favor of one over the other. Can the two battles be waged simultaneously, or does an advance on one front mean a setback on the other? First, what can be said for blackness taking precedence over femaleness?

The black-power movement assumes that the fate of the black woman is inextricably linked to that of the black man and that her interests will be served best by the promotion of his. It therefore concentrates on her role as wife and mother rather than as wage-earner. In this role she does not receive as much financial and emotional support as her white counterpart. Although considerable progress has been made in the last decade, the black man has not been able to achieve economic parity with the white man. He is prevented from doing this by the discrimination he encounters in the white opportunity structure—educational, occupational, legal, political, and so forth—and by a lack of achievement motivation and crushed feelings of manliness engendered by both discrimination and early childhood experiences in a matrifocal family in which he lacks an adequate male model and suffers other deprivations stemming from poverty. As long as black men are made to feel the mark of oppression, the black struggle will be stymied and black women will continue to share the oppression of black men. Therefore, in their own self-interest black women should concentrate their efforts on building up black men, even if this means a retreat into domesticity. Their burdens as blacks, both directly and as foisted upon them through the deficiencies of black males as husbands, fathers, and providers, are of far greater importance than the small advantages over black men that they have wrested from the white power structure or may hope to do in the future. They have far more in common with black men than with white women.

This approach would counsel black women to emulate the family patterns out of which many middle-class white women are now seeking to escape—with the exception that birth control through contraception or abortion should be resisted as genocide. Of course, although playing a traditional family role, black women would stand shoulder to shoulder with black men in the black liberation movement.

On the psychological side especially, black nationalism may be seen as improving the relationships between black men and black women. During the long generations in which they lived in the shadow of white society, their interaction was disrupted in two ways. First, having internalized white standards of attractiveness, they could not develop a concept of themselves as beautiful. The desirability of a woman grew in proportion to her approximation of white physical features. In extreme form this feeling led to the fantasy of converting blacks into whites, expressed so dramatically by Eldridge Cleaver through the character he dubs "the Lazarus."[65]

> You may not believe this . . . when I off a nigger bitch, I close my eyes and concentrate real hard, and pretty soon I get to believing that I'm riding one of those bucking blondes.

Second, the frustrations endured by black men could not be relieved in aggression toward the dominant whites but had to be vented against blacks—oneself, other black men, or black women. Black women retaliated with whatever weapons, physical or psychological, they had at hand. This sex antagonism, derivative of the color caste system, is well expressed in the following quotation:

> American society is patriarchal—white women suffer the slings and arrows of that system, in the first instance. Black women are victimized on two counts: they are women and they are Black, a clear case of double indemnity. For the duration of their lives, many Black women must bear a heavy burden of male frustration and rage through physical abuse, desertions, rejection of their femininity and general appearance. Having a job provides relief for her stomach but not for her soul, for a Black woman's successful coping with the economic problem (and we might throw in the education problem) enhances her rejection by Black men, or else invites acceptance in the form of exploitation. Stymied in his attempt to protect and free the Black woman (and himself), the Black man further degrades her. She, doubly powerless and vengeful, insults his manhood by whatever means at her disposal. Thus are many Black men and women hateful partners in a harrowing dance.[66]

The impression garnered from the black media, however, is that the black movement, with its "black is beautiful" emphasis, is bringing about a new honeymoon between black men and women. Helen H. King speaks of the new "lovemaking" between black men and women which leaves little room for women's liberation. Moreover, she refers to the open battle between black and white women as "second only to that triggered by black women's anger over that 'black man–white woman thing.' "[67] (Parenthetically, it may be remarked that the double standard in the black community takes the form of permitting black males to date and even marry white women, but ostracizes the black female who engages in the same behavior with white men.)

In addition to their hatred of white women as actual or potential sexual competitors, many articulate black women view the women's movement as a diversion from the more important struggle against racism, an avoidance behavior on the part of whites. Further, many blacks hold the white woman to be as much the enemy as the white man. She is the Miss Anne who has underpaid and demeaned the black woman in the kitchens of America. According to poet Nikki Giovanni, writing in *Ebony* in March 1971, the invitation extended by white women to black women to join the feminist movement is

> . . . just another attempt of white people to find out what black people are doing or to control what we are doing. . . . They [white women] want the "equality" to deal with black women because they've certainly dealt with black men. They're so upset about black women not coming in because they're ultimately trying to control us. There aren't any other reasons why they should be upset. Black people consider their first reality to be black and given that reality we know from birth that we are going to be oppressed —man, woman, or eunuch![68]

Other black women, such as Aileen Hernandez, Florynce Kennedy, Pauli Murray, are ardent feminists who believe that black people can't be free until women are.

We turn now to the views of those who do not believe that adopting or maintaining traditional (white) gender roles is required to advance the black cause, and that, indeed, pressing ahead as women will help black women to undermine white domination.

First, the argument goes, the damaging effects of the matrifocal family on sons has been exaggerated, as has the importance of the family in general for economic success. Mothers have described the male role to their sons or provided them with models in the form of lodgers, relatives, or lovers. Further, black boys are more subject to peer influences and have gained positive images from increases in black solidarity. Even when reared in intact families, Negro men have not been able "to translate their educational attainment into occupational achievement as effectively as do non-Negro men, [which suggests] that the explanation of the powerlessness of the Negro male must be sought outside the family structure."[69]

Studies have also shown that a man's future earnings are more affected by the education of his mother than by her marital status.[70] Far from castrating the black male, the matrifocal family has contributed to feelings of autonomy and collective effort.

> Daniel Moynihan and other government sociologists have correctly surmised that the absence of the patriarchal family among blacks has been instrumental in the development of "anti-social" (revolutionary) black consciousness. Actually, in the absence of the patriarchal family, which this society has systematically denied black people, a sense of community life and collective effort has developed. Among whites, individualism and competitiveness prevail in social relations, chiefly because of the propagation of the ideology of the patriarchal family. The new sense of collective action among women is fast destroying the decadent family ideology along with its ugly individualism and competitiveness and complacency. Our demand for collective public child care is throwing into question the private family (or individual) ownership of children.[71]

While Bert Adams[72] and Andrew Billingsley[73] praise the black family as a source of strength in the desperate struggle for survival, there is some ambiguity as to whether they are referring to the "matriarchate," extended family units, or the traditional husband-headed family.

Second, an important goal of the black struggle is the right to maintain and create a cultural identity in the manner of other ethnic groups. To achieve economic and social equality blacks should not be asked to give up their own distinctive forms of family and man-woman relationships, such as male-female egalitarianism, the sexual freedom of women, and the nonstigmatization of illegitimate children, especially since these may be considered superior to white practices.

> That there are parallels between being a woman and being black has not been denied, but that there are parallels between the black woman and the white woman has always been resisted, and the black woman has been set apart consistently from her white counterpart. We have instead been considered as a special subgroup

within the black community, which black men should try to deal with as their own private extensions. . . .

The family, as a white institution, has been held up to blacks as a desirable but somehow unattainable goal, at least . . . in the pure forms that whites have created. Witness the black middle class or pseudo-escapees into the mainstream. This group has assumed many of the institutional postures of the oppressor, including the so-called intact family, but even here we find a fantastically high divorce rate and the frustration on this domestic level has increased dissension between individual black men and women, when it should instead be a signal that something is radically wrong with the model they have chosen to imitate.[74]

Third, whether she is living with a husband or not, the black woman's earnings are crucial to herself and her family. Discrimination against her as a woman may be more significant than as a black. Generally, black women carry a larger share of the family financial burden than white women; partly because more black families are female-headed and partly because black husbands usually earn less than their white counterparts. Furthermore, blacks tend to have somewhat larger families than whites, which more strongly motivates black wives to contribute to the family finances. Among husband-wife families, 58 per cent of the black wives were working in 1970 compared with 45 per cent of white wives.[75] For families in which both husband and wife worked, wives on the average contributed 31 per cent of the family income among blacks and 26 per cent among whites.[76]

Although historically black women may have had an advantage over black men in finding and holding jobs and obtaining an education, today black males have more than caught up. Black men are better represented in the professions and in high-paying jobs, are more likely to have college and graduate degrees, and earn more money than black women.

Sonia Pressman Fuentes reports that black women are actually at the bottom of the economic scale. In 1967, the median earnings of year-round full-time workers by sex and race were as follows:

White men	$7,518
Black men	4,837
White women	4,380
Black women	3,268

In 1969, 44 per cent of nonwhite women of whom 93% were black were private-household workers or service workers outside the home. In 1967, the median wages of female full-time private-household workers was $1,298.[77]

Since black women bear heavy family responsibilities and have lower incomes than black males or white females, it is too much to ask them to sit back and wait for a black man to support them and their children. Additional force is added to this argument when we consider the fact that black girls and women over fourteen years old exceed black males by more than half a million.

> In the face of their multiple disadvantages, it seems clear that black women can neither postpone nor subordinate the fight against sex discrimination to the Black Revolution. Many of them must expect to be self-supporting and perhaps to support others for a considerable period or for life. In these circumstances, while efforts to raise educational and employment levels for black males will ease some of the economic and social burdens now carried by many black women, for a large and apparently growing minority these burdens will continue. As a matter of sheer survival black women have·no alternative but to insist upon equal opportunities without regard to sex in training, education, and employment. Given their heavy **family** responsibilities, the outlook for their children will be bleak **indeed** unless they are encouraged in every way to develop their potential skills and earning power.[78]

Robert Staples provides additional testimony on the scarcity of black males, which contributes to the large number of female-headed households among blacks: in the age range of greatest marriageability, twenty-five to sixty-four years, there are about 85 black males for every 100 black females. Further, the ranks of black males are disproportionately depleted by war, homicides, deaths in accidents, and imprisonment.[79]

Fourth, the freedom and independence of the black woman constitute a vital asset to the black movement. Using her as a "slave of a slave" has the effect of reinforcing the caste system by providing a safety valve for the frustrations of black men, who might otherwise channel their energies into the black struggle.

> I've heard it echoed by too many black full-grown males that black womanhood is the downfall of the black man in that she is "evil,"

"hard to get along with," "domineering," "suspicious," and "narrow-minded." In short, a black, ugly, evil you-know-what.

As time progresses I've learned that this description is used as the . . . excuse for the further shoving, by the black man, of his own head into the sand of oblivion. Hence, the black mother, housewife, and all-around girl-Thursday is called upon to suffer both physically and emotionally every humiliation a woman can suffer and still function.

Her head is more regularly beaten than any other woman's, and by her own man; she's the scapegoat for Mr. Charlie . . . her physical image has been criminally maligned, assaulted, and negated; she's the first to be called ugly and never yet beautiful, and as a consequence is forced to see her man (an exact copy of her, emotionally and physically) brainwashed and wallowing in self-loathing, pick for his own the physical antithesis of her (the white woman). . . . Then, to add guilt to insult and injury she (the black woman) stands accused as the emasculator of the only thing she has ever cared for, her black man. She is the scapegoat for what white America has made of the "Negro personality."[80]

Blacks need all the resources they can muster. The potential talents of black women must not be lost to home chores and babies.

Finally, it should be noted that beyond equal pay for equal work and other demands relating to economic opportunities, some of the specific planks of the feminist platform have special application to the situation of black women. These include: abortion on demand, 24-hour daycare centers, collectivization of social services, and redistribution of domestic tasks.

Still, it is undeniable that large numbers of black women have not been drawn into the female liberation movement, but neither, for that matter, have whites. While many middle-class black women are militantly opposed others are beginning to organize independent groups. It may well be that young radicalized black middle-class women are contributing their proportionate share to the movement. The movement has been characterized as being predominantly white and middle class, but the factor of age may be even more important. And even though they may not be activists, black women appear to be even more sympathetic to feminist strivings than white women. Some of the findings of a 1972 poll of a national cross-section of 3,000 women and 1,000 men conducted by Louis Harris and Associates for Virginia Slims are illuminating in this regard. They are presented in Table 10.

TABLE 10

ATTITUDES TOWARD FEMINIST STRIVINGS, BY SEX AND RACE

Attitude	Black		White	
	Women	Men	Women	Men
Favor efforts to strengthen or change women's status in society	62%	47%	45%	50%
Sympathize with efforts of women's liberation groups	67	50	35	40
Feel that being a woman has prevented me from doing some of the things I had hoped to do in life	18	—	6	—
Agrees frequently with following feelings:				
To get ahead in this world, a woman has to be twice as good at what she does as a man is	36	—	25	—
I hope that my daughter will have a more interesting career outside the home than I have had	42	—	19	—
My education is being wasted, since I never get to use what I learned in school in my everyday life	12	—	7	—
If I had been a man, I would have gotten a lot further in this world	17	—	8	—
Men are better at economics and business than women	39	—	50	—

Moreover, black women think a woman president would do a better job than men have done in dealing with problems of the poor, avoiding war, supporting the arts, handling criminals, managing the economy, and living up to her principles.

Summary

There seem to be three principal areas of dispute regarding the black family and black male-female relationships: the "authenticity" of black culture, the "pathology" or "normality" of the matrifocal family, and the relevance or irrelevance of the feminist movement to black women. More specifically, the following questions can be explored:

1. Is it possible to make an objective evaluation of the matrifocal family, or must defense of it be put down as rationalization and criticism of it as ethnocentricity or "male chauvinism"? Are

there any conditions in which the matrifocal family can be compatible with healthy child development?

2. Outside the ghetto, in what sense can black families be called "matriarchal"? In husband-present families, do black wives really have more power than white wives? The findings of studies on this question are conflicting.

3. Are experiences within the family or opportunities in the larger society more crucial for economic success? Or, to put it in another way, can a family form that is adapted to survival in the ghetto also be "functional" for rising out of the ghetto? Are girls less "damaged" than boys by matriarchy?

4. If the black movement were to realize the goal of complete parity with whites, what kind of family life would blacks be likely to have? Would they wish to retain "expressive" modes of behaving—"free love," male-female egalitarianism, etc.? Is it possible that the Black Muslim movement represents a revolt against women as much as against whites?

5. Did black women ever, and do they today, have an advantage over black men? Can they reconcile their problems as women with their problems as blacks?

No doubt the answers to these questions will be predicated upon developments in the environing white society and how far it moves toward male-female role interchangeability, with or without abandonment of an achievement orientation.

NOTES

1. Joseph Kahl, *The American Class Structure* (New York: Rinehart & Co., 1957), pp. 187 ff.
2. E. Digby Baltzell, *Philadelphia Gentlemen: The Making of a National Upper Class* (Glencoe, Ill.: Free Press, 1958), pp. 53 ff.
3. S. Foster Damon, *Amy Lowell: A Chronicle with Extracts from Her Correspondence* (Boston: Houghton-Mifflin, 1935), pp. 84–120.
4. E. Digby Baltzell, *The Protestant Establishment* (New York: Vintage Books, 1964), p. 351.
5. Nigel Nicolson, *Portrait of a Marriage* (New York: Atheneum, 1973).
6. Clifford Kirkpatrick, *The Family as Process and Institution*, 2d ed. (New York: Ronald Press, 1963), p. 168.
7. For insight into these wives, we are chiefly indebted to William H. Whyte, Jr., "The Wives of Management," *Fortune* (October 1951), pp. 86–88; reprinted in *Reflections on Marriage*, ed. William Stephens (New York: Thomas Y. Crowell, 1963), pp. 271–91.

8. John F. Cuber and Peggy B. Harroff, *Sex and the Significant Americans* (Baltimore: Penguin Books, 1966).
9. Helen Mayer Hacker, "The Feminine Protest of the Working Wife," *Indian Journal of Social Work* (1971), 31:4.
10. Talcott Parsons, "A Revised Analytical Approach to the Theory of Social Stratification," in *Essays in Sociological Theory*, rev. ed. (New York: Free Press, 1964), p. 423.
11. Robin M. Williams, Jr., *American Society: A Sociological Interpretation* (New York: Alfred A. Knopf, 1951), p. 59.
12. Joseph Veroff and Sheila Feld, *Marriage and Work in America* (New York: Van Nostrand Reinhold, 1970), p. 341.
13. See Frederick Elkin and Gerald Handel, *The Child and Society*, 2d ed. (New York: Random House, 1972), pp. 78–79, for a useful clarification of the neutral and the pejorative uses of the term "lower class."
14. Arthur B. Shostak, *Blue Collar Life* (New York: Random House, 1969).
15. Helen Mayer Hacker, "The New Burdens of Masculinity," *Journal of Marriage and Family Living*, 19:3 (1957), pp. 227–33.
16. Herbert J. Gans, *The Urban Villagers* (New York: Free Press, 1962), p. 51.
17. Ethelyn Davis, "Careers as Concerns of Blue-Collar Girls," in *Blue Collar World: Studies of the American Worker*, eds. Arthur B. Shostak and William Gomberg (Englewood Cliffs, N.J.: Prentice-Hall, 1964), pp. 154–64.
18. Lee Rainwater, Richard Coleman, and Gerald Handel, *Workingman's Wife* (New York: Oceana Publications, 1959), p. 102.
19. Ethelyn Davis, *op. cit.*, p. 155.
20. *Ibid.*, p. 162.
21. William Simon and John H. Gagnon, "On Psychosexual Development," in *The Sexual Scene*, eds. Gagnon and Simon (New York: Aldine, 1970), p. 37.
22. Shostak, *Blue Collar Life, op. cit.*, p. 127.
23. Mirra Komarovsky, *Blue Collar Marriage* (New York: Random House, 1962).
24. Rainwater *et al.*, *op. cit.*
25. Nathan Hurvitz, "Marital Strain in the Blue-Collar Family," in Shostak and Gomberg, *op. cit.*, pp. 107–8.
26. Shostak, *op. cit.*, p. 133.
27. Elizabeth Bott, *Family and Social Network*, 2d ed. (New York: Free Press, 1971).
28. Bennett M. Berger, *Working Class Suburb: A Study of Auto Workers in Suburbia* (Berkeley: University of California Press, 1960).
29. Gerald Handel and Lee Rainwater, "Persistence and Change in Working-class Life Style," in Shostak and Gomberg, *op. cit.*, p. 40.
30. Komarovsky, *op. cit.*
31. Susan Jacoby, "Feminism in the $12,000-a-Year Family: What Do I Do for the Next Twenty Years?" *New York Times Magazine* (June 17, 1973), pp. 10, 11, 39–49. See also, as an indication of the awakening of working-class women, Nancy Seifer, *Absent from the Majority: Working-Class Women in America* (New York: American Jewish Committee, 1973). As this book was going to press, the McFadden-Bartell Corporation released an excellent report on "Working-Class Women in a

Changing World," prepared by Social Research, Inc., which statistically confirmed many of Ms. Seifer's impressions and predictions.

32. Arthur B. Shostak, "Middle-Aged Working Class Americans at Home: Changing Expectations of Manhood." (Paper presented at 1972 meeting of the Eastern Sociological Society in Boston.)

33. A most comprehensive description of gender roles in the lower class may be found in Gail Putney Fullerton, *Survival in Marriage* (New York: Holt, Rinehart and Winston, 1970), pp. 189–210. Fullerton, however, does not consistently distinguish between working class and lower class or between white and nonwhite.

34. David Schultz, *The Changing Family: Its Functions and Future* (Englewood Cliffs, N.J.: Prentice-Hall, 1972), p. 123.

35. F. Ivan Nye and Felix M. Berardo, *The Family: Its Structure and Interaction* (New York: Macmillan, 1973), pp. 57–58.

36. Oscar Lewis, *The Children of Sanchez: Autobiography of a Mexican Family* (New York: Vintage Books, 1961), pp. xxiv–xxvii.

37. Elizabeth Herzog, "Is There a 'Breakdown' of the Negro Family?" *Social Work* (January 1966), 11:3–10.

38. S. M. Miller and Frank Riessman, "The Working Class Subculture: A New View," *Social Problems* (1961), 9:86–97.

39. Lee Rainwater, *And the Poor Get Children: Sex, Contraception and Family Planning in the Working Class* (Chicago: Quadrangle Books, 1960).

40. Jessie Bernard, *Marriage and Family Among Negroes* (Englewood Cliffs, N.J.: Prentice-Hall, 1966), p. 33.

41. E. Franklin Frazier, *The Negro Family in the United States*, rev. and abr. ed. (Chicago: University of Chicago Press, 1966).

42. Melville J. Herskovits, *The Myth of the Negro Past* (New York: Harper & Bros., 1941).

43. Bert N. Adams, *The American Family: A Sociological Interpretation* (Chicago: Markham, 1971), p. 119.

44. Stanley M. Elkins, *Slavery: A Problem in American Institutional and Intellectual Life* (New York: Grosset & Dunlap, 1963).

45. Adams, *op. cit.*, p. 119.

46. Frazier, *op. cit.*, p. 102.

47. *Ibid.*, pp. 102–3.

48. Patricia Robinson, "A Historical and Critical Essay on Black Women in the Cities," in *The Black Woman*, ed. Toni Cade (New York: Signet Books, 1970), p. 207.

49. In March 1965, the Office of Policy Planning and Research of the U.S. Department of Labor issued a 78-page document under the title *The Negro Family: The Case for National Action*. This document is better known as the Moynihan Report, after its chief author, Daniel Patrick Moynihan, who was Assistant Secretary of Labor at the time of writing.

50. U.S. Bureau of Census, Series P-23, No. 46, "The Social and Economic Status of the Black Population in the United States, 1972" (Washington, D.C.: U.S. Government Printing Office, 1973), p. 29.

51. Joe R. Feagin, "Black Women in the American Work Force," in *The Family Life of Black People*, ed Charles V. Willie (Columbus, Ohio: Charles E. Merrill, 1970).

52. Robert O. Blood, Jr., and Donald M. Wolfe, *Husbands and Wives: The Dynamics of Married Living* (New York: Free Press, 1960), p. 35.

53. *Ibid.*, pp. 182, 195, 214. See also Dolores E. Mack, "The Power Relationship in Black Families and White Families," *Journal of Personality and Social Psychology* (1974), 30:409–13. Using a different measuring technique, she found class, but no racial, differences in spousal power.
54. Robert Staples, "The Myth of the Black Matriarchy," *The Black Scholar* (January–February 1970), pp. 8–16.
55. Herbert H. Hyman and John Shelton Reed, "Black Matriarchy Reconsidered: Evidence from Secondary Analysis of Sample Surveys," *Public Opinion Quarterly* (1969), 33:346–55.
56. Feagin, *op. cit.*, pp. 23–35.
57. Helen Mayer Hacker, "A Functional Approach to the Gainful Employment of Married Women," unpublished Ph.D. dissertation, Columbia University (1961), chap. 7.
58. Leland J. Axelson, "The Marital Adjustment and Marital Role Definitions of Husbands of Working and Nonworking Wives," *Marriage and Family Living* (1963), 25:189–95.
59. Bernard, *op. cit.*, p. 6.
60. Carlfred Broderick, "Sociosexual Development Among Urban Negroes and Whites." (Paper presented at meetings of the National Council of Family Relations, Miami, 1964.)
61. Elliot Liebow, *Talley's Corner* (Boston: Little, Brown, 1967).
62. Reynold Farley, "Trends in Marital Status Among Negroes," Willie, *op. cit.*, pp. 172–83.
63. John H. Scanzoni, *The Black Family in Modern Society* (Boston: Allyn & Bacon, 1971), p. 312.
64. J. Richard Udry, "Marital Instability by Race, Sex, Education, Occupation, and Income," in Willie, *op. cit.*, pp. 143–55.
65. Eldridge Cleaver, *Soul on Ice* (New York: Delta, 1968), p. 161.
66. Jean Carey Bond and Patricia Peery, "Is the Black Male Castrated?" in Cade, *op. cit.*, pp. 116–17.
67. Helen H. King, *Ebony*, March 1971. See also Julia Mayo, "The New Black Feminism," in *Contemporary Sexual Behavior: Critical Issues in the 1970s*, eds. Joseph Zubin and John Money (Baltimore, Md.: Johns Hopkins University Press, 1973); and Toni Morrison, "What the Black Woman Thinks About Women's Lib," *New York Times Magazine*, August 22, 1972.
68. *Ibid.*
69. Beverly Duncan and Otis Dudley Duncan, "Family Stability and Occupational Success," in Willie, *op. cit.*, p. 165.
70. Charles V. Willie, "Intergenerational Poverty," in Willie, *op. cit.*, p. 319.
71. Roxanne Dunbar, "Female Liberation as the Basis for Social Revolution," in *Sisterhood Is Powerful*, ed. Robin Morgan (New York: Vintage Books, 1970), p. 487.
72. Adams, *op. cit.*
73. Andrew Billingsley, *Black Families in America* (Englewood Cliffs, N.J.: Prentice-Hall, 1968).
74. Kay Lindsey, "The Black Woman as a Woman," in Cade, *op. cit.*, p. 86.
75. U.S. Bureau of the Census, Series P-23, No. 39, "Differences Between Incomes of White and Negro Families by Work Experiences of Wife and Region: 1970, 1969, and 1959" (Washington, D.C.: U.S. Government Printing Office, 1971), p. 9.

76. *Ibid.*, p. 13.
77. Sonia Pressman Fuentes, "Job Discrimination and the Black Woman," in *Womankind: Beyond the Stereotypes,* ed. Nancy Reeves (Chicago: Aldine, 1972), pp. 288–89.
78. Pauli Murray, "The Liberation of Black Women," in *Voices of the New Feminism,* ed. Mary Lou Thompson (New York: Beacon Press, 1970), p. 101.
79. Robert Staples, *The Black Woman in America* (Chicago: Nelson-Hall, 1973), pp. 20–22. See also Jacquelyne J. Jackson, "But Where Are the Men?" *The Black Scholar* (1971), 3:30–41.
80. Abbey Lincoln, "Who Will Revere the Black Woman?" in Cade, *op. cit.*, p. 82.

6

Gender Roles from a Cross-Cultural Perspective

HELEN MAYER HACKER

In an earlier portion of this volume the legacy of American gender roles from Europe and ancient civilizations was examined. It is now time to shift our focus to consider current developments in the social roles of women and men in societies other than our own. Viewing variations in gender-role patterning will help to counter the tendency to confuse American gender-role definitions with what is right or "natural." Ideas concerning feminine delicacy, for example, would not survive the observation of women in India carrying loads of bricks on their heads to building-construction sites, nor would the attribution to women of greater emotionality and intuition hold up in Iran, where men are expected to be sensitive and poetic and women practical and logical. A look at other cultures may also disclose some universals, as well as alternatives, in gender roles that challenge explanation. If the things that men do are everywhere held in higher esteem than women's activities, the question of causation arises. That is, do men arrogate to themselves the more prestigious work, or does the higher status of the job stem simply from the fact that it is performed by men? Either answer, of course, requires additional explanation.

Further, intensive analysis of particular societies yields insight into the factors that shape and sustain gender roles. It increases our knowledge of the interrelationships among social institutions

185

that tend to keep things as they are and, conversely, the stresses and strains that make for social change.

On the practical side, social reformers may profit from the experience of other countries, both in assessing the possibilities for change in the United States and in devising suitable strategies for effecting such change.

For the purpose of placing gender roles in cross-cultural perspective, the nations of the world can be divided into two types: planned and unplanned. The more familiar usage of the word "planned" is in regard to the economy, but in the present context the term refers to a conscious attempt on the part of the government to change the traditional roles of the sexes in implementation of an ideology of sex equality. Modifications of gender roles may be occurring in other countries as a consequence of industrialization, urbanization, efforts at population control, or other factors, but since these changes may be viewed primarily as by-products of other processes, we do not consider them here.

Although differing in governmental form, official ideology, degree of industrialization, per capita income, and many other ways, the Israeli kibbutzim, the Soviet Union, the People's Republic of China, and Sweden have in common their expressed commitment to the liberation of women. None of these attempts as yet has succeeded. Why? Is it because such efforts are foredoomed to failure, or because of special circumstances that can be overcome in the future? We must analyze each case in turn.

The Kibbutz

The founders of the Israeli kibbutz movement more than sixty years ago were devoted to the principles of social and economic equality, including equality between men and women. To implement the socialist dictum of "from each according to his ability, to each according to his need," collective ownership of the land and other means of production was instituted, and all members shared equally in the joint income. Women were freed from economic as well as legal and social dependence upon a husband. To facilitate their equal participation in the collective work, communal dining rooms, laundry and clothing-repair services, and childcare facilities were established. In the one room occupied by a married couple, housekeeping was reduced to the minimum, and what simple tasks remained were shared by husband and wife.

Parental role differentiation also reached almost the vanishing point. Within one week of delivery the baby was placed in a "baby house," sharing a room with three or four other infants as close to its age as possible, and in the care of a "metapelet"—in effect a professional mother. (It should be noted that men are not assigned to childcare.) Although the biological mother breast-feeds her baby and both parents visit regularly, the main portion of the socializing process, including the disciplinary function, is assumed by the metapelet. The natural parents provide only nurturance and affection. Since the father has been stripped of his patriarchal role, he provokes no ambivalent feelings in his children. He is only a loving playmate and friend, to be admired for his productive role in the community. More hostility may be felt toward the mother, who, by virtue of her sex, is partially identified with the metapelet, who does command and punish. This situation presents an interesting role reversal from the stereotyped conception of Europe, with its emphasis on the mother-child bond.

Thus, childrearing practices in the early days of the kibbutzim present two interesting innovations: the downplaying of the maternal role, and the dedifferentiation of the maternal and paternal functions. With regard to the first, there has been an ongoing controversy concerning the importance of a constant maternal figure in infancy and early childhood. René Spitz and John Bowlby are representative of those social scientists who attach great importance to mothering and find "maternal deprivation"[1] to be a significant factor in the mental retardation and psychological impairment of institutionalized children. On the other hand, some psychologists, such as Bruno Bettelheim, have averred that the vital aspect of "constancy" is the provision of challenges and satisfactions in the light of a common value system, especially as mediated by the metapelet and peer group, rather than a fixed number of persons who take care of the child.[2] Many kinds of evidence point to the successful outcome of collective childrearing in Israel, including personality assessments of various kinds and the signal contributions the kibbutzniks have

made to the development of the country and their disproportionate representation in positions of leadership.

The second issue centers on the necessity of parental role differentiation for the correct gender-role identification and emotional
adjustment of the child. Talcott Parsons is the leading sociological
exponent of the view that "the mother figure is always the more
permissive and supportive, the father more denying and demanding."[3] Presumably the mother's indulgence gives the child emotional security, while the father's setting of achievement standards
equips him to cope effectively with the world of reality. Philip
Slater, however, has argued that such differentiation may lead to
conflicts in the self-perceptions of the child, with dysfunctional
consequences for both him and the society as a whole.[4] It should
also be noted that correct gender-role identification becomes less
problematic in societies lacking a strong demarcation of adult
gender roles.

Recent reports from Israel, however, indicate that parents, especially mothers, are making inroads on collective childrearing. They
are seeking more time with their children and want them to sleep
at home after the age of three. This trend is particularly marked
in the "Anglo-Saxon," more affluent, and right-wing kibbutzim. In
all, about 30 out of 280 kibbutzim have shifted in the direction of
greater emphasis on the nuclear family. In line with this reversion
to traditionality is a growing tendency to take meals at home, to
accumulate consumer goods, to elaborate homemaking as mainly
the wife's responsibility, and for women to seek to enhance their
sex appeal in dress, grooming, and cosmetics and to diminish their
participation in committee work and collective decision-making.

More important, the lines between men's and women's work
have become more sharply drawn. Men predominate in the "productive" or income-yielding branches while women are engaged in
the necessary but less prestigious service jobs in the kitchen, laundry, and clothing areas. They also monopolize the early education
of the children, a sector that has grown in importance and carries
considerable prestige, though little power. The nature of women's
work denies them access to the experience and knowledge requisite for economic policy-making.

Such an outcome, given the structural arrangements originally
made to overcome the occupational division between men and

women and the professed egalitarianism of the founding genera-tion, was unanticipated. Popular opinion supposes a female retreat from equality, but it would be more accurate to characterize this development as a retreat from the ideal of women's doing "mascu-line" work. Although a few men occasionally worked in the ser-vices, there was never any wholesale commitment to the concept of role interchangeability. Rather, the emphasis was on changing women's roles without any corresponding change in men's roles. If we accept the proposition that a superficial version of equality was imposed on an underlying traditional gender-role imagery, that only the semblance rather than the reality of equality be-tween the sexes existed in the pioneer stage, then the problem becomes one of explaining the sequence of events that led to the present situation rather than why the kibbutz failed in one of its avowed aims. Two basic perspectives—the biological and the socio-logical—are once again in conflict.

The first takes its cue from William Graham Sumner's famous essay "The Absurd Effort to Make the World Over," in which he asserts that social engineering cannot override "human nature."[5] In other words, woman's maternal instinct crushed to earth will rise again. The kibbutzim, so the argument runs, represented a noble experiment in sex equality, which flouted the biological basis of gender-role differentiation and thus could be maintained only in crisis conditions. The most modern and sophisticated protagonist of this point of view is Steven Goldberg,[6] who ex-plains the "failure" of the kibbutz to challenge successfully the universal gender-role distinctions as stemming from biological fac-tors, manifested, for example, in women's lower distress threshold for a baby's crying. If women are more strongly committed to child welfare than men are, one need not even invoke men's greater aggression, deriving from testosterone, to account for their usurpation of dominant political and economic positions.

According to this line of reasoning, the women pioneers never fully shared the ideological commitment of the men but were brainwashed by them. They accepted the collective childrearing arrangements, contrary to their heart's desire, because their work was urgently needed for community survival and because it is the essence of femininity to want to please men. But then, when cir-cumstances permitted, their submerged natural bent could be expressed. True, this re-emergence may not have occurred until the second or even third generation of kibbutzniks, but in a kind of return of the repressed, the older, European-born generation passed on the covert message to the young.

Indeed, adherents of the "natural differences" school explain the temporary abrogation of the primacy of men's provider role and women's maternal role as necessitated by the struggle for survival, in which labor resources had to be maximized. Women's sharing of heavy agricultural work with men was predicated on the relative scarcity of children. As the kibbutzim became economically and militarily more secure, two interrelated developments served to reintroduce the old polarization of labor between the sexes. First, the shift from an economy of necessity to one of comparative "luxury" made expansion of the services possible, and it was "natural" for women, rather than men, to be drawn into these branches. Second, the stability of the kibbutz both permitted and required an increase in the birthrate. The advent of children encouraged and expressed a familistic trend which further reinforced women's absorption in domestic and childcare activities. In addition, there was a growing tension between family and community as the kibbutzim became larger and more differentiated, and it was no longer so feasible to maintain the primary ties and camaraderie of a small, dedicated group. The growing proportion of children in the total membership enhanced the importance of education, which was considered an appropriate field for the expression of women's professional aspirations and served to contain any discontent they might feel as a result of their exclusion from top positions in the productive branches. The conclusion from the experience of the kibbutz is that the familial roles that were once imposed upon women, and only temporarily suspended, now come to be their free choice.

The sociological perspective considers, among other things, aspects of the value system that the pioneers sought to implement in their regained homeland. Of central importance was the elevation of manual over intellectual work and the higher prestige accorded the "productive" as compared to the "service" branches. Although at first women worked in the fields and orchards along with the men, they were gradually relegated to the communal kitchen, laundry, and nursery. This development was rationalized on the grounds of men's greater physical strength and, particularly in those kibbutzim near the frontiers, the need for field workers to take up arms at a moment's notice.

This approach tries to identify the key social factors in the transition from rough equality to the present differentiation of the sexes. It attempts to specify the "turning points" and the precise nature of the interplay between structural and attitudinal changes. Menachem Rosner[7] is representative of the school of thought that stresses the importance of images, conscious or unconscious, held by men and women concerning the aptitudes and inclinations of the two sexes. His contention is that no transformation of consciousness took place in the founding generation.

It is probable that the first generation of women resented being excluded from men's occupations; the second generation does not want to be part of the masculine world.* This generation sees no point in pretending to an equality that it does not have and that is not very rewarding, while losing the advantages of traditional femininity.

Rae Lesser Blumberg pinpoints the arrival of male, childless immigrants as the factor that promoted the erosion of sex equality in the kibbutz.[8] She argues that given the disparity in prestige between the productive and the service branches, the kibbutzim might have adopted a principle of seniority whereby the newcomers would enter at the bottom of the ladder. If these men had been assigned to the kitchen and the laundry, then the women they supplanted could have returned to the fields and other "productive" tasks. Such a step was not taken, according to Blumberg, because the new immigrants were overeducated for the jobs available in the kibbutz and could be lured only on the basis of their ideological commitment, an ideology that glorified tractors rather

---

* An amusing twist to women's renewed interest in personal appearance is given in Edwin Samuel, *The Structure of Society in Israel* (New York: Random House, 1969), p. 150: "At one time kibbutz women, in their puritanical fervor, despised frills, jewelry, even makeup. Now each established kibbutz has a well-equipped beauty parlor. Kibbutz stores stock cosmetics, on the theory that a woman's femininity and beauty are weapons in her fight for equality in a world dominated by men. Women see no reason why they should be unarmed." Samuel leaves unclear whether women are using sex appeal to wage war on the traditional home front or in the public domain, where they have always been accused of not competing like gentlemen. He brings no empirical evidence to bear upon this point.

than pots and pans. The young mothers whom they displaced were already committed to the kibbutz and, moreover, had hostages to it in the form of children. The question naturally arises as to why immigrant young men rather than young women had to be propitiated. The answer would have to invoke traditional gender roles in the rest of the world whereby males are more likely than females to embark on autonomous courses of action.

Blumberg's hypothesis overlooks the possibility that men as well as women could have been directed to the services to make room for the newcomers.[9]

Ideology in and of itself must be activated by real events in the real world. Given the psychological outlook of both sexes in regard to the aptitudes of the sexes, the official ideology of sex equality might have prolonged the initial sharing of the income-producing branches had it not been for certain types of events, both imminent and external.

The "privatization of women," then, represented a protective mechanism against greater inroads on their free time, already less than men's, and against unequal odds in competing with men. The women's struggle became one of the "transvaluation of values," of upgrading the castle as contrasted to the counting house. Jobs defined as primarily feminine should bring the same rewards as their masculine counterparts. The slogan became "equality of value achievement" or "equality of satisfaction," which implies recognition of a sexual division of labor. "Feminine" jobs might be in the collective services, but femininity might be even better upheld and revalued in the domestic domain.

It is evident that the kibbutz has not achieved its aim of equality of opportunity for men and women, although it has more nearly approximated this goal than any previous attempt has. Its shortcomings need not be attributed to the unachieveability of sexual equality but, rather, to specific social factors present at the outset in the settlements, coupled with subsequent developments. The chief factor was the identification of equality with the masculinization of both sexes. The ability of women to perform successfully in "masculine" pursuits depends upon the level of technological development, negating the importance of physical strength and the extent to which women are constrained by childrearing. Any other impediments to women's equality are imposed by the value system of the society.

MAINLAND CHINA

With respect to broad social change, including modifications in gender roles, Chinese history can be divided roughly into three periods: "traditional" China, China under Westernizing influences, beginning even under the Ch'ing dynasty toward the close of the nineteenth century and lasting through the establishment of the Republic in 1911 and the rule of the Kuomintang, and finally the Maoist regime, which came to power in 1949. It is a mistake to think of the Communist Revolution as initiating fundamental reforms in the family and the economy, but it did represent the first intensive use of political power and social influence to implement proclaimed policy.[10]

In thinking about China one must take care not to confuse the life-style of the minority gentry class with that of the great bulk of the Chinese peasantry. Few of the latter were able to realize the Confucian ideal of the many-generational extended family unified in a household economy living in the shadow of ancestors. Rather, their meager resources restricted the peasants to small nuclear families not unlike the American household farm families of the last century.

But whether born into the gentry or the peasantry, the Chinese woman has been called "the unhappiest creature on earth." Whatever her social class, throughout the persistence of the traditional family system for about two thousand years, she was completely subservient to men from birth to death. Indeed, suicide was her only mode of protest and escape. It is interesting to note that in *The Dream of the Red Chamber*, a famous novel written in the late eighteenth century, almost a dozen of the female characters die young, the aristocrats wasting away because of broken hearts, and the servants killing themselves because of "dishonor" or in devotion to a deceased mistress. All the male characters survive. The one woman who tries to lead an independent life by becoming a nun is abducted and sold into prostitution.

Let us compare the life chances of two archetypal females. The birth of a girl into a peasant home was no occasion for rejoicing. Indeed, in hard times she might not even be allowed to survive, either killed outright or neglected in childhood. Even the anticipated bride price might not warrant the cost of her maintenance. She was put to work as heavy as she could bear as early as possible and received no schooling. In times of famine or debt she might be sold into slavery or placed in the home of her future husband, whose family was thereby spared the bride price for their son. Similar circumstances might cause her husband to sell or pawn her in later life. In addition to sharing back-breaking labor in the fields, she had the further burden of producing children and taking care of them and the home. Owning nothing in her own right, the woman was herself a chattel. She owed unquestioning obedience and fidelity to her husband, though he might take other women at will. She also had to endure beating and brutality without complaint. Even if she did not suffer at the hands of her husband, she might be raped or otherwise abused by the landlord. These were the experiences that the women of rural China were encouraged to relate in the "Speak Bitterness" sessions organized in the 1940's by the Eighth Route (Communist) Army in an effort to revolutionize the roles of women and to arouse their support for the Communist Revolution.[11]

In comparison to the gentry, though, the peasant girl had greater opportunities for contact with men outside the family and for exploring the world with unbound feet. Most revealing in this regard is the beautiful anonymous love story "Six Chapters from a Floating Life," in which the hero defies convention by dressing his wife as a man so that she may accompany him in his travels, ascending mountains and visiting temples and gazing at the moon. Lacking such male conspiratorial help, the gently born woman may have been spared physical drudgery and even permitted to while away her leisure hours in writing poetry, but her physical world was circumscribed and her psychological servitude complete. Though in early childhood she may have basked in the tender warmth of her own family, she was early thrust out in an arranged marriage to a strange man whose first loyalty was to his own family and who inevitably sided with his mother in any conflict between her and his wife. Indeed, conjugal love posed a threat to the solidarity of the patrilineal family, in which only men were linked by important kinship ties. The young bride who came as a stranger into her husband's home could be divorced if she did not please his family. Her position became more secure when she bore a male child, but it was essentially one of "put up or shut up." She could not even count on economic security because of her complete dependence on her husband, who by caprice or extravagance might reduce the family to ruin.[12] At best she could look forward to becoming a mother-in-law herself, with dominion over her sons' hapless wives. Even in this role her authority in supervising the household was only delegated by a husband who was occupied with more important pursuits, or, if she was widowed, by the indulgence of other males in the family. And whatever her age, a widow had small possibility of remarriage.

The contrast between the two classes of women has been well put by Ray Baber:

> The Chinese lady did not soil her hands with labor, but she was actually much less free than the coolie's wife who labored by his side and of necessity had privileges not available to the lady behind the curtains. But each was doing what man told her to, whether pulling a plow side by side with a beast or making her body beautiful to please her lord.[13]

The hierarchical structure of old China according to generation, age, and sex, in which everyone progressed through his prescribed stations in life, began to be shaken by the impact of the Western world about the middle of the last century. Chinese students who had studied abroad came back with new ideas about democracy, liberalism, science, and the rights of youth and women. Foreign missionaries diffused Western outlooks in hospitals, schools, and churches. Most important, once China had been opened to foreign trade, industrial development began, bringing in its wake rationalistic, matter-of-fact attitudes toward life. Women, as well as men, were drawn into the factories in urban centers. Their new work roles required some education and an end to footbinding.

In this transitional period the physical as well as role segregation of men and women began to be eroded. The sexes, both married and unmarried, mixed in recreation. Chinese women became enthusiastic about cosmetics, new coiffures, and clothes designed to display their physical charms. A feminist movement emerged, symbolized by Madame Sun Yat-sen. Women's new economic contributions gave them a stronger voice in family affairs, but they also acquired many of the problems and burdens of Western women, such as chief responsibility for the care of children. (In old China the education of sons had been a paternal responsibility.)

These processes were accelerated by the overthrow of the Ch'ing dynasty when the leaders of the new republic called upon the Chinese people to enter the twentieth century. The Kuomintang, the main political party of the republic of China, founded chiefly by Sun Yat-sen in 1911 and led since 1925 by Chiang Kai-shek, promulgated many laws to improve the position of women and young people, including freedom of mate choice, increased rights of divorce for women, and elimination of footbinding, concubinage, child labor, and female slavery. The extent to which the new laws were implemented is another question.

Following the Communist seizure of power in 1949, a policy of sex equality was pursued with force and fervor as part of a concerted effort to break with the past domination of the traditional "li," or customary obligations, which subordinated the young to the old, both within and between generations, and women to men. No longer was the female to be subject to her father in childhood, her husband in marriage, and her son in widowhood. The Communist Family Law of May 1, 1950, was intended to bring family patterns into line with the new system of production and ownership.

Although the emancipation of women and youth was undoubtedly a part of the Communist ethos in its own right, the dominant consideration was the creation of an independent, mobile work force to make agriculture more productive, speed industrialization, and build socialism. The hedonistic ethic of the republican period was to be supplanted by a selfless dedication to the goals of the Communist regime. Thus, early marriage was frowned upon, not only as a measure of population control, but also to prolong the period of study and work untrammeled by family obligations. Women were encouraged to enter the labor force and to participate with men in political and economic decision-making, but for the good of the country, not primarily as a mode of self-expression. Comradely rather than romantic relationships between the sexes were encouraged. Sexual abstinence prior to late marriage was expected and largely obtained. In contrast to the transitional period, self-adornment of women was deplored and a unisex costume adopted.[14]

Certainly women are not regarded as sex objects in Communist China, nor do they suffer from a double standard of sexual morality. Discrimination against children born out of wedlock is legally forbidden, and both mother and father are held responsible for the care and maintenance of the child. Official policy calls for equality in employment opportunities and equal pay for equal work. The need for professionally trained workers has enabled women to overcome prejudice in filling formerly masculine positions.[15] The rise of paraprofessionals, such as "barefoot doctors," has also benefited women, helping them to make up for their educational handicaps in comparison to men in programs of rapid and intensive training.[16]

But with all these great leaps forward, can it be said that women and men are now equal in China? Consider first the relative economic status of the sexes. Although women are employed in many formerly male jobs on all skill levels and constitute half of all the doctors, a sexual division of labor still obtains. Most tedious, nonmechanized factory work is done by women. It is considered only natural that all the nursery and kindergarten teachers are women, and by the same token women are underrepresented in the more prestigious professions, most notably in university teaching. Nor do women hold the leadership positions in the professions. Whether they will attain them once the educational lag is overcome remains to be seen. Further, as in the United States, women form an industrial reserve army and are the first to be laid off when employment drops. Then of course, as happened in 1962, the wife reverts to her traditional homemaking role.

Despite the principle of equal pay for equal work, women earn less than men throughout China. This differential in reward results from the "work points" system, whereby the kinds of jobs men perform, particularly hard manual labor, receive more points than the work women do.

Turning to the home, we find that even though men help, women do more housework. In order to free women for productive work outside the home, the government initiated a program of nurseries and mess halls in both the factories and rural communes. Needless to say, "aunties," not "uncles," take care of babies in the nursing rooms of the factories. A few 24-hour-a-day nurseries have been established where children may stay until the age of seven, when they return home to enter primary school. These auxiliary services, however, do not begin to cover the millions of babies in China, and the Chinese wife and mother is still pinpointed as the person responsible for home and children. Though she is encouraged to work and to be active politically, the double burden becomes her patriotic duty.

The obvious consequence is that women cannot compete economically with men and that employers, in addition to their active discrimination, have a rational basis in terms of higher rates of turnover and absenteeism for preferring men. While women's marital power has been increased by their economic contribution to the home, no real concessions have been asked of the Chinese husband. If his wife does not cook his meals, he may eat in the public mess hall, but he is not required to lose face by performing any traditionally feminine services. Goode suggests that Chinese women would not have been so willing "to accept the new burden of work if they had already enjoyed the advantages of Western women, who, by remaining at home in traditional activities, enjoy far more social and material benefits and far fewer disadvantages than their Chinese sisters."[17] He concludes that although ideological egalitarianism has gone farther in China than in most Western societies, the family will be retained and that while female tasks may be upgraded, they will remain as always: laundry, food preparation, care of children, and so forth. In short, the Chinese family system and sex-role allocation will approximate those of the West. Goode's reasoning appears to be that a family system is required as an emotional haven and social support in any society, particularly a modern industrialized economy, whether authoritarian or bureaucratic. He implies, without supplying a theoretical rationale, that retention of the family is a bar to sex equality.[18]

Official policy in regard to women in China has taken a zigzag course, reflecting the recognition of popular resistance and changing perceptions of social and economic needs. In the early days of the Revolution, from about 1949 to 1955, women's rights were emphasized. They were to show themselves the equals of men in work, to marry for love or throw off unwanted husbands of arranged marriages, to become mistresses of their own fate. During this period labor heroines who vied with men in skill and accomplishments were held up as models. By 1954, however, governmental cognizance of male resistance, women's reluctance to accept work assignments and leave their children in nurseries, the disruption of family life by the rash of divorces, and the dearth of desirable jobs for urban women led to a reaffirmation of women's family roles as prerequisite to building socialism. Free love and self-fulfillment in work were denounced as bourgeois. On the other hand, complete absorption in motherhood and housewifery to the exclusion of political participation and study was also excoriated as feudal. A "socialist" home would be run with economy and diligence, permitting both spouses to play a fuller part in society. Harmony between the marital partners would flow from correct political views rather than from love or romance. Such harmony was not to be achieved, however, by the wife's deference to the superior political acumen of her husband; in the words of a report from Moscow, husbands and wives were to "build themselves up ideologically by battering one another with criticism."[19] The Soviet newspaper *Nedelva* further quoted the Chinese press as advocating "a permanent atmosphere of ideological struggle" and dismissing love as a "psychopathic occupation that wastes time and energy."

Mao's tactic for reconciling women's two roles was the "Great Leap Forward" into communes in both city and countryside. In the rural communes women were assigned the lighter, more menial agricultural chores so that men might be freed for heavier productive labor. In the urban communes women were organized in "housewives' factories" or "satellite enterprises" around the state factories, where they performed nonmechanized tasks, such as making small crates from old pieces of wood. Although women were paid less than men, for the first time they received their wages directly, not through their husbands. The communes gave women new feelings of self-respect and self-confidence, but, in marked contrast to the kibbutz, the lack of concern for social relations prevented them from becoming an adequate substitute for family life.

By 1962 it was acknowledged that neither work nor collectivized services had liberated Chinese women. In fact, the majority were not only still home-oriented but tainted by Western materialism. The release from Moscow quoted above further reports that "Chinese wives had been acting in an especially bourgeois fashion by worrying about food and clothes instead of ideology and Mao Tse-Tung's thoughts." The Party changed its focus from women's *rights* to women's *attitudes*.[20] In fighting imperialism and building socialism the "woman question" would disappear. Thus the Cultural Revolution initiated in 1966 enlisted women in the "true revolution" which "does not differ according to sex."

What is noteworthy in China's history so far is that women are told what they should be—and only 10 per cent of the Party's Central Committee, as of September 1973, are female. Leadership in the army, industry, the university, and political committees is still largely male, and popular attitudes still find women better suited by nature to jobs that represent extensions of their traditional homemaking activities. Those women who do occupy leadership positions are largely confined to authority over other women. Moreover, they are young women who have grown up since the Revolution. Yet although Chinese women are far from equal with men, they have made tremendous strides, and in comparison with the "bitter past," their accomplishments give many a feeling of exhilaration.

THE SOVIET UNION

In assessing the present status of Russian women and probable future trends, it is necessary to consider, as with mainland China, the "bitter past" of prerevolutionary days, the influence of Marxist ideology, and the changing economic, political, and military needs of the country.[21] Again, one must make distinctions among the various social classes of Russia.

As in China, peasants made up the vast majority of the Russian population, and until 1860 most of them were serfs attached to the land of their lord. Although both sexes shared a life of unremitting labor, women bore the additional burden of complete subservience to their husbands and were expected to endure their drunkenness and beatings without complaint. Among the well-to-do peasantry the extended patriarchal family was common, in which the wife came to live in her father-in-law's household, and both spouses were subject to his despotic decisions. Here, too, the wife suffered harassment from her mother-in-law. Marriages were arranged to consolidate property rather than to fulfill personal preferences, and girls, even more than boys, could be married without their consent. The situation is reminiscent of China except that the moral underpinning was provided by Tsarist law and the Greek Orthodox Church rather than the Confucian code and ancestor worship.

Among the poorer peasantry overcrowding on the land often prevented the father from being able to maintain his expanding family and forced him into long treks in search of employment, leaving his small allotment to be cultivated by his wife, aged parents, and children. (Separation of families for employment reasons was also common in China.) In this manner the patriarchal structure of the family was weakened. Mother-centered families also became a common phenomenon when peasant families moved to industrial centers because of the precariousness of the father's employment and the wife's need to obtain some income. The plight of the peasantry exchanging village poverty for urban slums is well portrayed in Gorky's *Mother*.

Classics of Russian literature also mirror husband-wife and father-child relationships in the gentry and merchant classes. In the former, alliances of property and prestige were frequently contracted, with subsequent estrangement of husband and wife. Women, though protected and rarely in want, had no scope outside the home and were financially and spiritually dependent on men. The merchant class was depicted as suffering even more under the heavy and conservative hand of the paterfamilias.[22]

From the middle of the nineteenth century the Russian intelligentsia called for equal rights for women as part of their general protest against slothful and autocratic Russian society. They subscribed to a populist rather than a Marxist socialism and saw husband and wife, chosen by mutual appeal cleansed of materialist motives, as equal partners in service to "the people." Freedom of divorce, forbidden by canon law until 1917, complemented freedom of choice in marriage. Eventually their vision of the ideal family was rounded out by family planning.

When the Bolsheviks came to power in 1917, they were moved by both ideological and practical considerations to transform the family and the role of women. Since the primary identification of women in societies for which written records exist has always been in terms of their family roles and responsibilities, fundamental changes in women's roles are predicated upon changes in the family system.

Marxist ideology proclaims class struggle as the moving force in human history, but underlying class antagonism and prototypical of it is the battle of the sexes. Though it originates in the sexual division of labor in reproduction, men's biological advantage over women does not bring about male dominance until a stage of economic development is reached, such as a pastoral economy, in which the accumulation of wealth makes property rights important. Then, with women tied to the home and the care of children, the economic and military pursuits that brought wealth and power were appropriated by men. As some men were more successful than others, class divisions grew up. Upper-class men had less need of their wives' services, either as workers or as sexual partners, since they could buy both in the lower classes. And from wives who have become dependents rather than partners, a standard of sexual fidelity can be demanded to which the husbands do not conform. Chastity of the wife became of supreme importance to a man in removing all doubt that the heir to whom he was bequeathing his property was indeed his son. So Engels argues in *The Origin of the Family, Private Property and the State*. He further sees women as the means of production of children controlled by men.

With the development of industrial capitalism, the insufficiency of working-class men's wages brought women directly into a money economy. While Marx deplored the degrading conditions of work foisted on women and children and the undermining of traditional family ties, he recognized that a materialist basis had been created for the emancipation of women by providing them with a source of earnings outside the home.[23]

The Soviet theoreticians believed that the integration of all women into the economy would liberate them from masculine bondage and foster relationships between men and women based on love and mutual respect. Women's biological burdens were to be relieved by maternity leaves and legal abortions. (Contraceptive devices seemed to be in short supply, and possibly Russian men were as reluctant as Chinese men to use condoms.) Women's domestic duties were to be transferred to new social institutions: nursery schools, boarding schools, public dining halls, laundries, and the like. As in China, the emphasis was on changing women's roles but not tampering with men's roles. Despite some mild exhortations about helping out at home, there was no real expectation that Russian men would assume equal responsibility for the care of the home and of children.

Other reforms of the early Soviet period included the legalization of common-law marriages, the destigmatization of unmarried mothers, the removal of legal distinctions between children born in or out of wedlock, and easy divorce by mutual consent or even at the wish of only one of the marital partners. But all these measures, designed to transform housewives, whose work in the home was considered "unproductive," into workers, did not succeed in placing women on an equal footing with men either in the home or in industry. As we have discovered in the United States, present equality of opportunity for previously disadvantaged groups does not wipe out the effects of past discrimination. Treating unequals equally leaves them still unequal. Women's personal relationships with men are closely intertwined with their economic independence. Although enjoying the majestic equality of the law, Russian women, hindered by illiteracy, lack of skills, their own ingrained attitudes, and male prejudice in hiring, did not achieve economic parity with men. In addition, military and economic exigencies forced the provision of collectivized services to a low place on the Soviet agenda. Wars, revolutions, and purges took a heavy toll of men, driving up their price in sexual bargaining. Scarce men were in a position to exploit women. Finally, old attitudes concerning masculine superiority die hard, and women could not risk alienating potential suitors and husbands by pressing economic or personal demands.

Like the state, the family did not wither away, but it did become disorganized. In practice, easy divorce and the abolition of alimony as degrading to women put the full burden of the support and rearing of children on divorced mothers. In the years immediately following the Revolution, homeless children roamed the roads. The New Economic Policy (NEP), which permitted some private industry, was followed in 1928 by serious attempts at industrialization. The bringing of large numbers of women into industry led to a falling birth rate. Thus, a variety of considerations led to Stalin's "New Family Policy" beginning in 1934, which denounced divorce, abortion, and sexual freedom. Efforts were made to stabilize the nuclear family as the transmitter of values of the new regime, to protect women from male exploitation, and to encourage motherhood through honorific titles and family allowances. It was recognized that state schools could not meet the problem of childrearing and, under the influence of Makarenko, the Russian Dr. Spock, that parents were the best suppliers of a loving but firm authority in preparing the new generation for Communism and overcoming juvenile delinquency.

The main dilemma, however, remained: how to achieve maximum participation of women in the labor force without restricting their childbearing or causing them to shirk their homemaking duties. In addition, the Soviet woman rejected the revolutionary, sexless styles and aspired to feminine charm via cosmetics and clothes.

Since Russian women experience the same role conflict as Western women, one would not expect them to demonstrate economic equality with men, and indeed "they are underrepresented in the occupations that embody directive, managerial, decision-making, and executive functions and . . . overrepresented in the subordinate and junior positions and in the menial jobs."[24] Much has been made of Russian women's better showing in such professions as medicine and engineering in comparison with Western women, but their entry into these professions was facilitated by a manpower vacuum and male preference for more technical occupations. The proportion of women in medicine and teaching has already begun to decline.

Furthermore, although a favored minority are engaged in professional work, Russian women make up 80 per cent of the industrial sector, including the heavy, dirty, strenuous jobs in coal mining, asphalt paving, stevedoring, and foundry work, for which they are considered natural candidates. In the allocation of jobs between men and women we find a complex interplay of social values and technological factors.

Lenin reputedly said that every cook could govern, and by cooks he presumably meant women. Even the briefest review of gender roles in the Soviet Union should inquire into women's participation in political life. Obviously, the Communist Party is the most important center of power in the Soviet Union. Currently, women constitute about 20 per cent of Party members, but they are largely concentrated in the lower ranks. In regard to the soviets, which are more façade than fact of political power, women are not represented proportionately, but their role is in striking contrast to both prerevolutionary Russia and the contemporary United States.

From the Russian experience to date no conclusions can be drawn with regard to the future of gender roles either in the Soviet Union or in other industrialized societies. Certainly the Soviet case provides no refutation of the possibility of the abolition of the family or of the social and economic equality of men and women.

SWEDEN[25]

In contrast to the recent history of China and the Soviet Union, that of Sweden does not reveal dramatic changes of policy dictated by a small group of policy makers, nor was there ever any attempt to abolish the nuclear family. Although more serious about social reforms, more committed to social democracy, and more homogeneous in its population than the United States, Sweden is close to our own country in its governmental structure and economic development, and it too has adopted measures that sometimes conflict with each other and reflect different interest groups in the society. In Sweden, both debate about gender roles and legislative action concerning them have antedated, and achieved greater salience, than those in the United States.

In regard to social change and feminist thinking, four periods may be identified. First, in the early nineteenth century Sweden was still a predominantly agricultural and rural society, but the traditional rewards accruing to the gender roles of the patriarchal family were threatened by a population explosion, which touched off attacks on conventional marriage. The early stages of industrialization mark the second period, when migration to the towns began and economic necessity prompted women as well as men to seek employment in the mills and factories. Laws and customs stemming from the old agrarian barter economy persisted, however, and women suffered many disadvantages. Before the Marriage Act of 1921, women were considered the wards of their husbands and had no right to their own earnings. Education beyond the elementary school was denied to all but the wealthy few. Both government and industry discriminated against women in a variety of ways. This period, though, saw the beginning of a strong feminist movement, sparked by the writing of Frederika Bremer and Ellen Key. Public consciousness was also raised by the plays of the Norwegian Henrik Ibsen, most notably *A Doll's House*, which protested the submergence of the wife's identity into that of her husband. August Strindberg, a penetrating chronicler of the war of the sexes, came out for equality in the rights and obligations of marital partners in the preface to the first volume of *Married*, published in 1884. Although he advocated payment by the husband to his wife for domestic services, he did not consider the reverse situation.

The effects of industrialization on gender roles varied according to social class. Lower-class women either contributed to the support of the family or became self-supporting, while upper- and middle-class wives supervised servants in the activities which lower-class women carried as a double burden. Their position was protected, privileged, parochial, and provincial.

As in other Western countries, the state took over many of the protective functions formerly performed by the agrarian family. In its collective provisions for old age, sickness, unemployment, and other exigencies of life Sweden is most advanced, but both political authority and economic power were reserved for men. In this third stage of advanced industrialization women achieved a superficial equality; that is, they obtained equal political and educational rights. Their place in the labor force was acknowledged and protected by various legislative reforms, such as the prohibition against being discharged on the grounds of marriage or pregnancy.

The 1960s in Sweden initiated the fourth period of heightened debate concerning ideal gender roles and the means required to realize them. What may be unique to Sweden is the emphasis on changing men's roles as well as women's. Thus, there is agitation for a reduction in men's work time to encourage greater investment in their husband, father, and homemaker roles. This is termed "male emancipation." The demand is also heard that women should not profit in any way from marriage, for example, through tax policies that discriminate against unmarried persons or pensions for widows but not for widowers. It is recognized that no fundamental change in women's roles can be brought about without corresponding alterations in men's roles and that, indeed, some reforms made in the name of child welfare have served to tie women more closely to the home rather than to expand their freedom of choice. Conflicts and confusion of policies reflect divergent interests and outlooks in the society. While the moderates would upgrade the housewife role and assist those wives who desire an additional work role with vocational training, job placement, and collectivized services, the radicals would eliminate all differences in social expectations for the two sexes in that neither the parenting nor the provider role would be more the province of one sex than the other. It can be fairly said that consciousness is more elevated in Sweden than in the United States, but the lag in implementation of sex equality is no less.

Although labor-force participation rates for Swedish married women vary from something more than a fourth to almost two-thirds, depending on the number and ages of their children, the occupational segregation of Swedish men and women is such that they are essentially noncompeting groups. Thus, during the postwar years Sweden has simultaneously suffered from labor shortages in certain "masculine" occupations and female unemployment. Women's entry into male occupations is hindered by employer prejudice, residential immobility, lack of vocational guidance and training, lower levels of aspiration, and many other factors that continue to operate in Sweden as in the United States. Men are not tempted into traditional female occupations because of their lower pay and prestige. In 1966, for full-time employees, the average Swedish woman's wage was about three-fourths that of the average Swedish man. The comparable figure is 59 per cent for American women.[26]

Although Swedish women won the right to vote in 1920 and

vote in as high a proportion as men, they are poorly represented in elective bodies. In 1968 they constituted less than 10 per cent of the Riksdag, admittedly a better showing than that of American women in Congress. Their participation at regional and municipal levels is low.

One might suppose that the high level of interest in gender roles in a self-proclaimed welfare state, the intensive scrutiny of all executive and legislative measures in terms of their effects on the full integration of women into the economy, and the tremendous social effort invested in implementing sex equality might have produced more spectacular results. The fact is, though, that facilities for childcare, the construction of service apartments, and other reforms to help working mothers not only have lagged far behind the need but have hardly approached the growth in child allowances, student grants, and general economic expansion. Part of the explanation may be found in the persistence of social attitudes that look askance at father's sharing half or more of the parenting role, and the continued expectation on the part of employers that the man's salary will also cover the otherwise unpaid domestic services of the wife. The perpetuation of such attitudes is projected into the future by the differential socialization of Swedish boys and girls into sex-typed self-concepts and life aspirations.

SUMMARY AND CONCLUSIONS

What can be concluded from this brief review of governmental efforts to achieve sex equality? Can any generalizations be made about its feasibility or the factors, both temporary and permanent, that foster or hold back achievement of the full human potentialities of both women and men? As a preliminary to answering these questions, it may be useful to summarize both the common and the distinguishing features of the Israeli kibbutzim, Red China, the U.S.S.R., and Sweden.

Stage of Economic Development

The Soviet Union and China were predominantly agricultural when their revolutions occurred. Women's work was needed both for more efficient agriculture and to industrialize the country. No doubt the Communists in both countries were sincere in their wish to emancipate women, but chiefly to make women equal with men in political and economic obligations to the state. Therefore, equal access to jobs and equal pay for comparable skill took second place to economic productivity.

In Israel the kibbutzim began as primarily agricultural, although many later added industrial enterprises. The pioneers did not come from the peasantry, however, but were craftsmen, small businessmen, and scholars. Nevertheless, they too felt the necessity of making the optimum allocation of labor power, which they defined as freeing women from domestic and childrearing responsibilities to engage in "productive" work and reserving men for jobs which it was felt they could perform better than women. To what extent their categorization of jobs as either masculine and feminine corresponded to objective differences between the sexes is debatable.

Sweden also was primarily agrarian when the debate on gender roles began, but although the development of an industrial economy undermined women's traditional roles in the old agricultural barter economy, there was no pressing need for their menial labor either in the fields or in industry. Therefore, no external pressure was exerted on Swedish women to work full-time outside their homes, nor did the government have to face the dilemma of reconciling the divergent social needs for women's public and private services.

Strategies for Tapping Woman Power

Both China and the Soviet Union passed through a phase of emphasis on individual freedom for women, an all-out effort to snap the chains of their feudal bondage. Thus, marriage on the basis of love, divorce by mutual consent or even at one spouse's petition, abortion on demand, no stigmatization of children born out of wedlock or of unwed mothers, paternal responsibility for child support, and the promise of collectivized childcare, cooking, and laundry facilities were among the measures calculated to permit women to act as free agents. Further, women were urged, either as labor heroines in China or as Stakhanovites in Russia, to vie with men in their creativity on the job, production records, and performance of physically demanding jobs. Men were exhorted to overcome traditional prejudices in their attitudes toward women workers and to relinquish masculine prerogatives in the home.

This policy was subsequently modified in both countries because it did not accomplish the primary purpose of enhanced female productivity and, moreover, came into conflict with other goals of the regime, such as stability of family life and, in the U.S.S.R., a higher birthrate. Since the emancipation of women was viewed as part and parcel of the class struggle, it required little ideological juggling on the part of the leadership to castigate the feminist movement as bourgeois and to counsel women to postpone their demands or subordinate them to the construction of a socialist society secured against its enemies. In varying degrees the traditional family, with its implications of a double standard and gender-role segregation, was rehabilitated, partly in recognition of the unchanged consciousness of the bulk of the people, of the lag in collectivized services, and of the need for the protection of women, who remained unequal competitors with men economically and in personal relations.

Both China and the U.S.S.R. appear to be moving in the direction of the United States and Western Europe. As the economy grows more productive and illiteracy of women is overcome, they will be increasingly released from full-time, unskilled manual labor. Some relief from the double burden of domestic duties plus outside work, which women now carry, will be provided by the extension of part-time jobs and the redefinition of the homemaker role as socially productive, as well as by the expansion of childcare facilities and social services. There is little evidence of a serious attempt to magnify men's homemaking and childcare roles or to encourage them to enter occupations now dominated by women (with the possible exception of medicine). In the meantime women are not exonerated from their work and civic obligations and enjoy less free time than men. Still, the government wages a losing battle against bourgeois contentment. Much like blue-collar women in the United States, the masses of Chinese and Russian women do not find their work rewards in prestige and pay sufficient to offset the temptations of a higher level of living and shifting of the main economic burden to men. Altruistic ideals keep the pioneer generation at its post, but once minimal needs are assured, rising expectations sharpen women's perception of the inequalities in the opportunity structure, which make at least a partial retreat into traditional home routines a desirable alternative. Both the ideological and the economic bases for gender-role interchangeability in China and the U.S.S.R. are still lacking.

The kibbutzim went farther than either China or the U.S.S.R. in breaking down the patriarchal family and in making women economically independent of their husbands, but their value system gave priority to the production of goods, not to services. Further, despite the "ideal" norms of sex equality, members held stereotyped conceptions of the kinds of work best suited to each sex. In the early days these attitudes were masked by the need for women to work in the fields so that their labor power would not be sacrificed to childbearing and childrearing. Continuity of the group was accomplished mainly through the recruitment of new members. However, as the kibbutzim grew in wealth and numbers, children were desired as guarantors of community survival. This development affected women in two ways. First, pregnant women and nursing mothers were transferred to light and later part-time tasks in order to be near their babies, a move dictated in part by an ideology of gallantry not observed in the early days of industrialism in England or in many peasant societies. Second, the diversification and need for leadership in the kibbutz seemed to require a job continuity undisrupted by women's temporary abstentions. That these considerations were not wholly "objective" is attested by the community's willingness to overlook men's periods of absence for military purposes and the fact that the division of labor by sex in the kibbutz extended far beyond any limitations that might be imposed by women's comparative physical weakness or maternal functions. Thus, women might be assigned to the orchards but not to the carpentry shop, or to teach in the elementary school but not the high school. In contrast to the United States and possibly Sweden, Chinese, Russian, and kibbutz women were made to feel guilty if their family obligations interfered with their community and work responsibilities, but there is no difference among these societies with respect to the social expectation that men need not share equally in the functions of maintenance of the home and primary socialization of the children.

Need we conclude from the experience of those societies in which official policy supported an integration of feminine and masculine gender roles that no institutional framework can be engineered which provides equally for the expressive and economic desires of men and women, that there are inherent limitations on such equality arising either from the social consequences of biological differences between men and women or from the functional prerequisites of any type of social organization? Not necessarily, since it is evident from the foregoing survey that all four societies lacked one or more of the essential conditions for genuine equality of the sexes.

What are these preconditions? They would seem to spring from a complex interplay of social values and technological factors, both internal and external to the society. Let us look first at real social values, as opposed to ideal social values or ideology. It is possible to give lip service to official or prescribed norms, but not to believe in them in a concrete way or in specific instances. On the other hand, "real" ideals too may not correspond to actual behavior, so that we are dealing with three levels: (1) what people think they should hold as ideal, (2) what their ideals really are, and (3) discrepancies between their "real" ideals and their ability to put them into practice. The following discussion is pitched at the second level of "real" ideals. The ideological preconditions for sex equality, then, are

1. Internalized values that do not ascribe different interests and aptitudes on the basis of sex. This does not preclude observation of empirical differences between the "average" man and "average" woman but does not accord these differences greater importance than those obtaining within each sex.

2. Internalized values that give equal worth to production for use (including reproduction and services) and production for exchange—those that establish equivalency between men's and women's traditional functions, which in the contemporary context means upgrading activities monopolized by women to the extent that (1) women will derive self-esteem from them; (2)

men, except for childbearing, will be attracted to them; and (3) under the principle that, as men bear arms for the state, women bear children, social arrangements will be made to compensate women for childbearing, including "mother's preference" on civil service examinations, scholarships, no loss of seniority, pension rights, or even the job itself. On the other hand, women are to derive no benefit from the wifely status, nor will women receive special consideration for "masculine" types of job turnover which also entail loss of seniority, risks of discontinuity, etc.

3. A dominant value system that does not have efficiency at its apex but treasures quality of life and interpersonal relationships as highly as getting the most for the least.

4. Most important, but almost too obvious to mention, popular consensus on the desirability of making biological sex an irrelevant criterion in filling any status in the society. With no prejudgments on a categorical basis, all positions will be filled on the basis of individual merit, regardless of sex or any other group characteristic.

Such a transformation of the value system, however, must be sustained by certain key technological, economic, and political factors:

1. A physical plant that does not require more muscular power than is possessed by the average woman. (On the whole, women have 70 per cent of the muscular strength of men, but the average man does not use more than 20 to 40 per cent of his muscle power on the majority of industrial jobs.) Present machinery can be adjusted to a woman's height and hand size. Increasingly, automation opens up new jobs to women. A dramatic case in point is the substitution of the ignition key for the hand crank in starting automobiles, an invention that made every woman a potential driver. Increased mechanization of jobs that are now performed chiefly by women, particularly in "developing" countries, would have the further effect of raising productivity and thus helping bridge the earnings gap between men and women.

2. Sufficient capital accumulation to permit an "adequate" diversion of productive capacity into consumer goods and services. Such capital accumulation, however, is usually a concomitant of the technological development discussed in the preceding point.

A capital surplus is needed both to build machinery and to transfer family functions to other agencies. Further, in an economy of sheer survival, social values that ignore the physical advantages of men are not likely to be maintained. Thus, it has been the experience of rural communes in the United States that a traditional division of labor by sex develops as a condition of group subsistence.

3. These technological and economic requisites will not suffice unless they are predicated on a world in which military expenses are minimal. Although historically wars have given women their greatest opportunities, they have not permanently altered their status as an industrial reserve army.

In conclusion, it is possible that these three "materialist" and "ideological" conditions may come about as unanticipated consequences of unplanned social change, but it is more likely that they will have to be abetted by a strong feminist movement supported by both men and women.

NOTES

1. John Bowlby, *Maternal Care and Mental Health* (Geneva: World Health Organization Monograph, 1951); René Spitz, "Hospitalism: An Inquiry into the Genesis of Psychiatric Conditions in Early Childhood," in *The Psychoanalytic Study of the Child* (New York: International Universities Press, I, 1945), pp. 53–74.
2. Bruno Bettelheim, *Children of the Dream* (New York: Avon Books, 1970), pp. 211–16.
3. Talcott Parsons and Robert F. Bales, *Family, Socialization and Interaction Process* (New York: Free Press, 1955), p. 80.
4. Philip Slater, "Parental Role Differentiation," *American Journal of Sociology*, 67:3 (1961), pp. 296–311.
5. William Graham Sumner, *Social Darwinism* (Englewood Cliffs, N.J.: Prentice-Hall, 1963), chap. 12.
6. Steven Goldberg, *The Inevitability of Patriarchy* (New York: William Morrow, 1973), p. 126.
7. Menachem Rosner, "Women in the Kibbutz: Changing Status and Concept," *Asia and African Studies* (1967), 3:35–68.
8. Rae Lesser Blumberg, "Women of the Kibbutz: Retreat from Sexual Equality." (Paper presented at meetings of the Society for Applied Anthropology, Tucson, Arizona, April 1973.)
9. Personal conversation with Menachem Rosner, May 1974.
10. William J. Goode, *World Revolution and Family Patterns* (New York: Free Press, 1970), p. 270.

11. Ruth Sidel, *Women and Child Care in China* (Baltimore: Penguin Books, 1973), p. 17.
12. Marion J. Levy, Jr., *The Family Revolution in Modern China* (New York: Atheneum Press, 1968), p. 150.
13. Ray E. Baber, *Marriage and the Family*, 2d ed. (New York: McGraw-Hill, 1953), p. 332.
14. Myra Roper, *China: The Surprising Country* (New York: Doubleday, 1966), reports the laughter that greeted her purchase of a jacket identifiable as masculine rather than feminine solely by virtue of its having four rather than two pockets.
15. Levy, *op. cit.*, p. 320.
16. Sidel, *op. cit.*, p. 181.
17. Goode, *op. cit.*, p. 303.
18. *Ibid.*, p. 304.
19. *New York Times* (February 18, 1973).
20. Charlotte Bunny Cohen, "Women of China," in *Sisterhood Is Powerful*, ed. Robin Morgan (New York: Random House, 1970), pp. 385–417. See also Janet Weitzner Salaff and Judith Merkle, "Women and Revolution: The Lessons of the Soviet Union and China," *Socialist Revolution*, 1:4 (1970), pp. 39–72.
21. See Bernice G. Rosenthal, "The Roles and Status of Women in the Soviet Union," paper presented at the 1973 meeting of the American Anthropological Association for a delineation of three distinct periods (1917–28, 1928–53, and 1953 to the present) in the evolution of Soviet policy toward women corresponding to economic and political changes in Russian society and the negative consequences of previous policies.
22. Philip Mosely, "The Russian Family: Old Style and New," in *The Family: Its Functions and Destiny*, ed. Ruth Nanda Anshen, rev. ed. (New York: Harper & Row, 1959), pp. 105–22.
23. Karl Marx, *Capital: A Critique of Political Economy* (New York: Modern Library 1906), p. 536.
24. Mark G. Field and Karen I. Flynn, "Worker, Mother, Housewife: Soviet Woman Today," in *Sex Roles in Changing Society*, eds. Georgene H. Seward and Robert C. Williamson (New York: Random House, 1970), p. 262.
25. The discussion of Sweden is especially indebted to *The Changing Roles of Men and Women*, ed. Edmund Dahlstrom (Boston: Beacon Press, 1971).
26. Herbert Stein, "Women's Second Economic Revolution," *Ladies' Home Journal*, October 1972.

7

Beyond Masculinity: Liberating Men and Their Relationships with Women

*WARREN T. FARRELL**

Mention men's liberation in the United States, and it is rhetorically connected to women's liberation. There is little understanding of how men change or why they might want to change. Little effort is made to examine the problems resulting from the normal socialization of a male in our society. Most of the questioning of the stereotyped gender roles comes from the perspective of women. The implication is that liberation is a problem of women and that men, at best, might "help" women to become liberated. Yet in Sweden, where "women's liberation" has made the most progress, the gender-role problem is recognized as one that involves both sexes, in which women and men can learn from each other. But before men and women can learn from one another, closer attention must be given to the barriers to change in men's everyday life and attitudes and the specific ways in which these barriers can be overcome.

BARRIER TO CHANGE: SEPARATISM IN THE WOMEN'S MOVEMENT

One such barrier is the tendency to separate men and women within the liberation movement. Some women's groups take

* This chapter has been adapted by the author from his book *The Liberated Man*, subtitled *Beyond Masculinity: Freeing Men and Their Relationships with Women* (New York: Random House, 1974).

vehement exception to the possibility that men can be allied with women's liberation and can interact with women from their own perspective during the process of liberation. This feeling frequently results from the joint participation of men and women in women's liberation meetings. What often happens in such meetings is that men assume the very roles that have previously limited women's development. For example, men tend to stand up and give speeches. They attempt to solve problems rather than ask questions. They tend to take charge. Yet, joint meetings constitute a laboratory in which problems of the sexes could be worked on in practice rather than just talked about in theory.

The need for total separatism within the women's movement is sometimes defended as analogous to the black movement's need to discover and develop black consciousness. There is some validity to this analogy when groups are first organizing. Men and women *do* need to meet separately to find out who they are and to develop parts of themselves that have been suppressed. But the analogy breaks down at this point. It is possible for white persons and black persons to go through their entire lives quite separately, without sharing emotional contact. But almost every woman, black or white, has had some form of intimate association with a man, be it her father, brother, friend, husband, lover, or son. The women's movement is the only revolution in which the so-called oppressed shares a love relationship and children with the oppressor. The intimacy of this relationship makes it much more possible for the growth of one person to benefit the other. Conversely, the relationship between men and women may be damaged by a segregated women's movement. An important goal of gender-role change is to lessen the influence on women of men's attitudes. If this goal is to be achieved, women must become secure enough to resist the temptation of dependency, and to permit themselves the psychological freedom to control their own lives. Neither women nor men can break out of the straitjacket of gender roles if they are not aware of their participation in creating it. If fathers and mothers do not question their own gender roles, their children will continue to learn the same stereotypes. A men's liberation movement must occur simultaneously with a women's movement to eliminate existing barriers to gender-role changes.

BARRIER TO CHANGE: MEN'S ATTITUDES

Men's reactions to women's liberation on the abstract level are about equally divided in favor and in opposition. In a study of 240 men from four social groups (employers, state legislators, college students, and a random sample), I found that the closer proposed changes in gender roles came to the home environment, the more the men opposed it. For example, 82 per cent of the men were in favor of the Equal Rights Amendment (ERA), which few men see as affecting their personal lives. However, only 63 per cent of the men favored an end to sex-differentiated tracking in the school system, something coming a bit closer to home, and still fewer (31 per cent) favored childrearing without regard to traditional gender-role stereotypes. The same study measured whether men could alter their attitudes, by giving half of the subjects women's liberation literature to read and then a lengthy questionnaire to complete, and the other half the questionnaire only. It was found that as a result of reading the literature, every group of men tested changed in a positive direction except Jewish men (who were more liberal than most of the groups to begin with). Perhaps the more significant finding is that the men changed even in the areas that hit close to home. They went from 31 per cent in favor of rearing children without regard to stereotypes to 54 per cent in favor; from 63 per cent to 82 per cent in favor of eliminating gender roles in the classroom; and from 82 per cent to 89 per cent in favor of ERA.

Most of the respondents, however, had difficulty accepting proposals for concrete changes. For example, when asked if a *specific* toy would be appropriate for their son's or daughter's birthday, the average change among the men who read the literature was only about 5 per cent—often too small to be statistically significant. It was virtually impossible for men to accept giving dolls to their sons (only two men out of the 240 could envision a doll as a "most appropriate" gift, and only 7 per cent considered it even "fairly appropriate"). It was easier for men to contemplate giving their daughters a baseball bat (8 per cent felt that was "most appropriate" and another 18 per cent felt it was "fairly appropriate"). More significantly, though, the men not only were strongly in favor of traditional roles as regards giving dolls to boys, but were not willing to change. Eight per cent of the men would not even consider giving their sons dolls whether or not they read the literature, whereas, after they read the literature, the percentage of men willing to give their daughters baseball bats increased from 27 per cent to 37 per cent. In short, it was fine for their daughters to adopt the traditional masculine value system; it was more difficult to think of their sons preparing for parenthood (the feminine value system) by playing with dolls. Most men, in fact, were blocked from even considering that possibility by their fear that it might encourage homosexuality—probably the single biggest fear that fathers have about their sons.

In these observations, a relationship between attitude and behavior can be observed. To give one's son a doll is a behavior—that is, it constitutes putting an attitude into practice. To be in favor of ERA, however, is an attitude that does not require a behavior (except, perhaps, to vote for ERA). The behavioral commitment in giving one's son a doll is clear and personal; in favoring the ERA it is distant and probably never personally applicable. Men reach a plateau in their ability to change attitudes when the attitude and close personal behavior are linked. Thus 77 per cent of the men studied either approved of their wives or women friends joining a consciousness-raising group or felt it was "worth a try" for them to do so. But only 41 per cent felt that they themselves should join such a group. Both questions are closely linked to personal behavior, but their own joining is obviously closer and therefore meets much more opposition. In both of these areas, reading the literature had minimal effect, encouraging only 7 per cent more men to join the men's group and 3 per cent more men to approve of their women friends joining the women's group.

The most important single variable related to a man's attitude toward women's liberation was his knowledge about it. *Not one man in the entire sample who had a high degree of knowledge about women's liberation fell into the opposition category.**

* References to high, medium, or low knowledge or to agreement or disagreement (opposition) with women's liberation are based on the Knowledge Scale and on the Women's Liberation Agree-Disagree Scale, respectively. Each scale is divided into three categories to indicate degree of knowledge or agreement.

Some backlash was expected from men who were originally opposed to women's liberation, for some of the articles were quite radical, but the men who were originally most opposed to women's liberation ended up changing the most. Even the political conservatives who read the literature became much more favorable. Among Nixon voters, for example, 45 per cent who did not receive literature opposed women's liberation, but among those reading it, only 12 per cent were opposed. This is an enormous difference.

It had been expected that the men who would take the time to read the literature would be biased in favor of women's liberation, but in fact they were slightly more conservative in their original disposition toward the subject, which makes their eventual changes even more significant. Yet almost none of them would agree that they had changed or learned anything from the literature.

The effect of reading the literature was obviously quite different for different groups of men. Among religious groups, Catholics were originally the least positive toward women's liberation (only 10 per cent agreed who did not read the literature). They changed the most, to 18 per cent agreement, but this was still short of the agreement of Protestants and Jews who did not read the literature (23 per cent for both groups). The Protestants and Jews also made favorable changes, to 26 and 27 per cent, respectively.

The level of a man's education made a significant difference. Men with little education were strongly opposed to women's liberation. However, the literature had a very strong impact. Half of these men who did not read the literature were opposed to women's liberation, but not one man in the group reading the literature was opposed. This huge shift has broad implications for the potential of the women's movement among working-class families. Almost none of the working-class men interviewed had previously been exposed to women's liberation except in the mass media.

Married men are more hostile toward women's liberation than single men. But when married men read the literature, they change more than single men, perhaps because of their ability to relate the literature directly to their personal experience. A man with children, for example, can see the immediate relevance of articles pointing out the underlying significance of giving girl children nursing kits and boy children baseball bats. Agreement with the tenets of women's liberation among married men increased from 11 per cent to 23 per cent. Most of the remainder were in the mixed or moderate category.

BARRIER TO CHANGE: THE MASCULINE VALUE SYSTEM

The dominant group in a society generally supplies the values adopted by the majority. In America, masculine values (for example, values of competitiveness rather than cooperation) have become the society's values. Therefore, men have the ability to prevent women from seeking a whole range of alternatives unless the women play the game by masculine rules. Men control hiring and firing on jobs. They have the upper hand in choosing a mate, a career, the time and place of sexual relations, where the family will live, and for how long they will stay. It is mainly men who make the laws concerning abortion, marriage and divorce, adoption, inheritance, child custody, and birth control. They define what are "normal" and legal sexual relations. Men control, in essence, a woman's freedom in relation to a man and make laws regarding even her most personal possession, her own body.

Men control this system so completely that women who enter it find it easier to adopt masculine values, even in regard to other women. For example, a woman may seek equality on the job by becoming an aggressive salesperson, questioning neither the function of aggression nor the assumption that she is a sales*man*. (Our language [see Chapter 3] is just one example of society's taking the dominant value system for granted.) Liberation will mean little for men or women if women enter men's world with men's values.

What are some of these masculine (societal) values that are assumed to be superior to traditional feminine values? The male ideal exalts being a good talker rather than a good listener, logic as opposed to emotion, conflict and adventure rather than constructive and incremental growth, self-confidence rather than humility and modesty, quick decision-making rather than thoughtful pondering, charisma and dynamism more than long-term credibility, active striving for power rather than a general desire to achieve even if power does not accompany the achievement, politics or business as an end in itself rather than a human concern as an end, a tough, aggressive approach instead of a soft, persuasive approach, responsiveness to external rewards (money, trophies, votes) rather than internal satisfaction, sexuality rather than sensuality.

In the "real" world, female values, which are closer to human values, are considered nice but "unrealistic." It is the masculine system of values that determines realities. In almost every occupation, "realism" is cited in support of masculine values. Journalists, for example, contend that they must report crimes extensively because "crime is reality"—to ignore it would be "unrealistic." Yet the reality of *growth* is either ignored or placed on what used to be called the "Woman's Page." In education, for example, reality is how students learn best, or how effective teachers teach, not just how a few male union leaders conduct a strike. Yet strikes make the front pages more often. A strike is conflict and combat. Normal education is growth. The strike is male-conducted. Normal education tends to be female-conducted.

The public and the journalists, both operating in the masculine value system, assume that reality is found in the conflict that surfaces rather than in the events and nonevents beneath the surface. "Stories" mean conflict, and conflict gets "covered." Watts made more headlines during its few weeks of burning than in the fifty years of peace preceding or the ten years since. As long as there was conflict and adventure it was considered news; what happened since is less conflicted, less adventurous. The real news is defined by the masculine value system as "no news." Good news is no news.

Journalists balk at suggestions that crimes be listed in small type, as are obituaries, or that an obituary page and a crime page be put at the back of the paper. They protest, "But obituaries do make the front page when an outstanding person dies." Crimes, however, make the front page when any person commits them as long as they involve violence and blood. With white-collar crimes the participants must be important or the conflict value great before they are extensively covered. (Watergate had both important participants and conflict value and was therefore covered extensively.) With crimes of violence, though, the participants can be insignificant. Men treat conflict and combat as all-important processes of life. This is their reality. Women treat growth as all-important. The human value is clearly growth.

THE PROFESSIONAL WORLD

A look at the business world and how it functions demonstrates how men's attitudes and values prevent women from seeking alternatives unless they play the game by men's rules. Women are forced to take a double dose of the masculine value of aggressiveness to overcome the special barriers to success placed in their way. They thus fulfill the male accusation that "women who make it are bitches." (Generally followed by, "What they really need is a good roll in the hay.") If a woman continues to act aggressively, she provokes fear; if she returns to feminine values, she provokes laughter. The woman finds herself burdened by the requirement of "proving herself," not solely on competence, but also in accordance with the masculine value system. Meanwhile, the corporation and the men in it forfeit the human qualities women might otherwise have brought with them into their jobs.

The effectiveness of women operating in a masculine value system is often overlooked because their very position is supportive—their effectiveness is meant to bring credit to someone else. Further, women's power has limited scope. A woman is usually limited to influencing one man. She must choose to influence in the areas in which the man chooses to have influence, according to his timetable (or that of more influential men) and his priorities. The focus is on the man and the final word is his. The situation is the same in marriage. The man recognizes his wife's "invaluable help" as he does his secretary's, but the focus is still on *his* career and *his* ideas. On the job, in the home, and in bed, it is the woman who provides the services to help the man perform.

But men are also greatly lacking in freedom. A man's occupational choice is narrowed by masculine-value considerations of prestige and external rewards. Once he "chooses" his occupation his decisions are limited by his position within the corporation or factory and the limited focus of the corporation itself. Yet, instead of looking to the source of his own unhappiness—male-imposed corporate goals and bureaucratic power-seeking—the threatened male often complains about "those women's libbers."

How Masculine Values Develop

The male socialization process (Chapter 2) begins at an early age. Boys see models of men who display material success, detachment or coolness, physical and psychological strength, leadership, and apparent invulnerability. Boys learn to admire and aspire to be like the role models—to be pragmatic, know all the answers, never seek help, be tough, independent, powerful, ambitious, and physically and sexually aggressive. The goal in general is to be better than other men preferably, and certainly all women. If Moses or John Wayne were to hand down the "Ten Commandments of Masculinity," they might look like this:

Ten Commandments of Masculinity

1. Thou shalt not cry or in other ways display fear, weakness, sympathy, empathy, or involvement before thy neighbor.
2. Thou shalt not be vulnerable but shalt honor and respect the "logical," "practical," or "intellectual"—as thou definest them.
3. Thou shalt not listen for the sake of listening—it is a waste of time.
4. Thou shalt not commit introspection.
5. Thou shalt be condescending to women in every way.
6. Thou shalt control thy wife's body and all its relations.
7. Thou shalt have no other breadwinners before thee.
8. Thou shalt not be responsible for housework or childcare.
9. Thou shalt honor and obey the straight and narrow path to success: job specialization.
10. Thou shalt have an answer to all problems at all times.

The stereotype of masculinity that a given culture accepts is inculcated into a boy from the day he is born. Goldberg and Lewis, who studied six-month-old infants, found that the mothers touched the girls much more than the boys, breast-fed the girls significantly more than the boys, and vocalized to girls significantly more.[1] The importance of these findings can be seen months later. "The more physical contact the mother made with a boy at six months, the more he touched the mother at thirteen months. Similarly, at thirteen months, those girls who had been touched and talked to more than the boys at six months touched and talked to their mothers more than boys did." The self-fulfilling prophecy of stereotyped masculinity is flourishing by the time a child is thirteen months old.

The image of masculinity is pervasive and much more important than any individual tendency toward aggressiveness or passivity. The California Gender Identity Center has discovered that in dealing with an adolescent male who has been brought up as a female, it is easier to change his sex surgically, making him a woman, than to undo the social and cultural conditioning that has led him to behave like a woman.[2]

It is easy to understand how an incomplete conclusion—that the child needs mothering—can be drawn from the Goldberg and Lewis findings. But the study, like almost all other studies that come to "maternal instinct" conclusions are of mothers only. It cannot therefore reach any conclusions about the effects of fathering. Yet these studies have been used to support the view that mothers should not work outside the home, while fathers can get away with giving lip service to a desire to spend more time with their children. The male again severs himself from opportunities to develop traits of warmth, kindness, and love.

The second stage in the development of masculinity may create even greater damage than the early stages described by Goldberg and Lewis. The preschool and early-school-age boy is given a very clear message as to what it takes to be a boy as opposed to a girl.* In a study of 2,760 stories in 134 children's books, a NOW Task Force found that boys' and girls' roles were clearly differentiated.[3] NOW's conclusion was that the image of women presented in these books was so damaging as to make it a major women's liberation issue, yet it largely ignored the negative implications for men of the male image the books presented.

In order to be a real boy, a boy must not be caught being at all like a girl. A fundamental disrespect for everything that is associ-

---

* It should be recognized, however, that parts of the learning process, such as discipline and sitting still and listening, do *not* encourage traditional masculine values.

ated with a girl permeates these books. Boys feel that they have to live up to all the characteristics the books say a boy is supposed to have. In this drive to avoid resembling a girl, even those "masculine" traits that could be positive, such as self-confidence, become obsessive. As a boy gets somewhat older (late grammar and junior high), his fear of appearing "like a girl" increases.

The extent to which these images become part of a boy's early concept of what a girl is and what a boy ought to avoid being is graphically demonstrated by an examination of children's books. The NOW study found: "There were sixty-seven stories in which one sex demeaned the other; sixty-five of these were directed against girls, only two against boys."

The study continues:

> Girls are attacked as a class. *The negative behavior* [of the boys] always goes unpunished and *is never commented upon as such*. The way to gain a sense of superiority, albeit a highly immature one, is to make someone else seem unimportant. Possibly this is a misguided attempt on the part of the readers to butter up the boys, since they have more difficulty learning to read.[4]

Pretending that boys are superior in order to mask their underlying deficiency (reading difficulty) is the beginning of the building of the false male ego structure—something a secure man does not need. Yet the reading difficulty itself is perpetuated by the fear of studying and the insecurity by the fear of appearing like a girl. The basis for the ego-building is so weak that it is no wonder a man's ego becomes his second most fragile instrument.

The girls, though, learn that their role is to contribute to a man's false ego by self-mockery. The female characters in the stories consistently demean other girls and themselves with such comments as "It's easy. Even I can do it. And you know how stupid I am," "Who wants to eat dinner with a lot of girls anyway?" and "Women sure are funny." In one story, "Jerry always ran away when his friends walked with girls," and in another, "Women's advice is never worth two pennies. Yours isn't worth even a penny." Yet another series says, "When you mix the clay [to make a woman], mix in guile and cunning, a shameless mind, a deceitful nature."

No children's book in current use would claim that a black

boy's advice isn't worth two pennies or that he is made up of a shameless mind and a deceitful nature or that "blacks sure are funny" or ask "Who wants to eat dinner with a lot of blacks anyway?" Yet comments like these, found in almost every book, can make the fear of femininity a potent force for society to use against boys.

The damage of stereotyping is even greater for the boy than for the girl. When boys learn stereotyped male behavior there is a 20 per cent better chance that it will stay with them for life than when girls learn stereotyped feminine behavior.[5] This implies an even greater need to think through the results of a stereotyped upbringing for boys than for girls. A common element in both high-achieving and highly creative boys and girls is that neither adopts traditional gender roles.[6] Kagan and Moss find that academically high-achieving girls remain tomboys the longest—they are "fearless, independent, and competitive. Girls who were bold and daring from ages ten to fourteen became the most intellectual women as adults."[7]

As children progress in the educational process, the stereotyped themes continue. NOW's study found that the stories pictured men in 166 occupations but women in only twenty-five. In over 2,700 stories there was not one girl who became a doctor, lawyer, professor, astronaut, engineer, computer operator, or even a salesperson. Among the twenty-five options for girls are witch, cleaning lady, baby sitter, queen, and circus fat lady. No wonder boys run away from femininity and tomboys are among the most intelligent girls![8]

Children have already picked up their dislike for the woman's role by the age of four.[9] By kindergarten about half the girls prefer the father's role and about a quarter of the boys prefer the mother's role.[10] By the sixth and seventh grades, girls who act like boys are much more socially accepted than boys who act like girls.[11] Among adults, 20–31 per cent of women prefer the male social role while only 2.5–4 per cent of men prefer the woman's role.[12] It is apparent that each sex gradually accepts the stereotype, but the men almost unanimously recognize the relative advantages of their role.[13]

What happens, then, to this positive masculine role? The options open to men at large become cut off as each man specializes.

The opportunities at the top become expectations for which one must strive, creating anxiety and neuroticism.

THE CORE OF THE MASCULINE MYSTIQUE: THE STRIVERS

Most boys find that they must choose between the two basic images of what a man is and can be—images which are apparent from both the children's books and numerous other stimuli. One image is the "physical striving" man, the other is the "job-striving" man. The job-striving man is often a "leadership striver" when in school and not infrequently a "student striver" as well.

The "physical striving" man is often the choice of the boy who is not getting rewards from the classroom. This is not always the less intelligent boy; it can also be the boy whose environment places little emphasis on education or a high emphasis on sports. He is more often the product of a working-class background than the student striver. This is the boy for whom making the Little League and later the school wrestling, weightlifting, football, basketball, or skiing team take such priority that much of his self-concept is obviously wrapped up in such an achievement. If he fails, he must quickly find a new achievement.

Achievement for the physical striving boy is strongly related to approval from his peers, which is related to his proof of masculinity, and is dependent at least partially on his apparent success with women. Regarding the relationship between these phenomena, Miller writes, "Gang members fight to secure and defend their honor as males; to secure and defend the reputation of their local area and the honor of their women; to show that an affront to their pride and dignity demands retaliation. Combat between males is a major means of attaining these ends."[14] One gang member described his feeling as follows:

> I have my mind made up I'm not going to be in no gang . . . then here come all my friends coming to me . . . then they tell me what they gonna do. Like, "Man, we'll go out here and kill this cat." I say, "yeah." They kept on talkin' about what they gonna do, I said, "Man, I just gotta go with you." Myself, I don't want to go, but when they start talkin' about what they gonna do, I say "So, he isn't gonna take over my rep. I ain't gonna let him be known more than me." And I go ahead just for selfishness.[15]

A boy will often employ violence to demonstrate that he is somebody. Gang members use violence for upward mobility to acquire prestige or raise their "rep."[16] When a gang member has "made it," the need for him to engage in illegal violence is diminished. In his studies of gangs, Miller found that lower-status gang members committed crimes between four and six times as frequently as higher-status members.[17] This is the same relationship that occurs in suicide squads in football. The insecure rookie is the most likely recruit. The major rewards of the physical striving boy, then, come from his peers; he considers it masculine not to care about what his teachers think.

The job-striving boy at this stage is usually a student striver or class-leadership striver. His major rewards stem from his teachers. However, the student striver is still concerned about what his peers think of him. "How much you can get away with" is far more masculine than an enthusiastic "look how much I learned!"* The physical striver is not required to do well in even one subject. The irony is that it is the books in use by the school that reinforce the boy's need to be masculine, which leads to his rebellion against the school, against femininity, and his association of the school with femininity.

While leadership and job striving are essentially male problems, student striving is endemic to both men and women until the late college years, when women often substitute husband striving. As a woman learns that grades in college will not determine the essence of her future, she becomes less a prisoner of that system. She will still achieve, but not at the expense of almost all other values. Yet as she gives up the need to be a winner, she substitutes the need to have a winner. The man's side of the coin is "living it and winning it"; the woman's side is "living it vicariously and winning it vicariously." The entire coin is tarnished.

Student strivers write exams according to their appraisal of the teacher's biases. They are manipulated by the system through their own striving to manipulate the system. Rather than choosing to write and analyze the way they want to, they confine them-

---

* Another difference between these types is the physical strivers' preference for contact sports such as boxing at about a 4:1 ratio to student strivers. Noncontact sports such as tennis are preferred by the student strivers. See, for example, Sexton, *op. cit.*, p. 69.

selves to "psyching out" someone else's wishes. They often choose a college on the basis of what others will think of them should they obtain a degree from that college. Once in college, the student strivers stick to easy teachers or "name" teachers. They choose, in essence, a teacher who will give them the grade or the status they believe someone else will require them to have. They perform in whatever way is demanded for the currency of a grade.

The student-striving male uses the questioning process to prove his prowess as the physical-striving male uses athletics: to give the impression of self-confidence and invulnerability. The poorly educated physical striver makes absolute statements often bordering on the authoritarian. In this way, he feels no one dares challenge him. The student striver learns to hedge his statements so carefully as never to be vulnerable. He does not mind being challenged because this gives him an opportunity to articulate further, to explain that he already thought of that. In fact, the more he is challenged, the more attention he gets, and the more people can admire his ability to respond. He stops short of asking questions to which he does not already know the answer. But both strivers are concerned with proving themselves right rather than discovering what is right. In the process, the original purpose of questioning—to learn, keeping a critical but open mind—is lost.

It is not a long jump from searching for the teacher who gives the easiest grade or the most prestige to searching for the job that offers the most status. Again, the need to climb breeds caution. A man cannot question on a job unless he feels the questioning will please. If the questioning is encouraged, he then becomes a questioner; if it is discouraged, he keeps quiet. Either way, he allows society to manipulate him by his own need to appear more a man by holding a higher position in his male role as breadwinner. As one psychologist observed: "He may have been a hero in high school—president of the student body or a star athlete, that sort of thing. But then he gets out into the world and becomes a cog in the organization, and he comes home feeling defeated."[18]

While striving on the inside, the student striver must not appear to care too much; it's respectable to have intelligence, but not respectable to "plug." He must remain aloof from his work and have it "just come naturally." To prove that he's not a "sissy" he had better have at least one sport in which he can do well.

There is no parallel requirement that the physical striver succeed academically.

The physical striver proves his success by muscle building, the job striver by leadership building. Leadership is the educated man's proof of muscle. His self-worth depends on leadership of a contingent of campus radicals, student government, the literary journal. Whatever his ideology, he must stand out. The leadership striver must have the solution to all problems. If he espouses women's liberation, he is the one who speaks up at NOW meetings and tells "the girls" the best way to dress for a demonstration.

If the leadership striver is a radical, he is quick to endorse the latest line with great fervor. He is able to "change," but only by making speeches proclaiming, "I *used* to believe that way, too, until I realized . . ." with a new self-righteousness based on an "I've been through it all" (often reminiscent of the father he may have rebelled against). If he is a student-government type, much of his interest in people is based on what they can do for him. He loses the ability to know them except insofar as they relate to his election or organization. The radical leadership striver confines his friendships to adherents; he cannot be friends with a non-ideologue unless he is a member of the working class with potential for conversion.

DIMENSIONS OF CONTEMPT I: THE SEX-OBJECT TRAP

From the male perspective, the need for a woman to look beautiful in order to attract a man leads him into a "sex-object trap," which makes him resent her even more. The "sex-object trap" catches the man as follows: He chooses her for her looks, invests time and money so as to get her to bed, and once he finally gets his physical satisfaction, starts looking for mental satisfaction. It is only by coincidence that he finds it (if he does), since he made his initial selection from among the most physically attractive women rather than by actively seeking out an interesting woman and then finding himself attracted to her physically as well. From his perspective, the woman's flaw may be her bourgeois interests, her lack of logic, or the fact that she is not thinking on his intellectual level (as defined by him). He finds he wants to back out —gracefully. If his investment in her is great and if she finds him attractive, he may feel trapped. His resentment increases the longer he plays the game.

Eventually he does get out, but not without a mark on him and his feelings toward women. He is determined not to make the same mistake again, but he doesn't know how he made the mistake in the first place. Now he knows only that the last weeks of the relationship were without sex. And so he repeats the process— he looks for a beautiful woman and again he invests his time and money. A woman ("broad") who initiates physical relationships or goes to bed with him the first night is still regarded at least quizzically. She is suspected of being a whore, a nymphomaniac, oversexed and insatiable. The trapped man's contempt for women increases. The woman, on the other hand, must either deny her sexuality or risk his contempt.

DIMENSIONS OF CONTEMPT II:
HUSBAND AND BREADWINNER-PROTECTOR

It has often been argued that the image of a husband presented in the media is almost as poor as the woman's image. Commercials that picture married men doing domestic chores like the family wash downgrade the men by presenting them as "gushing-housewife types."[19] The mockery of men doing women's work is really a mockery of women. Invariably these are married men—men who are subject to mockery and contempt because they have allowed themselves to be trapped and controlled by women, their inferiors. Single men are portrayed as individualistic, rugged, and able to get the sex women provide without getting caught by the woman. An analysis of comic-book characters finds that in these sources too the married man is the subject of mockery.[20]

The male breadwinner role creates strong pressure on men to achieve economically and creates a simultaneous disrespect for women, who are largely prevented from similar achievement. When Wills pointed out that "the mystique of earning has inflicted a crippling sense of inferiority on our nation's nonearners," he was speaking of the nation's welfare poor.[21] The same truth applies to the nation's women, most of whom are nonearners despite the fact that they do work, receiving money from their husbands as if it were welfare. Men usually think of breadwinning as part of their protective function, but the power to protect implies the power to leave unprotected. The protector, on a personal level or a national level, almost always looks down on those he is protecting (e.g., the "underdeveloped" nations). Men find themselves in the same position—pressured to prove themselves adequate protectors while simultaneously condescending to those they protect.

Possible solutions to this problem are for husband and wife to share both the breadwinning and the childcare roles or to pay the person who stays at home half the income of the household, as a salary. Neither solution will be accomplished without overcoming substantial barriers, as I found when I surveyed male employers. I asked if they would ever consider taking a year off to care for their children. A typical response was: "Personally I would like to do it, but I could really endanger myself here at work—imagine telling my boss I'm going to be a mother for a year!" If I agreed that might be impractical and asked, "Would you actively support a childcare center here in your company?" a standard reaction was, "If I keep pushing for things like that I'll end up Vice-President in Charge of Girls" (laughter). If I posed a situation that made his taking care of the children practical, a typical response was, "Well, I guess I could do it, but I'd have to have something important to do, too." Over and over, the men seemed afraid to be a part of anything out of the ordinary, particularly if it associated them with something "weaker," like women, or showed weakness, like self-examination. They never perceived the corporation as controlling their lives but were terrified to do anything that would deviate from its norms—especially if they could be laughed at.

DIMENSIONS OF CONTEMPT III: THE SEX STRIVER

The physical, student, leadership, and job strivers have in common another major area that simultaneously limits them and hurts women. They are usually sex strivers. The pressures to "score" with girls, to "make" as many as possible, to "see how far you can get" do not encourage a young man to concentrate on a woman's intellectual and human qualities, or on his own.

Many a college man is quick to claim that he is liberated from all this, but his every motion betrays dominance. He may not call

it "dating," but he still initiates "getting together" whenever there
are sexual overtones in a relationship. Even on a casual stroll with
a woman he will lead. He will drive unless the woman specifically
asks to do so, and will suggest where they might go, although in-
sisting, "I'll do anything you want." He still initiates the first
physical contact in each area—from handholding to genital caress-
ing. At a dance, college men still ask women to dance more than
the reverse. If they do something that costs money, the woman
may volunteer to pay her share, but she, unlike the man, never
starts out assuming that she might pay for both, unless special
circumstances require a deviation. In each instance a woman is in
the position of reacting or falls back on coyness or coquetry to
initiate interest. This behavior in turn reinforces men's contempt
for her, the male performance ethic, and the fragile male ego.
Most important, it forces the man to be the aggressor—to plan
and calculate his sexual advances.

THE CONFINES OF MASCULINITY

Redefining Impotence

One of the limitations of masculinity is, ironically, an inability
to enjoy the sexual activity for which the "masculine" man has
allegedly been clamoring. The psychology of many women has
changed so that sexual enjoyment is now possible for many more
of them. According to Dr. Herbert A. Otto, chairman of the National Center for the Exploration of Human Potential, many men
become impotent the moment women show an overt desire for
sex. He observes that men are beginning to perceive the woman as
"sexually demanding and possibly insatiable, since the fear of
pregnancy which has acted as a deterrent to her sexual appetite
has been removed."[22]

What causes this impotence? According to Dr. B. Lyman Stew-
art of the American Urological Association, one factor is an unconscious hostility toward women,[23] which becomes acute when a
woman becomes liberated enough to stop denying her sexuality
and challenges the male prerogative of initiating sex. His penis
was used to rising to the challenge of conquering. Now that the
challenge is over, the penis has no reason to rise—unless a new

challenge can replace the old. Perhaps he can control her, play teacher, and excite himself by exciting her with his ability to introduce new sexual techniques. It is, of course, even possible to please the woman with each form of experimentation, but by the emphasis on control he is restricting himself. He has no resources for knowing how to be dependent on a woman. He has never thought of a woman that way; fear sets in. He cannot become excited by her excitement unless it is controlled by him. He fears her and fears his supposed loss of masculinity. In this position he is insecure and afraid.

A man also cannot perform sexually if he worries about his ability to get an erection. Men's sexuality is still a penis-centered sexuality. It is, in fact, a narcissism of the penis. Therefore, a man's pride is devastated when he cannot will an erection. Once he "fails," his self-consciousness keeps him unable to perform. His impotence is compounded by the fear of impotence. His penis-centeredness blinds him to sexuality that is not penis-centered. Germaine Greer puts the problems of penis-centeredness succinctly:

> The man who is expected to have a rigid penis at all times is not any freer than the woman whose vagina is supposed to explode with the first thrust of such a penis. Men are as brainwashed as women into supposing that their sexual organs are capable of anatomical impossibilities. . . . Women must humanize the penis, take the steel out of it and make it flesh again. . . . Men are tired of having all the responsibility for sex; it is time they were relieved of it . . . the emphasis should be taken off male genitality and replaced upon human sexuality.[24]

It is obvious that men must take the bulk of the responsibility to integrate the penis into sexuality rather than integrate sexuality into the penis. Some cultures have, in fact, developed a rich and varied sex life without even having intercourse.[25] Some men who have worked on this problem in consciousness-raising groups have developed the ability to enjoy sex after orgasm, something they formerly believed only women could do. I feel a man can develop this ability concurrently with the ability to share emotions. When emotional flow is added to semen flow, the woman ceases to be a semen receptacle to be discarded after use, because the emotions are still with him when the semen is with her.

Greer addresses this problem from the parallel perspective of the clitoris:

> Women's continued high enjoyment of sex, which continues after orgasm, observed by men with wonder, is not based on the clitoris, which does not respond particularly well to continued stimulus, but is a general sensual response. If we localize female response in the clitoris we impose upon women the same limitation of sex which has stunted the male's response.[26]

Effecting the change from penis-centeredness requires a drastic shift from impotence-centeredness. Whether impotence is defined as premature ejaculation or the lack of an erection, it puts a premium on performance. It also, as noted, leads to nervousness, which in turn fulfills the man's fears of impotence. A new word—"readiness"—should replace "potence." A lack of readiness on the woman's part is less easily observable except in the extreme. Her comparative lack of vulnerability in this area gives her greater psychological freedom than the man. It puts less pressure on her to perform. In the man such pressure can be overcome only if the penis is not considered essential to lovemaking and if its softness is only considered a sign of lack of readiness for intercourse *per se*. Redefining impotence, then, means eliminating the pressure on the penis to be erect.

The Clockwork Executive: High-Level Mediocrity

A man's need for an erect penis is paralleled by the need to be upwardly mobile in his career. The pressure on the man to appear successful compels him to make others appear unsuccessful. An otherwise honest man is pressured into small dishonesties. Men find themselves playing these roles in order to rise in the hierarchy.

To overcome the pressure to perform is not to return to mediocrity; it is to gain the freedom to escape mediocrity. It is not to give up achievement but to avoid being locked into one type of achievement. To perform without choosing the way one performs is to become, in Anthony Burgess's phrase, a clockwork orange. An orange develops according to a certain schedule, or clockwork; it becomes an orange blossom first and then an orange.

Some oranges may be bigger than others, some may get there faster, and some types may be more valued than others, but the orange itself has little choice. This is what the average man is doing in his striving for a higher level. He is trying to make himself big by being a bigger orange, not by questioning the type of orange he wants to be or whether or not he wants to be an orange at all. Not only does he respond reflexively to *having* to achieve, he does little to question his need to achieve. The criterion for success is established by someone else, according to someone else's clockwork. He is a clockwork executive.

Kafka portrayed the ordinary man as tepid, narrow, and distinguished only in his mediocrity—a man who wants merely to "do his job" or "get through the day." Men today who believe they are not mediocre because they have achieved are often merely high-level mediocrities. Society suggests that men should achieve by being productive in certain areas and by achieving a certain position, and men have gone scampering in just those directions.

If the status game preserved men's health or happiness, it might be worth the self-deception, but it is the man on the way up who needs status symbols to prove to himself that he is successful. He covers his increasing nervousness by drinking more or buying more expensive cars and his increasing insecurity by switching to a more expensive brand.

The need to continue despite the consequences is perpetuated by an image of the male executive as independent, assertive, and creative.

A considerable number of men in the larger corporations seem to be more assertive in their jobs than they really are. Fence-sitting is often developed into a specialty that sees a man through many long years of steady advancement. Decision-making by committee or computer or both can take the edge off individual responsibility. . . . The corporation man sometimes emerges as much less than heroic to the one person in a real position to know—his secretary, on whom he often becomes markedly dependent. He may rely on her completely. She stalls people he doesn't want to see. She fields for him when his superiors are pressing him for a decision he'd rather avoid making. She buys his wife's birthday or wedding anniversary gift for him. In extreme cases she presses his clothes in the office and makes sure that his tie is on straight.[27]

Part of men's liberation means breaking down roles so that men can gain the freedom to make creative mistakes on their jobs, switch jobs, or even just resist on their jobs without risking the entire family income. The ability to resist can be an important aspect of creating a sense of self, as Erving Goffman notes: "Our sense of selfhood can arise from the little ways in which we resist the pull. Our status is backed by the solid buildings of the world, while our sense of identity often resides in the cracks."[28]

Thou Shalt Not Be Vulnerable; Thou Shalt Specialize

It is difficult for men to discover this sense of self. It will remain difficult as long as they are not free to be vulnerable, to admit they are wrong without thinking less of themselves. Fear of self-examination, fear of vulnerability are limitations of masculinity which are exacerbated by the job striver's concern for external rather than internal rewards. The fear is characteristic of men in all classes. It is an essential aspect of the striving male.

If this is not a problem of all males or only males, it is a problem emanating from the male system of values, which places success above vulnerability. For example, most top-level bureaucrats are men—men highly protective of their expertise, lest their function be eliminated. A highway commissioner is not likely to support an investigation which might conclude that mass transportation is more valuable than highways. Seeking the truth is secondary to retaining the position so carefully acquired. This can become a lockstep into which man forces himself to march. Can William Buckley, for example, really open his mind to a liberal position now that his whole life-style is based on his conservatism? Could Jerry Rubin or Eldridge Cleaver afford to concede even one point to William Buckley? If Gerald Ford were persuaded that Communism was really superior to capitalism, could he make a reversal while President? Why were Clark Clifford and Dean Rusk unable to act on their feelings about the war in Southeast Asia? These are all men operating in an environment which discourages close examination of one's consciousness.

The bureaucratic specialist is further discouraged from questioning his own conclusions because his expertise discourages others from questioning him. To maintain that aura, he must never admit weakness or fault, never submit to emotional outbursts, always maintain a "cool hand on the switch." These demands are especially clear in the political world.

What do George Romney, Edmund Muskie, and Thomas Eagleton have in common? Each had a promising political career that was severely damaged by an admission or revelation of weakness. George Romney admitted to having been brainwashed; Edmund Muskie allowed tears to escape his eyes; Thomas Eagleton admitted to having been treated for depression. American society reacted to each indication of vulnerability as its own shock treatment. Romney's admission in the 1968 primary campaign of having been brainwashed by White House briefings about the war in Vietnam made him "unfit for the Presidency," where he could presumably be brainwashed by anybody. The public's reaction was not "here is a man big enough to recognize when he is wrong and admit it in the middle of a primary," "too bad Lyndon Johnson, Dean Rusk, and Clark Clifford could not admit their mistakes while they were in office," but, rather, a nationwide torrent of criticism exacerbated by the press, which forced Romney to withdraw from the primary race against a man less willing to admit vulnerability, Richard Nixon.

In the primary campaign of 1972, a similar event occurred. Edmund Muskie broke into tears while countering a slur on his wife. The incident led to nationwide speculation about Muskie's emotional stability. The *New York Times* reported that Muskie "showed himself here, in the view of many politicians, to be a man who tires easily and tends toward emotional outbursts under pressure."[29] To keep weakness to oneself is the American way. It is the masculine mystique in all of us that prevents us from electing leaders who can admit to having been brainwashed or admit fault in Vietnam. It is this mystique that allowed some Americans to rationalize the Watergate affair—even after the wiretappers are found guilty and directly connected to the Office of the President. We can accept scandal with cynicism—because cynicism is an emotion we know how to express. The masculine mystique is the masculine mistake.

If the cases of Romney and Muskie are important, that of Thomas Eagleton is even more so. Eagleton was forced to resign as a Vice-Presidential candidate after it was revealed that he had received electric shock treatments for depression, even though the last shock treatment was six years prior to his candidacy and there was no recent evidence of depression. The fact of his vulnerability indicted him.

Males in bureaucracies reinforce one another's tendency toward specialization and protect one another's safe bastion of expertise. As they specialize and protect, their personalities adapt. Max Weber's description of the development of bureaucracy has striking application to the male personality: "Its specific nature . . . develops the more perfectly the more bureaucracy is 'dehumanized,' the more completely it succeeds in eliminating from official business love, hatred, and all purely personal, unrational and emotional elements which escape calculation."[30] In this atmosphere, men cannot help but be either emotionally incompetent (unable to handle emotions expressed by others) or emotionally inhibited (unable to express their emotions) or both.[31] One wonders—is there such a thing as a liberated top executive, or does the trip through the bureaucracy maim them all?

When a man does question the criteria for success or the reflexive need for a schedule of achievement, he often does so in the form of a socially accepted cocktail cynicism: "Anyone who wants my job can have it!" Cynicism is a man's emotional outlet. Real emotions are retained in his system. He does not have the strength to carry out the logical conclusion of his cynicism—open protest. His defense is the same as an unliberated woman's: "The risks are too great." They are both insecure.

If the emotionally restrained man acknowledges that he has emotions, he certainly cannot show them. A cardinal tenet of the masculine mystique is that a man must not cry. Many men, when confronted with this edict say, "If a man wants to express himself crying or what have you, no one's stopping him." It is not easy to find a man who has tested this proposition in public. The overt liberalism expressed toward crying is like the overt liberalism once expressed by Northern whites toward integration: people were free to do it until they did it.

A friend told me that he had broken down and cried in front of a colleague at the office after some personal tragedies and office frustrations. He explained, "The news of my crying was all over the office in an hour. At first no one said anything. They just sort of looked. They couldn't handle the situation by talking about it. Before this only girls had cried. One of the guys did joke, 'Hear you and Sally been crying lately, eh?' I guess that was a jibe at my masculinity, but the 'knowing silence' of the others indicated the same doubts. What really hurt was that two years later, when I was doing very well and was being considered for a promotion, it was brought up again. My manager was looking over my evaluations, read a paragraph to himself and said, 'What do you think about that crying incident?' You can bet that was the last time I let myself cry."

Dependency Inhibition

A man's emotional inhibition is supplemented by his dependency inhibition. The job and leadership striver thinks of himself as independent, but the very characteristics which make him appear independent—his success, money, and status among peers— are the things on which he is dependent: success, money, and peer-group approval. His dependence on success may lead to assertiveness at work, but it saps his energy to the point of his being passive with his family. He refuses to admit his dependency because his identity is attached to everything on which he is dependent. The vicious cycle makes dependency an important topic for consciousness-raising groups.

While dependency is less acute among men in consciousness-raising groups than among men in general, because entering a consciousness-raising group in itself is a sign of willingness to ask for help and engage in introspection, examples of dependency still occur at almost every meeting. Some men cannot let their wives or woman friends drive without feeling uncomfortable; others avoid doctors until it is proved they are sick. To see a psychiatrist is especially threatening, for it means to admit not only weakness but mental weakness, the kind "real men" supposedly don't have. To enter a consciousness-raising group is even harder for some men, since it entails trusting equals and opening up before them. For this reason, consciousness-raising and psychotherapy are usually good preparation for each other. It is the freedom to examine oneself, growing out of a willingness to be vulnerable on a number of levels, that is the most important preliminary to men's liberation.

Redefining Fatherhood

Once men perceive the limitations of the masculine role of sole breadwinner, they can see how sharing with a liberated woman the responsibility for earning the family income can take pressure off them. It enables the man to question on his job because if he is fired his family does not at once go to the poorhouse. It also enables him to take a job that pays less but interests him more. Many a man who is better suited to be a teacher than an administrator has found himself striving to become an administrator because of the extra income and prestige. If his wife were sharing the responsibility for earning the family income he would be freed monetarily to be a teacher, provided that he could overcome the feeling that he needs to prove his masculinity by striving to rise in his occupation.

Once the breadwinning role is shared by the woman, sharing childcare and housework becomes a part of the man's role. Many men have no problems *helping* in the raising of children—on weekends and in the evenings—when they happen to be free. But when it comes to *sharing the responsibility* a lot of old myths arise. The mother, it is maintained, has a special maternal instinct. The child would be hurt by not having the full attention of the mother during the early years. In fact, the children are hurt by the full attention of the mother combined with the normal "after hours" participation of the father. The normal "full participation" role of the mother encourages the mother to live vicariously through the child, dominating and controlling it. Girls actually develop a higher IQ when they are relatively free from the restrictions of a dominant mother—free to explore, develop, and be creative.[32] Boys who have dominant mothers, and fathers who are generally absent, develop anxieties about their male role. They are more anxious and more likely to become homosexual.[33] Inadequate fathering is twice as common a problem among juvenile delinquents as inadequate mothering.[34] In sum, the normal

American method of childrearing, with a dominant mother and an absentee father, has negative effects on both boys and girls.

If the father and mother both work, does this mean that the child will have inadequate parenting? Under some conditions, yes; under others, no. It is important that the process of nurturance and discipline be shared among all those who care for the children—mother, father, or the equivalent of a childcare center. The parents should be with the child often enough to provide a long-term source of stability to the child and should be attentive, with both nurturance and discipline, when they are with the child. The surrogate parent should share basic values or methods of caring for the children with the parents.

These conditions take time and effort to find or develop. Sharing the childrearing means sharing the responsibility to look for adequate care and even to stay home to care for the children in the event such care cannot be found.

This balance of the roles of the mother, father, and substitute parent in the family has the effect of producing healthy children and of making the father, for the first time, a member of the family (rather than "head of household"). For the individual family, though, the sharing of these roles presents many obstacles that could be alleviated by changes on the societal level, to make work schedules and childcare arrangements more flexible and less sexist. For this reason, NOW's National Task Force on the Masculine Mystique has advocated a number of concrete alternatives. Such as the four-day, forty-hour work week, staggered hours, childcare centers at the place of employment, communes, paternity leaves, male birth control, childless families, and homemaker payments.

CONCRETE ALTERNATIVES

The four-day, forty-hour work week enables both the mother and father to have three days per week free, thereby needing the services of a surrogate parent for only one day per week. Staggered hours enable the man, for example, to work from seven o'clock to three and the woman from twelve to eight. If this schedule were used on a normal five-day-per-week basis, the parents would need a substitute for only three or four hours a day (depending on commuting time). If staggered hours and a four-day, forty-hour week were combined, childcare facilities would be needed only a few hours for only one day per week.

A father can gain more time with his child if childcare centers are located at the place of employment. Because most men work, if they spend an hour commuting each way every day, this gives the man an extra two hours with the children he would not otherwise have. It also enables him to check on the children at lunch time—in essence, to share *responsibility* for them. For the company, childcare centers at the place of employment are among the few fringe benefits that also benefit the company, by cutting down turnover and absentee rates.

Communes are a viable alternative which need not be limited to youth or the left counterculture. A commune can consist of as few as three or as many as a dozen or more adults, sharing the care of children, rotating cooking, cleaning, and shopping—affording everyone more private time when desired and the companionship of persons gathering in the central living areas when companionship is desired. If the parents provide a stable source of intimate contact, the child can develop both the capacity for intimacy and the balanced view of life resulting from multiple role models.

As fathers assume responsibility for children, it is likely that paternity leaves and male birth control in the form of vasectomy and semen storage banks will take on stronger priority. Men will also be more cautious about wanting children merely for the image of being a family man or proof of their fertility.

Finally, the option of staying at home should be available to either parent without his or her feeling that he or she must come to the spouse working outside the home for money as a welfare recipient. Half the income of the person working outside the home should be sent automatically to the person working inside the home, as a way of giving the person in the home a legitimate and independent source of income. Homemaker payments are an important aspect of men's liberation, since they encourage men to take time off to retrain for another occupation, look for a more fulfilling job, or care for the children without feeling they must come to their wives for every penny of their income during that time.

THE MOVEMENT BEYOND MASCULINITY

Throughout the United States the men's liberation movement is growing. More than three hundred groups are already meeting to make themselves more aware of the problems and the alternatives that can be applied to their own lives. Most men's consciousness-raising groups meet separately from women's groups for a two- or three-month period and then meet alternately together with and apart from women's groups.* In June 1974, a national Conference on the Masculine Mystique was sponsored by NOW's Task Force on the Masculine Mystique to train facilitators throughout the country to start such groups. Research and writing on masculinity are being encouraged by a nationwide Men's Anthology Collective. In numerous universities, courses on women's studies are being expanded to become courses on gender roles, and men's liberation courses are beginning to develop. New magazines, such as *Brother* in Berkeley, are additional signs of the movement to reach beyond masculinity.

CONCLUSION

Getting beyond masculinity means getting beyond the concrete barriers to sharing roles, but it also means the achievement of new freedoms—freedom from proving oneself, from worrying about appearances—on the playing field or in the office; in earned degrees or job titles; in clothes, status, or swagger. It is getting beyond condescension and contempt for women, the need to be in control, to have an answer to all problems at all times, specializing past the point of diminishing returns, the need to become the expert, to be the sole breadwinner. It means learning how to listen to others rather than dominate a conversation, to be personal as well as intellectual, to be vulnerable rather than construct false façades of infallibility, to feel and show emotions rather than be emotionally constipated, to be dependent as well as independent, to value internal, human rewards as well as external rewards. It means recognizing the trap involved in treat-

* The last few chapters of my book *The Liberated Man* deal exclusively with how to run men's and joint consciousness-raising groups.

ing women as sex objects. Going beyond masculinity, then, means overcoming the pressures that make us try to appear "masculine" rather than get in touch with our humanity.

NOTES

1. Susan Goldberg and Michael Lewis, "Play Behavior in the Year-Old Infant: Early Sex Differences," *Child Development*, 40:1 (New York: International Universities Press, 1956), p. 356.
2. See Kate Millett, *Sexual Politics* (New York: Doubleday, 1970).
3. NOW's study is by Women on Words and Images (Central New Jersey National Organization for Women), *Dick and Jane as Victims: Sex Stereotyping in Images* (1972). Earlier studies even found females portrayed as morally inferior to males. See I. L. Child, E. H. Potter, and E. M. Levine, "Children's Textbooks and Personality Development," *Psychological Monographs*, 60 (1946), 1–7:32.
4. Child et al., *op. cit.*, p. 33.
5. P. H. Mussen, "Some Antecedents and Consequents of Masculine Sex-Typing in Adolescent Boys," *Psychological Monographs* (1961), 75:2 (Whole No. 506), and P. H. Mussen, "Long Term Consequents of Masculinity of Interests in Adolescence," *Journal of Consulting Psychology*, 26 (1962), pp. 432–40, both cited in Jerome Kagan, "Acquisition and Significance of Sex Typing and Sex Role Identity," in *Review of Child Development Research*, eds. Martin L. Hoffman and Lois Wladis Hoffman.
6. Jerome Kagan and Howard A. Moss, *From Birth to Maturity*, is the source for the high achievers; for the highly creative, it is E. P. Torrance, "Sex-Role Identification and Creative Thinking," *Research Memo* BER-S9-10 (Minneapolis: Bureau of Education Research, University of Minnesota, 1959).
7. Cited in Patricia Cayo Sexton, *The Feminized Male* (New York: Random House, 1969), p. 93, citing Kagan and Moss, *op. cit.*
8. *Ibid.*
9. Kagan, *op. cit.*, p. 162.
10. J. A. C. Brown, "Masculinity, Femininity . . . ," pp. 197–202, cited in Sexton, *op. cit.*, p. 100.
11. Susan W. Gray, "Perceived Similarity to Parents and Adjustment," *Child Development* (1959), 30:91–107, in Sexton, *op. cit.*
12. Fortune Survey, *Fortune* (August 1946), in Sexton, *op. cit.*
13. M. Raban, "Sex-Role Identification in Young Children in Two Diverse Social Groups," *Genetic Psychological Monograph*, 42 (1950), pp. 81–158, cited in Kagan, "Acquisition and Significance," *op. cit.*, p. 153.
14. Walter B. Miller, "Violent Crimes in City Gangs," in Thomas Dye, *Politics in the Metropolis* (Columbus, Ohio: Charles E. Merrill, 1967), p. 141.
15. Lewis Yablonsky, *The Violent Gang* (New York: Macmillan, 1963), p. vi.
16. *Ibid.*, p. 8.
17. Walter B. Miller, in "Violent Crimes in City Gangs," *op. cit.*, p. 133.
18. Psychotherapist Jeanne Knakal, in a conversation with Myron Brenton,

quoted in Brenton, *The American Male* (London: Unwin Brothers Ltd., 1967), pp. 142–43.

19. Myron Brenton, *op. cit.*

20. Jhan and June Robbins, "Why Young Husbands Feel Trapped," *Redbook* (March 1962), cited in *ibid.*, p. 142.

21. Gary Wills, *Nixon Agonistes* (New York: New American Library, Signet Books, 1971), p. 541.

22. Interview reported in Sunday St. Louis *Star-Ledger* (October 31, 1971), p. 64.

23. Reported in Sunday St. Louis *Star-Ledger* (October 31, 1971), Health and Medicine section.

24. Germaine Greer, *The Female Eunuch* (New York: McGraw-Hill, 1971), p. 3.

25. Ruth Free, "Cross-cultural Sex Roles: An Anthropological View." (Paper delivered at Seton Hall University Symposium on *Sex Roles and Social Change*, March 22, 1972).

26. Greer, *op. cit.*, p. 34.

27. Brenton, *op. cit.*, pp. 22–23.

28. Erving Goffman, *Asylums: Essays on the Social Situation of Mental Patients and Other Inmates* (Garden City, N.Y.: Doubleday Anchor Books, 1961), p. 386.

29. *New York Times* (March 9, 1972), p. 32.

30. Max Weber, *Essays in Sociology*, trans. H. H. Gerth and C. W. Mills (New York: Oxford University Press, 1946), p. 214.

31. See Louis J. Cutrona, Jr., "What Goes On Inside a Men's Liberation Rap Group," *Glamour* magazine (August 1971).

32. Eleanor E. Maccoby, *The Development of Sex Differences*, pp. 36–37.

33. L. M. Terman and C. C. Miles, *Sex and Personality: Studies in Masculinity and Femininity* (New York: McGraw-Hill, 1936). See also I. Beiber *et al.*, *Homosexuality: A Psychoanalytic Study* (New York: Basic Books, 1962).

34. A. L. Chinn, "A Brief Survey of Nearly 1,000 Juvenile Delinquents," *British Journal of Educational Psychology* (1938), 8:78–85.

Afterword

The women's liberation movement is a redefinition of female and male statuses and roles in society. In an achievement-oriented society, women are usually given the housekeeping and parenting roles, which place them at a distinct disadvantage economically and socially. The changing female consciousness, however, is now motivating women to seek achievement outside the home, in the occupational, educational, and political spheres of society. Such a movement, if it can be sustained, could close the gap in status between men and women to the point where they could relate to each other on a truly equal level.

There are today in the United States many women who have renounced traditional feminine roles and moved into the world "out there." These women are replacing their former particularistic roles with universalistic roles. Because their actions are publicized and highly visible, traditional women are slowly emulating them. Certainly not all women will become liberated, but the trend is without question in the direction of nontraditional roles for as many women as can and will accept them.

Nevertheless, we are still a long way from success. (I almost said "from home," but that would be exactly the opposite of what I mean!) True, fewer and fewer women will be likely to accept second-class statuses passively, but it will continue to be difficult to root out of our consciousness, our ideology, and our institutions those deeply entrenched notions and attitudes that have for centuries defined women and their place in society.

At the present time we are in a transitional stage, and women have devised four major ways of responding to the discrepancy between their life-styles as currently institutionalized and as they hope they will and can be. Some, probably the majority, *accept*

249

the supportive role, partly because they do not know how to reject it or because they are afraid to reject it. Some *compromise* by accepting housekeeping as the primary female responsibility and at the same time pursuing careers on a part-time basis. Others *compensate* by giving the feminine role an aura, a mystique. These women emphasize femininity and its alleged qualities and claim that womanhood is actually superior to manhood. Finally, there are those women who totally *reject* second-class status and who are redefining themselves and their lives. Such women claim equal status with men. They are refusing the role of the "other." They are self-actuating women who are fulfilling their potentialities as human beings.

Gloria Steinem speculated on what the world would be like if the women's liberation movement were wholly successful. First of all, women would not want to turn the tables and oppress men. They would want an economic system that would provide equal opportunities and rewards to the sexes. They would try to discourage men's warlike and aggressive proclivities. They would be willing to share the problems of supporting families. In short, Steinem writes, "Men and women won't reverse roles; they will be free to choose according to individual talents and preferences."[1]

Furthermore, equality for women would mean the end to sexual hypocrisy. Men would no longer need to worry about whether women find them attractive for themselves or for the security they offer. Nor will men be required any longer to live with domineering wives, emasculating women, overprotective mothers, or dependent child-women.

American children, too, would benefit. If parental responsibility were truly shared, children would have less "mothering" and more "fathering." Better still, they would have less interaction with either parent and more with peers in daycare centers. Women, contrary to popular sexist belief, are not interested in abolishing the family. Instead, they realize that equality with their men will strengthen the family ties because children will have the companionship of two parents who interact with them because they want to do so, not because one has no choice but to overinteract and the other has no choice but to underinteract.

Steinem believes that men's health is likely to improve when the stresses of masculinity are removed. There should be fewer heart attacks, fewer ulcers, and a lowered male suicide rate. Acceptance of women in the higher levels of the clergy might result in a radical redefinition of sin. There will be less sexism in literature, especially in children's books. Men and women will dress for comfort rather than to emphasize sexual characteristics. Feminine beauty will become less important, with the corollary that both men and women will be able to enjoy maturity without feeling inferior. In short, Steinem concludes, "If women's lib wins, perhaps we all do."

Sociology claims that personality is a reflection of others' opinions. It also claims that, when a situation is defined as real, it is real in its consequences. If these claims are true, women develop inferior personalities because society views them as inferior. Women act inferior because they have been so defined. We have an opportunity now to alter the social context and redefine our gender roles, giving both males and females a chance to explore themselves without being confined by sex distinctions. The real issue is choice. Neither sex should be maneuvered into a position that is predetermined and contrary to individual preferences and talents. All of us should be free to select the life-style that will enlarge our horizons and grant us contentment as individuals.

NOTE

1. Gloria Steinem, "What It Would Be Like if Women Win," *Liberation Now!* (New York: Dell, 1971), pp. 55–61.

Bibliography

ADAMS, BERT N. *The American Family: A Sociological Interpretation.* Chicago: Markham, 1971.

ADORNO, T. W.; ELSE FRENKEL-BRUNSWIK; DANIEL J. LEVINSON; and R. NEVITT SANDFORD, *The Authoritarian Personality.* New York: Harper & Bros., 1950.

ALBJERG, PATRICIA. "Women in Academe." *Science* 169 (1970): 3952.

ANGRIST, SHIRLEY S. "Changes in Women's Work Aspirations During College (Or Work Does Not Equal Career)." Paper read at Ohio Valley Sociological Society, Akron, Ohio, May 1970.

ARDREY, ROBERT. *African Genesis.* New York: Atheneum, 1966.

————. *The Territorial Imperative.* New York: Atheneum, 1966.

ARNOTT, CATHERINE C. "Husbands' Attitude and Wives' Commitment to Employment." *Journal of Marriage and the Family* 34 (1972):4.

————. "Married Women and the Pursuit of Profit: An Exchange Theory Perspective." *Journal of Marriage and the Family* 34 (1972):1.

AXELSON, LELAND. "The Marital Adjustment and Marital Role Definitions of Working and Non-Working Wives." *Marriage and Family Living* 25 (1963).

BABER, RAY E. *Marriage and the Family.* 2d ed. New York: McGraw-Hill, 1953.

BAKER, ELSWORTH F. "Our Sex-Negating Culture." *Social Behavior,* December 1972.

BALTZELL, E. DIGBY. *Philadelphia Gentlemen: The Making of a National Upper Class.* Glencoe, Ill.: Free Press, 1958.

————. *The Protestant Establishment.* New York: Vintage Books, 1964.

BARDIS, PANOS D. "Family Forms and Variations Historically Considered." In *Handbook of Marriage and the Family,* ed. Harold T. Christensen. Chicago: Rand McNally, 1964.

BARRON, NANCY. "Sex-typed Language: The Production of Grammatical Cases." *Acta Sociologia* 14 (Winter 1971).

BARRY, H.; M. BACON; and I. L. CHILD. "A Cross-cultural Survey of Some Sex Differences in Socialization." *Journal of Abnormal and Social Psychology* 55 (1957).

253

BEIBER, I., et al. *Homosexuality: A Psychoanalytic Study.* New York: Basic Books, 1962.

BELL, ROBERT R. *Marriage and Family Interaction.* 3d ed. Homewood, Ill.: Dorsey Press, 1971.

BELL, ROBERT R., and MICHAEL GORDON, eds. *The Social Dimension of Human Sexuality.* Boston: Little, Brown, 1972.

BEM, SANDRA L., and DARYL J. BEM. "Training the Woman to Know Her Place: The Power of a Nonconscious Ideology." In D. J. Bem, *Beliefs, Attitudes, and Human Affairs.* Belmont, Calif.: Brooks/Cole, 1970.

BENSON, LEONARD. *Fatherhood: A Sociological Perspective.* New York: Random House, 1968.

BERG, IVAR. *Education and Jobs: The Great Training Robbery.* New York: Praeger, 1970.

BERGER, BENNETT M. *Working Class Suburb: A Study of Auto Workers in Suburbia.* Berkeley: University of California Press, 1960.

BERNARD, JESSIE. *Marriage and Family Among Negroes.* Englewood Cliffs, N.J.: Prentice-Hall, 1966.

————. "My Four Revolutions: An Autobiographical History of the ASA." *American Journal of Sociology* 78 (1973):4.

BETTELHEIM, BRUNO. *Children of the Dream.* New York: Avon Books, 1970.

BILLINGSLEY, ANDREW. *Black Families in America.* Englewood Cliffs, N.J.: Prentice-Hall, 1968.

BLACK, IRMA SIMONTON, ed. "After School." In *Around the City: The Bank Street Readers.* New York: Macmillan, 1965.

BLOCH, RAYMOND. *The Etruscans.* Trans. Stuart Hood. New York: Praeger, 1958.

BLOOD, ROBERT O., JR. "Long-Range Causes and Consequences of the Employment of Married Women." *Journal of Marriage and the Family* 27 (1965).

BLOOD, ROBERT O., JR., and DONALD M. WOLFE. *Husbands and Wives.* New York: Free Press, 1960.

BLUMBERG, RAE LESSER. "Women of the Kibbutz: Retreat from Sexual Equality." Paper presented at meetings of the Society for Applied Anthropology, Tucson, Arizona, April 1973.

BOND, JEAN CAREY, and PATRICIA PEERY. "Is the Black Male Castrated?" In *The Black Woman,* ed. Toni Cade. New York: Signet Books, 1970.

BONDURANT, SUSAN. "It's All Right, Doc—I'm Only Dying." *Rough Times* 3 (1972):1.

BOTT, ELIZABETH. *Family and Social Network.* 2d ed. New York: Free Press, 1971.

BOWLBY, JOHN. *Maternal Care and Mental Health.* Geneva: World Health Organization Monograph, 1951.

————. *Child Care and the Growth of Love.* Geneva: World Health Organization, 1952.

BRADWAY, KATHERINE P., and CLARE W. THOMPSON. "Intelligence at Adulthood: A Twenty-five-Year Follow-Up." *Journal of Educational Psychology* 53 (1962).

BREMER, J. *Asexualization: A Follow-Up Study of 244 Cases.* New York: Macmillan, 1959.

BRENTON, MYRON. *The American Male.* London: Unwin Bros., Ltd., 1967.

BRIM, O. G., JR. "Socialization Through the Life Cycle." In O. G. Brim, Jr., and S. Wheeler, *Socialization After Childhood.* New York: John Wiley, 1966.

BRODERICK, CARLFRED. "Sociosexual Development Among Urban Negroes and Whites." Paper presented at meetings of the National Council on Family Relations, Miami, 1964.

BRODY, SYLVIA. *Patterns of Mothering.* New York: International Universities Press, 1956.

BROVERMAN, D. M., *et al.* "Roles of Activation and Inhibition in Sex Differences in Cognitive Abilities." *Psychological Review* 75 (1968).

BROVERMAN, INGE K., *et al.* "Sex-Role Stereotypes and Clinical Judgments of Mental Health." *Journal of Consulting and Clinical Psychology* 34 (1970):1.

BROWN, J. A. C. *Freud and the Post-Freudians.* Baltimore: Penguin, 1961.

BURGESS, ERNEST W., and HARVEY J. LOCKE. *The Family.* New York: American Books, 1953.

CAIN, GLEN S. *Married Women in the Labor Force.* Chicago: University of Chicago Press, 1966.

CANTRIL, HADLEY. *Public Opinion, 1935–1946.* Princeton, N.J.: Princeton University Press, 1951.

CAPLOW, THEODORE. *The Sociology of Work.* New York: McGraw-Hill, 1954.

CARROLL, MARGARET. "The Working Wife and Her Family's Economic Position." *Monthly Labor Review* 85 (1962).

CHAFE, WILLIAM HENRY. *The American Woman.* New York: Oxford University Press, 1972.

CHILD, I. L.; E. H. POTTER; and E. M. LEVINE. "Children's Textbooks and Personality Development." *Psychological Monographs* 60 (1946).

CHINN, A. L. "A Brief Survey of Nearly 1,000 Juvenile Delinquents." *British Journal of Educational Psychology* 8 (1938).

CLEAVER, ELDRIDGE. *Soul on Ice.* New York: Delta, 1968.

COHEN, CHARLOTTE BUNNY. "Women of China." In *Sisterhood Is Powerful*, ed. Robin Morgan. New York: Random House, 1970.

COHEN, MALCOLM S. "Married Women in the Labor Force: An Analysis of Participation Rates." *Monthly Labor Review* 92 (1968).

COLLINS, RANDALL. "A Conflict Theory of Sexual Stratification." *Social Problems* 19 (1971):1.

COOLEY, C. H. *Social Organization.* New York: Scribner's, 1909.

COOPER, GEORGE. "Women and Employment Benefits." In *Women's Role in Contemporary Society*, ed. Eleanor Holmes Norton. New York: Avon Books, 1972.

COULANGES, FUSTEL DE. *The Ancient City.* Trans. Willard Small in 1873. This edition published by Doubleday Anchor Books, New York, no date.

CRAWLEY, ERNEST. *The Mystic Rose.* Vol. 1. New York: Meridian Books, 1960.

CROW, DUNCAN. *The Victorian Woman.* New York: Stein & Day, 1971.

CUBER, JOHN F., and PEGGY B. HAROFF. "The More Total View: Relationships Among Men and Women of the Upper Middle Class." In *Marriage, Family, and Society,* ed. Hyman Rodman. New York: Random House, 1965.

———. *Sex and the Significant Americans.* Baltimore: Penguin Books, 1966.

CUTRONA, LOUIS J., JR. "What Goes On Inside a Men's Liberation Rap Group." *Glamour Magazine,* August 1971.

DAHLSTROM, EDMUND, ed., *The Changing Roles of Men and Women.* Boston: Beacon Press, 1971.

DAMON, S. FOSTER. *Amy Lowell: A Chronicle with Extracts from Her Correspondence.* Boston: Houghton-Mifflin, 1935.

D'ANDRADE, R. G. "Sex Differences and Cultural Institutions." In *The Development of Sex Differences,* ed. Eleanor E. Maccoby. Stanford, Calif.: Stanford University Press, 1966.

DAVIS, ANN E. "Women as a Minority Group in Higher Academics." *American Sociologist* 4 (1969):2.

DAVIS, ELIZABETH GOULD. *The First Sex.* Baltimore: Penguin Books, 1971.

DAVIS, ETHELYN. "Careers as Concerns of Blue-Collar Girls." In *Blue Collar World,* eds. Arthur B. Shostak and William Gomberg. Englewood Cliffs, N.J.: Prentice-Hall, 1964.

DAVIS, KATHERINE B. *Factors in the Sex Life of 2200 Women.* New York: Harper & Row, 1929.

DEMOS, JOHN. *A Little Commonwealth.* New York: Oxford University Press, 1970.

DIAMOND, M. "A Critical Evaluation of the Ontogeny of Human Sexual Behavior." *Quarterly Review of Biology* 40 (1965).

DICKINSON, ROBERT L., and LURA BEAN. *A Thousand Marriages.* New York: Century, 1932.

DORNBUSCH, SANFORD M., and DAVID M. HEER. "The Evaluation of Work by Females, 1940–1950." *American Journal of Sociology* 63 (1957).

DOUVAN, ELIZABETH. "Employment and the Adolescent." In *The Employed Mother in America,* ed. F. Ivan Nye and Lois Wladis Hoffman. Chicago: Rand McNally, 1963.

DUNBAR, ROXANNE. "Female Liberation as the Basis for Social Revolution." In *Sisterhood Is Powerful,* ed. Robin Morgan. New York: Vintage Books, 1970.

DUNCAN, BEVERLY, and OTIS DUDLEY DUNCAN. "Family Stability and Occupational Success." In *The Family Life of Black People,* ed. Charles V. Willie. Columbus, Ohio: Charles E. Merrill, 1970.

ECKERT, RUTH, and JOHN E. STECKLEIN. "Academic Women." *Liberal Education* 45 (1959).

EHRMANN, WINSTON W. *Premarital Dating Behavior.* New York: Holt, Rinehart, and Winston, 1959.

ELKIN, FREDERICK, and GERALD HANDEL. *The Child and Society.* 2d ed. New York: Random House, 1972.

ELKINS, STANLEY M. *Slavery: A Problem in American Institutional and Intellectual Life.* New York: Grosset & Dunlap, 1963.

ELLIS, H. *Studies in the Psychology of Sex.* Vol. 1. New York: Random House, 1936.

EPSTEIN, CYNTHIA FUCHS. "Women Lawyers and Their Professions: Inconsistency of Social Controls and Their Consequences for Professional Performance." Paper presented at the 64th annual meeting of the American Sociological Association, San Francisco, September 1969.

————. *Woman's Place*. Berkeley: University of California Press, 1970.

ERON, LEONARD D., *et al.* "Comparison of Data Obtained from Mothers and Fathers on Childrearing Practices and Their Relation to Child Aggression." *Child Development* 32 (1961).

FAHO, SOPHIA LYON, and DOROTHY T. SPOERL. "A Boy Full of Troubles." In *Beginnings: Earth, Sky, Life, Death*, eds. Helen M. Robinson *et al.* Chicago: Scott, Foresmann, 1965.

FEAGIN, JOE R. "Black Women in the American Work Force." In *The Family Life of Black People*, ed. Charles V. Willie. Columbus, Ohio: Charles E. Merrill, 1970.

FELD, SHEILA. "Feelings of Adjustment." In *The Employed Mother in America*, eds. F. Ivan Nye and Lois Wladis Hoffman. Chicago: Rand McNally, 1963.

FELDMAN, FRANCES. "Supplementary Income Earned by Married Women." In National Manpower Council, *Work in the Lives of Married Women*. New York: Columbia University Press, 1958.

FERRISS, ABOTT L. *Indicators of Trends in the Status of American Women*. New York: Russell Sage Foundation, 1971.

FIELD, MARK G., and KARIN I. FLYNN. "Worker, Mother, Housewife: Soviet Woman Today." In *Sex Roles in Changing Society*, eds. Georgene H. Seward and Robert C. Williamson. New York: Random House, 1970.

FILLER, W., and N. DREZNER. "The Results of Surgical Castration in Women Under 40." *American Journal of Obstetrics and Gynecology* 47 (1944).

FLACELIÈRE, ROBERT. *Daily Life in Greece at the Time of Pericles*. Trans. Peter Green. New York: Macmillan, 1965.

FRAZIER, E. FRANKLIN. *The Negro Family in the United States*. Rev. and abr, ed. Chicago: University of Chicago Press, 1966.

FREE, RUTH. "Cross-cultural Sex Roles: An Anthropological View." Paper delivered at Seton Hall University Symposium on Sex Roles and Social Change, March 22, 1972.

FRIEDAN, BETTY. *The Feminine Mystique*. New York: Norton, 1963.

FRIEDMANN, GEORGES. *The Anatomy of Work*. New York: Crowell-Collier, 1961.

FROMM, ERICH. *Escape from Freedom*. New York: Avon Books, 1941.

FUENTES, SONIA PRESSMAN. "Job Discrimination and the Black Woman." In *Womankind: Beyond the Stereotypes*, ed. Nancy Reeves. Chicago: Aldine, 1972.

FULLERTON, GAIL PUTNEY. *Survival in Marriage*. New York: Holt, Rinehart, and Winston, 1972.

GANS, HERBERT J. *The Urban Villagers*. New York: Free Press, 1962.

GARLAND, T. NEAL. "The Better Half? The Male in the Dual Professional Family." In *Toward a Sociology of Women*, ed. Constantina Safilios-Rothschild. Lexington, Mass.: Xerox, 1972.

GARN, S. M. "Fat, Body Size, and Growth in the Newborn." *Human Biology* 30 (1958).

GARN, S. M., and L. C. CLARK, JR. "The Sex Differences in the Basic Metabolic Rate." *Child Development* 24 (1953).

GOFFMAN, ERVING. *Asylums: Essays on the Social Situation of Mental Patients and Other Inmates.* Garden City, N.Y.: Doubleday Anchor Books, 1961.

GOLD, M. A. *A Social Psychology of Delinquent Boys.* Ann Arbor, Mich.: Institute for Social Research, 1961.

GOLDBERG, PHILIP. "Are Women Prejudiced Against Women?" *Trans-action* 5 (April 1968).

GOLDBERG, STEPHEN. *The Inevitability of Patriarchy.* New York: William Morrow, 1973.

GOLDBERG, SUSAN, and MICHAEL LEWIS. "Play Behavior in the Year-Old Infant: Early Sex Differences." *Child Development* 40 (March 1969):1.

GOODE, WILLIAM J. *World Revolution and Family Patterns.* New York: Free Press, 1970.

GORNICK, VIVIAN, and BARBARA K. MORAN, eds. *Woman in Sexist Society.* New York: Basic Books, 1971.

GOVER, DAVID M. "Socio-economic Differentials in the Relationship Between Marital Adjustment and Wife's Employment Status." *Journal of Marriage and the Family* 25 (November 1963).

GOY, R. W. "Organizing Effects of Androgen on the Behavior of Rhesus Monkeys." In *Proceedings of the London Conference: Endocrines and Human Behavior,* ed. R. P. Michael, 1968.

GRAHAM, ALMA. "The Making of a Nonsexist Dictionary." *Ms. Magazine,* December 1973.

GRAY, HORACE. "The Trapped Housewife." *Marriage and Family Living* 24 (1962).

GRAY, SUSAN W. "Perceived Similarity to Parents and Adjustment." *Child Development* 30 (1959).

GREENWOOD, ERNEST. "Attributes of a Profession." In *Man, Work, and Society,* eds. Sigmund Nosow and William H. Form. New York: Basic Books, 1962.

GREER, GERMAINE. *The Female Eunuch.* New York: McGraw-Hill, 1971.

GROSS, EDWARD. "*Plus ça change . . . ?* The Sexual Structure of Occupations over Time." *Social Problems* 16 (1968).

HAAN, NORMA. "Proposed Model of Ego Functioning: Coping and Defense Mechanisms in Relationship to I.Q. Change." *Psychological Monographs* 77, no. 571 (1963).

HACKER, HELEN MAYER. "The New Burdens of Masculinity." *Journal of Marriage and Family Living* 19 (1957):3.

———. "A Functional Approach to the Gainful Employment of Married Women." Unpublished Ph.D. dissertation. New York: Columbia University, 1961.

———. "The Feminine Protest of the Working Wife." *Indian Journal of Social Work* 31 (1971):4.

HAFSTROM, JEANNE L., and MARILYN M. DUNSING. "A Comparison of Economic Choices of One-Earner and Two-Earner Families." *Journal of Marriage and the Family* 27 (August 1965).

HAMILTON, GILBERT V. *A Research in Marriage.* New York: Albert and Charles Boni, 1929.

HAMPSON, J. L. "Determinants of Psychosexual Orientation." In *Sex and Behavior*, ed. F. S. Beach. New York: John Wiley, 1965.

HAMPSON, J. L., and J. G. HAMPSON. "The Ontogenesis of Sexual Behavior in Man." In *Sex and Internal Secretions.* Vol. 2, ed. W. C. Young. Baltimore: Williams and Wilkins, 1961.

HANDEL, GERALD, and LEE RAINWATER. "Persistence and Change in Working-Class Life Style." In *Blue Collar World*, eds. Arthur B. Shostak and William Gomberg. Englewood Cliffs, N.J.: Prentice-Hall, 1964.

HAWKES, JACQUETTA. *The Dawn of the Gods.* New York: Random House, 1968.

HAYS, H. R. *The Dangerous Sex.* New York: Pocket Books, 1966.

HEER, DAVID M. "Dominance and the Working Wife." In *The Employed Mother in America*, eds. F. Ivan Nye and Lois Wladis Hoffman. Chicago: Rand McNally, 1963.

HERKOVITS, MELVILLE J. *The Myth of the Negro Past.* New York: Harper & Bros., 1941.

HERZOG, ELIZABETH. "Is There a 'Breakdown' of the Negro Family?" *Social Work* 11 (January 1966).

HOFFMAN, LOIS. "The Decision to Work." In *The Employed Mother in America*, eds. F. Ivan Nye and Lois Wladis Hoffman. Chicago: Rand McNally, 1963.

HOLMSTROM, LYNDA LYTLE. *The Two-Career Family.* Cambridge, Mass.: Schenkman, 1972.

HORNER, MATINA. "The Motive to Avoid Success and Changing Aspirations of College Women." In *Readings in the Psychology of Women*, ed. Judith M. Bardwick. New York: Harper & Row, 1972.

HORNEY, KAREN. "The Neurotic Personality of Our Time." Reprinted in J. A. C. Brown, *Freud and the Post-Freudians.* Baltimore: Penguin Books, 1961.

HUGHES, HELEN MACGILL, ed. *The Status of Women in Sociology.* Washington, D.C.: The American Sociological Association, 1972.

HURVITZ, NATHAN. "Marital Strain in the Blue-Collar Family." In *Blue Collar World*, eds. Arthur B. Shostak and William Gomberg. Englewood Cliffs, N.J.: Prentice-Hall, 1964.

HYMAN, HERBERT H., and JOHN SHELTON REED. "Black Matriarchy Reconsidered: Evidence from Secondary Analysis of Sample Surveys." *Public Opinion Quarterly* 33 (1969).

JACOBY, SUSAN. "Feminism in the $12,000-a-Year Family: What Do I Do for the Next Twenty Years?" *New York Times Magazine*, (June 17, 1973).

KAGAN, JEROME. "Acquisition and Significance of Sex Typing and Sex Role Identity." In *Review of Child Development Research*, vol. 1, eds. Martin L. Hoffman and Lois W. Hoffman. New York: Russell Sage Foundation, 1964.

KAGAN, JEROME, and HOWARD A. MOSS. *From Birth to Maturity.* New York: John Wiley, 1962.

KAHL, JOSEPH. *The American Class Structure.* New York: Rinehart, 1957.

KALLMAN, F. J. "Comparative Twin Study of the Genetic Aspects of

Male Homosexuality." *Journal of Nervous and Mental Diseases* 115 (1952).

————. "Twin and Sibship Study of Overt Male Homosexuality." *American Journal of Human Genetics* 4 (1952).

————. "Genetic Aspects of Sex Determination and Sexual Maturation Potentials in Man." In *Determinants of Human Sexual Behavior*, ed. G. Winokur. Springfield, Ill.: Charles C. Thomas, 1963.

KANOWITZ, LEO. *Women and the Law*. Albuquerque: University of New Mexico Press, 1969.

KARLEN, ARNO. *Sexuality and Homosexuality*. New York: Norton, 1971.

KING, HELEN H. *Ebony*, March 1971.

KINSEY, ALFRED C.; WARDELL B. POMEROY; and PAUL H. GEBBARD. *Sexual Behavior in the Human Male*. Philadelphia: Saunders, 1948.

————. *Sexual Behavior in the Human Female*. Philadelphia: Saunders, 1953.

KIRKPATRICK, CLIFFORD. *The Family as Process and Institution*. 2d ed. New York: Ronald Press, 1963.

KLEIN, VIOLA. *The Feminine Character*. London: Paul, Trench, Trubner, 1946.

KLUCKHOHN, FLORENCE. "Cultural Factors in Social Work Practice and Education." *Social Service Review* 25 (March 1951).

KNOP, C. A. "The Dynamics of Newly Born Babies." *Journal of Pediatrics* 29 (1946).

KOEDT, ANNE. "The Myth of the Vaginal Orgasm." In Deborah Babcox and Madeline Belkin, *Liberation Now!* New York: Dell, 1971.

KOHLBERG, LAWRENCE. "A Cognitive-Developmental Analysis of Children's Sex-Role Concepts and Attitudes." In *The Development of Sex Differences*, ed. Eleanor E. Maccoby. Stanford, Calif.: Stanford University Press, 1966.

————. "Stage and Sequence: The Cognitive Development Approach to Socialization." In *Handbook of Socialization Theory and Research*, ed. David A. Goslin. Chicago: Rand McNally, 1969.

KOMAROVSKY, MIRRA. *Women in the Modern World*. Boston: Little, Brown, 1953.

————. *Blue Collar Marriage*. New York: Random House, 1962.

KOSA, JOHN. "Women and Medicine in a Changing World." In *The Professional Woman*, ed. Athena Theodore. Cambridge, Mass.: Schenkman, 1971.

KOSA, JOHN, and ROBERT E. COKER, JR. "The Female Physician in Public Health: Conflict and Reconciliation of the Sex and Professional Roles." *Sociology and Social Research* 49 (1965):3.

KRAFFT-EBING, R. *Psychopathia Sexualis*. New York: Physicians and Surgeons Book Co., 1922.

KROGER, WILLIAM S. "Sexual Frustration." *Sexual Behavior*, December 1972.

LeMASTERS, E. E. *Parents in Modern America*. Homewood, Ill.: Dorsey Press, 1970.

LEVINE, S. N. "Sex Differences in the Brain." *Scientific American*, April 1966.

LEVINE, S. N., and R. F. MULLINS, JR. "Hormonal Influences on Brain Organization in Infant Rats." *Science* 152 (1966).

LEVY, MARION J., JR. *The Family Revolution in Modern China.* New York: Atheneum, 1968.

LEWIS, EDWIN C. *Developing Women's Potential.* Ames: Iowa State University Press, 1968.

LEWIS, OSCAR. *Five Families: Mexican Case Studies in the Culture of Poverty.* New York: Basic Books, 1959.

————. *The Children of Sanchez: Autobiography of a Mexican Family.* New York: Vintage Books, 1961.

LIEBOW, ELLIOT. *Talley's Corner.* Boston: Little, Brown, 1967.

LINCOLN, ABBEY. "Who Will Revere the Black Women?" In *The Black Woman,* ed. Toni Cade. New York: Signet Books, 1970.

LINDSEY, KAY. "The Black Woman as a Woman." In *The Black Woman,* ed. Toni Cade. New York: Signet Books, 1970.

LINTON, ROBERT. *The Study of Man.* New York: Appleton-Century-Crofts, 1936.

LIPSITT, L. P., and N. LEVY. "Pain Threshold in the Human Neonate." *Child Development* 30 (1959).

LOPATA, HELENA Z. "The Secondary Features of a Primary Relationship." *Human Organization,* 1965.

————. *Occupation: Housewife.* New York: Oxford University Press, 1971.

LORENZ, KONRAD. *On Aggression.* New York: Harcourt, Brace and World, 1966.

LUNDBERG, FERDINAND, and MARYNIA FARNHAM. *Modern Woman: The Lost Sex.* New York: Harper & Row, 1947.

MACCOBY, ELEANOR E., ed. *The Development of Sex Differences.* Stanford, Calif.: Stanford University Press, 1966

MACDONALD, J. "Manners, Customs, Superstitions, and Religions of South African Tribes." *Journal of the Anthropological Institute* 20 (1891).

MACDOUGALL, PRISCILLA RUTH. "Married Women's Common Law Right to Their Own Surnames." *Women's Rights Law Reporter* 1 (Fall–Winter 1972–73), Newark.

MACK, DOLORES E. "The Power Relationship in Black Families and White Families," *Journal of Personality and Social Psychology,* 30:3 (1974), 409–13.

MCLAUGHLIN, LORRIE. "Out of Her Shell." In *More Roads to Follow,* ed. Helen M. Robinson *et al.* Chicago: Scott, Foresman, 1965.

MASON, W. A. "The Social Development of Monkeys and Apes." In *Primate Behavior,* ed. I. DeVore. New York: Holt, Rinehart, and Winston, 1965.

MASTERS, WILLIAM H., and VIRGINIA E. JOHNSON. *Human Sexual Response.* Boston: Little, Brown, 1966.

MAYO, JULIA. "The New Black Feminism," in *Contemporary Sexual Behavior: Critical Issues in the 1970s,* eds. Joseph Zubin and John Money. Baltimore, Md.: Johns Hopkins University Press, 1973.

MEAD, GEORGE HERBERT. *Mind, Self, and Society.* Chicago: University of Chicago Press, 1934.

MEAD, MARGARET. *Sex and Temperament in Three Societies.* New York: William Morrow, 1935.

————. "Cultural Determinants of Sexual Behavior." In *Sex and*

Internal Secretions, vol. 2, ed. W. C. Young. Baltimore: Williams and Wilkins, 1961.

MERRIAM, CHARLES, and HERBERT GOSNELL. *Non-Voting.* Chicago: University of Chicago Press, 1924.

MILLER, CASEY, and KATE SWIFT. "One Small Step for Genkind." *New York Times Magazine,* April 16, 1972.

MILLER, DANIEL R., and GUY E. SWANSON. *The Changing American Parent.* New York: John Wiley, 1958.

MILLER, S. M., and FRANK RIESSMAN. "The Working Class Subculture: A New View." *Social Problems* 9 (1961).

MILLER, WALTER B. "Violent Crimes in City Gangs." In Thomas Dye, *Politics in the Metropolis.* Columbus, Ohio: Charles E. Merrill, 1967.

MILLETT, KATE. *Sexual Politics.* New York: Doubleday, 1970.

MONEY, J. "Components of Eroticism in Man: The Hormones in Relation to Sexual Morphology and Sexual Desire." *Journal of Nervous and Mental Diseases* 132 (1961).

————. "Sex Hormones and Other Variables in Human Eroticism." In *Sex and Internal Secretions,* vol. 2, ed. W. C. Young. Baltimore: Williams & Wilkins, 1961.

MONEY, J.; J. L. HAMPSON; and J. G. HAMPSON. "An Examination of Some Basic Sexual Concepts: The Evidence of Human Hermaphroditism." *Bulletin of the Johns Hopkins Hospital* 97 (1955).

MONTESQUIEU. *The Spirit of the Laws,* vol. 1. Trans. Thomas Nugent. New York: Hafner, 1949.

MORRISON, TONI. "What the Black Woman Thinks about Women's Lib," *New York Times,* August 22, 1972.

MOSELY, PHILIP. "The Russian Family: Old Style and New." In *The Family: Its Function and Destiny,* ed. Ruth N. Anshen. New York: Harper & Row, 1959.

MOSS, H. A. "Sex, Age, and State as Determinants of Mother-Infant Interaction." *Merrill-Palmer Quarterly* 13 (1967).

MULLAHY, PATRICK. *Oedipus: Myth and Complex.* New York: Grove Press, 1948.

MURPHY, LOIS B., et al. *The Widening World of Childhood.* New York: Basic Books, 1962.

MURRAY, PAULI. "The Liberation of Black Women." In *Voices of the New Feminism,* ed. Mary Lou Thompson. Boston: Beacon Press, 1970.

MUSSEN, P. H. "Some Antecedents and Consequents of Masculine Sex-Typing in Adolescent Boys." *Psychological Monographs* 75 (1961):2.

————. "Long Term Consequents of Masculinity of Interests in Adolescence." *Journal of Consulting Psychology* 26 (1962).

NAGEL, STUART, and LENORE J. WEITZMAN. "Double Standard of American Justice." *Trans-action* 9 (1972): 1–2.

New York Law Journal, January 15, 1974.

New York Times, March 9, 1972.

————, February 18, 1973.

————, July 11, 1973.

NICOLSON, NIGEL. *Portrait of a Marriage.* New York: Atheneum, 1973.

NOTTINGHAM, ELIZABETH. "Toward an Analysis of the Effects of Two World Wars on the Role and Status of Middle Class Women in the English-speaking World." *American Sociological Review* 12 (December 1947).

NOW. *Dick and Jane as Victims: Sex Stereotyping in Images.* 1972.

NYE, F. IVAN. "Maternal Employment and Marital Interaction." *Social Forces* 40 (1961).

NYE, F. IVAN, and FELIX M. BERARDO. *The Family: Its Structure and Interaction.* New York: Macmillan, 1973.

NYE, F. IVAN, and LOIS WLADIS HOFFMAN, eds. *The Employed Mother in America.* Chicago: Rand McNally, 1963.

O'NEILL, WILLIAM L. *The Woman Movement.* Chicago: Quadrangle Books, 1969.

OPPENHEIMER, VALERIE KINCAIDE. *The Female Labor Force in the United States: Demographic and Economic Factors Governing Its Growth and Changing Composition.* Berkeley: Institute of International Studies, University of California, 1970.

ORDEN, SUSAN, and NORMAN BRADBURN. "Working Wives and Marriage Happiness." *American Journal of Sociology* 74 (1969).

PARRISH, J. B. "Professional Womanpower as a National Resource." *Quarterly Review of Economy and Business,* 1961.

PARSONS, TALCOTT. "The Kinship System of the Contemporary United States." In *Essays in Sociological Theory.* New York: Free Press, 1954.

———. "A Revised Analytical Approach to the Theory of Social Stratification." In *Essays in Sociological Theory.* Rev. ed. New York: Free Press, 1964.

PARSONS, TALCOTT, and R. F. BALES. *Family Socialization and Interaction Process.* Glencoe, Ill.: Free Press, 1955.

PETERSON, ESTHER. "Working Women." In *The Woman in America,* ed. Robert Lifton. Boston: Beacon Press, 1964.

PETRAS, JOHN W. *Sexuality in Society.* Boston: Allyn & Bacon, 1973.

PLATO. *The Republic.* Trans. W. H. D. Reuss. New York: New American Library, 1956.

POLOMA, MARGARET M. "Role Conflict and the Married Professional Woman." In *Toward a Sociology of Women,* ed. Constantina Safilios-Rothschild. Lexington, Mass.: Xerox, 1972.

POLOMA, MARGARET M., and T. NEAL GARLAND. "The Myth of the Egalitarian Family: Familial Roles and the Professionally Employed Wife." In *The Professional Woman,* ed. Athena Theodore. Cambridge, Mass.: Schenkman, 1971.

PORTER, SYLVIA. *New York Post,* February 14, 1972.

Prime Time 2 (January 1974):1. " 'Social Security'—A Gross Misnomer, Especially for Women."

PROPPER, ALICE MARCELLA. "The Relationship of Maternal Employment to Adolescent Roles, Activities, and Parental Relationships." *Journal of Marriage and the Family* 34 (1972):3.

PULLUM, CARLA A. "Women, Medicine, and Misconceptions." *Journal of American Medical Women's Association* 18 (1963).

RABAN, M. "Sex-Role Identification in Young Children in Two Diverse Social Groups." *Genetic Psychological Monograph* 42 (1950).

RAINWATER, LEE. *And the Poor Get Children: Sex, Contraception and Family Planning in the Working Class*. Chicago: Quadrangle Books, 1960.

RAINWATER, LEE; RICHARD COLEMAN; and GERALD HANDEL. *Workingman's Wife*. New York: Oceana Publications, 1959.

REISS, IRA R. *The Family System in America*. New York: Holt, Rinehart, and Winston, 1971.

RENNE, KAREN S. "Correlates of Dissatisfaction in Marriage." *Journal of Marriage and the Family* 32 (1970):1.

REYNOLDS, MYRA. *The Learned Lady in England, 1650–1750*. Gloucester, Mass.: Peter Smith, 1964.

RIDLEY, CARL A. "Exploring the Impact of Work Satisfaction and Involvement on Marital Interaction When Both Partners Are Employed." *Journal of Marriage and the Family* 35 (1973):2.

RIESMAN, DAVID, and WARNER J. BLOOMBERG. "Work and Leisure: Fusion or Polarity?" In *Research in Industrial and Human Relations*, ed. C. M. Arensberg *et al*. New York: Harper, 1957.

ROBBINS, JHAN, and JUNE ROBBINS. "Why Young Husbands Feel Trapped." *Redbook*, March 1962.

ROBINSON, PATRICIA. "A Historical and Critical Essay on Black Women in the Cities." In *The Black Woman*, ed. Toni Cade. New York: Signet Books, 1970.

ROBY, PAMELA, and VIRGINIA KERN. "The Politics of Prostitution." *The Nation*, April 10, 1972.

ROPER, MYRA. *China: The Surprising Country*. New York: Doubleday, 1966.

ROSENBERG, B. G., and BRIAN SUTTON-SMITH. *Sex and Identity*. New York: Holt, Rinehart, and Winston, 1972.

ROSENTHAL, BERNICE. "The Roles and Status of Women in the Soviet Union." Unpublished paper.

ROSNER, MENACHEM. "Women in the Kibbutz: Changing Status and Concept." *Asia and African Studies* 3 (1967).

ROSSI, ALICE S. "Equality Between the Sexes: An Immodest Proposal." *Daedalus*, Spring 1964.

ROSTOW, EDNA. "Conflict and Accommodation." In *The Woman in America*, ed. Robert Lifton. Boston: Beacon Press, 1964.

ROTHCHILD, ELLEN. "Emotional Aspects of Sexual Development." In *Sexual Development and Behavior*, ed. Anne McCreary Juhasz. Homewood, Ill.: Dorsey Press, 1973.

SAFILIOS-ROTHSCHILD, CONSTANTINA. "Marital Expectations and Marital Experience: Why Such a Discrepancy?" Paper read at the ICOFA meetings in Rennes, France, April 1969.

———. *The Sociology and Social Psychology of Disability and Rehabilitation*. New York: Random House, 1970.

SALAFF, JANET WEITZNER, and JUDITH MERKLE. "Women and Revolution: The Lessons of the Soviet Union and China." *Socialist Revolution* 1 (1970):4.

SAMUEL, EDWIN. *The Structure of Society in Israel*. New York: Random House, 1969.

SCANZONI, JOHN H. *The Black Family in Modern Society*. Boston: Allyn & Bacon, 1971.

SCHAEFER, E. S., and NANCY BAYLEY. "Maternal Behavior, Child Behavior, and Their Intercorrelations from Infancy Through Adolescence." *Monographs of the Society for Research in Child Development* 28 (1963).

SCHLEGEL, W. S. "Die konstitutionsbiologischen Grundlagen der Homosexualität." *Zeitschrift für menschliche Vererberung: Konstitutionslehre* 36 (1962).

SCHNEIDER, JOSEPH W., and SALLY L. HACKER. "Sex Role Imagery and the Use of the Generic 'Man' in Introductory Texts." Paper read at the American Sociological Association meetings, New Orleans, August 1972.

SCHULTZ, DAVID. *The Changing Family: Its Functions and Future.* Englewood Cliffs, N.J.: Prentice-Hall, 1972.

SCOTT, ANN. "The Equal Rights Amendment: What's in It for You?" *Ms. Magazine,* July 1972.

———. "The Value of Housework." *Ms. Magazine,* July 1972.

SCOTT, J. P. "The Naked Ape: A Zoologist's Study of the Human Animal by Desmond Morris." *Contemporary Psychology* 15 (1970).

SEARS, ROBERT R., *et al. Patterns of Child Rearing.* Evanston, Ill.: Row, Paterson, 1957.

SEIFER, NANCY. *Absent from the Majority: Working-Class Women in America.* New York: American Jewish Committee, 1973.

———. "Big Losers in the Hot Stove League." *New York Times,* April 10, 1974.

SEXTON, PATRICIA CAYO. *The Feminized Male.* New York: Random House, 1969.

SHERR, LYNN. "Teaching Kit to Free Vowels from Chauvinist Consonants." *New York Times,* February 20, 1972.

SHOSTAK, ARTHUR B. *Blue Collar Life.* New York: Random House, 1969.

———. "Middle-aged Working Class Americans at Home: Changing Expectations of Manhood." Paper presented at the Eastern Sociological Society meeting, Boston, 1972.

SHOSTAK, ARTHUR B., and WILLIAM GOMBERG, eds. *Blue Collar World: Studies of the American Worker.* Englewood Cliffs, N.J.: Prentice-Hall, 1964.

SIDEL, RUTH. *Women and Child Care in China.* Baltimore: Penguin Books, 1973.

SIMON, WILLIAM, and JOHN H. GAGNON. "On Psychosexual Development." In *Handbook of Socialization Theory and Research,* ed. David A. Goslin. Chicago: Rand McNally, 1969.

SKOLNICK, JEROME P. *Justice Without Trial: Law Enforcement in Democratic Society.* New York: John Wiley, 1966.

SLATER, PHILIP. "Parental Role Differentiation." *American Journal of Sociology* 68 (1961):3.

SMIGEL, ERWIN O. *The Wall Street Lawyer.* 2d ed. Bloomington: Indiana University Press, 1969.

SMITH, PAGE. *Daughters of the Promised Land.* Boston: Little, Brown, 1970.

SOBOL, MARION G. "Commitment to Work." In *The Employed Mother in America,* eds. F. Ivan Nye and Lois Wladis Hoffman. Chicago: Rand McNally, 1963.

SONTAG, L. W.; C. T. BAKER; and VIRGINIA A. NELSON. "Mental

Growth and Personality Development: A Longitudinal Study." *Social Research in Child Development Monograph* 23, no. 68 (1958).

SPITZ, RENÉ. "Hospitalism: An Inquiry into the Genesis of Psychiatric Conditions in Early Childhood." In *The Psychoanalytic Study of the Child.* New York: International Universities Press, 1945.

STAPLES, ROBERT. "The Myth of the Black Matriarchy." *The Black Scholar,* January–February 1970.

————. "The Black Woman's Burden: Racism and Sexism." In *The Black Woman in America,* ed. Robert Staples. Chicago: Nelson-Hall, 1973.

STEIN, HERBERT. "Women's Second Economic Revolution." *Ladies' Home Journal,* October 1972.

STEINEM, GLORIA. "What It Would Be Like If Women Win." In Deborah Babcox and Madeline Belkin, *Liberation Now!* New York: Dell, 1971.

STOLL, CLARICE STASZ, ed. *Sexism: Scientific Debates.* Reading, Mass.: Addison-Wesley, 1973.

SUMNER, WILLIAM GRAHAM. *Social Darwinism.* Englewood Cliffs, N.J.: Prentice-Hall, 1963.

TAYLOR, G. RATTRAY. *Sex in History.* New York: Ballantine Books, 1954.

TERMAN, L. M., and C. C. MILES. *Sex and Personality: Studies in Masculinity and Femininity.* New York: McGraw-Hill, 1936.

THEODORE, ATHENA, ed. *The Professional Woman.* Cambridge, Mass.: Schenkman, 1971.

TIGER, LIONEL. *Men in Groups.* New York: Random House, 1969.

TORRANCE, E. P. "Sex-Role Identification and Creative Thinking." *Research Memo* BER-S9-10. Minneapolis: Bureau of Education Research, University of Minnesota, 1959.

TROPMAN, JOHN E. "The Married Professional Social Worker." *Journal of Marriage and the Family* 30 (1968).

TURNBULL, COLIN. *The Mountain People.* New York: Simon & Schuster, 1972.

TURNER, RALPH. "Some Aspects of Women's Ambition." *American Journal of Sociology* 70 (1964).

UDRY, J. RICHARD. "Marital Instability by Race, Sex, Education, Occupation, and Income." In *The Family Life of Black People,* ed. Charles V. Willie. Columbus, Ohio: Charles E. Merrill, 1970.

U.S. Bureau of the Census. Census of 1960. Vol. 1.

————. Census of 1963. Vol. 1.

————. Series P-23, no. 39, *Differences Between Incomes of White and Negro Families by Work Experience of the Wife and Region: 1970, 1969, and 1959.* Washington, D.C.: U.S. Government Printing Office, 1971.

————. Series P-23, no. 46, *The Social and Economic Status of the Black Population in the United States, 1972.* Washington, D.C.: U.S. Government Printing Office, 1973.

U.S. Department of Labor. *The Negro Family: The Case for National Action.* Washington, D.C.: Office of Policy Planning and Research, 1965.

VALENSTEIN, E. S. "Steroid Hormones and the Neuropsychology of Development." In *The Neuropsychology of Development: A Symposium*, ed. R. L. Isaacson. New York: John Wiley, 1968.

VAN DEN BERGHE, PIERRE L. "The Two Roles of Women." *American Sociologist* 5 (1970).

VEROFF, JOSEPH, and SHEILA FELD. *Marriage and Work in America.* New York: Van Nostrand Reinhold, 1970.

WASHAY, DIANA W. "Sex Differences in Language Style." In *Toward a Sociology of Women*, ed. Constantina Safilios-Rothschild, Lexington, Mass.: Xerox, 1972.

WAXMAN, RUTH. Article in *Women's Role in Contemporary Society*, ed. Eleanor Holmes Norton. New York: Avon Books, 1972.

WEBER, MAX. *Essays in Sociology.* Trans. H. H. Gerth and C. W. Mills. New York: Oxford University Press, 1946.

WEINMAN, MARTHA L. "Q—If You Rape a Woman and Steal Her TV, What Can They Get You For in New York? A—Stealing Her TV." *New York Times Magazine*, January 30, 1972.

WEISS, ROBERT S., and NANCY M. SAMUELSON. "Social Roles of American Women: Their Contribution to a Sense of Usefulness and Importance." *Journal of Marriage and Family Living* 20 (November 1958).

WEISSTEIN, NAOMI. "Psychology Constructs the Female." In *Woman in Sexist Society*, eds. Vivian Gornick and Barbara K. Moran. New York: Basic Books, 1971.

WHITE, JAMES J. "Women in the Law." *Michigan Law Review* 65 (1967):6.

WHYTE, WILLIAM H., JR. "The Wives of Management." *Fortune* (October 1951).

———. "The Corporation and the Wife." *Fortune* (November 1951).

———. *The Organization Man.* Garden City, N.Y.: Doubleday, 1956.

WILLIAMS, JOSEPHINE J. "Patients and Prejudice: Lay Attitudes Toward Women Physicians." *American Journal of Sociology* 51 (1964).

WILLIAMS, ROBIN M., JR. *American Society: A Sociological Interpretation.* New York: Alfred A. Knopf, 1951.

WILLIE, CHARLES V. "Intergenerational Poverty." In *The Family Life of Black People*, ed. Charles V. Willie. Columbus, Ohio: Charles E. Merrill, 1970.

WILLS, GARY. *Nixon Agonistes.* New York: New American Library, Signet Books, 1971.

WISE, GENEVIEVE M., and DON C. CARTER. "A Definition of the Role of Homemaker by Two Generations of Women." *Journal of Marriage and the Family* 27 (1965).

WOLFF, KURT H., ed. and trans. *The Sociology of Georg Simmel.* Glencoe, Ill.: Free Press, 1950.

"Women in Prisons." *Women's Yellow Pages.* Boston: Women's Collective, 1972.

Woman's Bureau. *Bulletin 296* (Washington, D.C.: U.S. Department of Labor, 1970).

———. *The Fuller Utilization of the Woman Physician.* (Washington, D.C.: U.S. Department of Labor, 1968).

―――. *1969 Handbook on Women Workers.* Washington, D.C.: U.S. Department of Labor, 1969.

YABLONSKY, LEWIS. *The Violent Gang.* New York: Macmillan, 1963.

YOUNG, W. C. "The Organization of Sexual Behavior by Hormonal Action During the Prenatal and Larval Periods in Vertebrates." In *Sex and Behavior,* ed. F. A. Beach. New York: John Wiley, 1965.

Index